Inclusive Christ and Broken People

Christian Heritage Rediscovered

The Series, as the name suggests, is meant to focus on Christian Faith & Living vis-à-vis topics like Literature & Poetry, Indigenous Philosophizing, Ethical response towards Agriculture, Health & Healing, Science & Technology, Eco-feminist Theology, Sociological approach towards Human Rights, Law & Politics, Arts, History of Ideas, Ancient Civilizations, Cultural Contiguity, Religious Cosmologies & Mysticism, Footsteps of famous Theologians, World Peace & Harmony, Global Capitalism, Network Marketing, Cybertheology, Population & Demographics, Epigraphic Studies, Contextualized Education, and many others. We welcome a Mss. on any topic/s mentioned, whether they are original works, scholarly monographs, collections of conference papers, revised dissertations, or translations of historical documents. Through the Series we, the Publishers, are striving to put forward published works that may help Institutions, Academic Bodies, Researchers, Scholars and the World at large in furthering their respective knowledge and understanding on the concerned subject. We welcome your comments on our efforts and further suggestions on how we can foster the upcoming thought provoking theologically grounded books.

Christian Heritage Rediscovered - 67

Inclusive Christ and Broken People

Towards a Dalit Christology in the Light of the Early Church Faith Confession

Josfin Raj S. B

CWI

Christian World Imprints™

First Published in 2018 by

Christian World Imprints™
Christian Publishing & Books from India
H-12 Bali Nagar, **New Delhi-110015**
info@christianworldimprints.com
www.ChristianWorldImprints.com
Phone: +91 11 25465925

ISBN: 978-93-5148-280-2 (HB) ISBN: 978-93-5148-281-9 (PB)

Cataloging in Publication Data--DK
Courtesy: D.K. Agencies (P) Ltd. <docinfo@dkagencies.com>

Raj, Josfin, 1989- **author.**
Inclusive Christ and broken people : towards a dalit Christology in the light of the early church faith confession / Josfin Raj.
pages cm. -- (Christian heritage rediscovered ; 67)
Includes bibliographical references.
ISBN 9789351482802 (hardback)
ISBN 9789351482819 (paperback)

1. Dalits--India--Religion. 2. Liberation theology--India. 3. Creeds. 4. Jesus Christ--Person and offices. I. Title. II. Series: Christian heritage rediscovered ; 67.

LCC BL1237.58.D36R35 2018 | DDC 305.56880954 23

Printed in India

Contents

Foreword

It is not important to accept the views expressed in a book as there might be agreements and disagreements. However, considering seriously the concerns of the author is very significant. This book *Inclusive Christ and Broken People* is an attempt of Rev. Josfin Raj to examine the dalit Christology in the light of early church's confession. He tries to bring the dalit theological materials to our attention to argue that present dalit Christology is very rigid and exclusive. He feels that the dalit Christology holds a rejectionist approach in relation to the other communities. He opposes this standpoint and tries to develop an inclusive dalit Christology, which he feels more adequate and acceptable in relation suiting to early Christian understanding.

It is important to note that there are reactionary elements in dalit theology which are the result of centuries long suffering and oppression they had undergone. This may not mean the total rejection and annihilation of other communities. But the annihilation of caste and its pollutive elements are essential factors.

This book draws our attention to a vast amount of dalit theological resources which enable the readers to have some in-depth understanding of the dalit roots and their condition. It is, of course, a valuable contribution to dalit theology.

Dr. M. Stephen
Principal
Faith Theological Seminary
(Senate of Serampore)
Manakala, Adoor
Kerala

Acknowledgement

In my post-graduate study, I had been motivated to continue my saga with Dalit Christology which I had started from my undergraduate studies at New Life Biblical Seminary, Kollam. During this research endeavour, I had been going through a 'dalit' experience. When I started my thesis journey, unexpectedly, my father (Rev. N. S. Balaraj) passed away– an experience of brokenness. Towards completing this research, I have found (not I found, but God prepared) my life partner waiting for me – an experience of wholeness. When I give this manuscript for publishing, I am blessed with God's gift in our life – Jeevan (son).

This is the meaning of dalit…
It is not the caste that makes me dalit
It is not the birth that makes me dalit
The Anubhava that makes me dalit
Being Broken and Striving for Wholeness

The process of brokenness to wholeness (Dalit) was not a onetime activity. I am also not claiming that I have reached the condition of wholeness. In this dalit journey, I have to stop for a moment, look back and realise that I have to say thank you to many.

This book was originally a thesis submitted to Luther New Jr. Theological College (NTC), Dehradun during my M.Th. studies. Special thanks to M.Th./ Post-Graduate faculty panel of NTC for granting permission to publish the same. The present form is revised with a change in title and also certain additions and corrections in content. Therefore, I am responsible for the revised format of this work and its changed title.

It gives me great pleasure to record my deep sense of gratitude to my thesis mentor Rev. Dr. Jacob Mathew, then Dean of Post-Graduate Studies, Luther W. New Jr. Theological College (NTC), Dehradun, for his sincere help, generous support, personal interest, creative insights and great availability at every stage of my research.

I express my profound gratitude to Uncle George and Aunty Leela, Dr. Simon Samuel, Dr. Santhosh Sahayados, Dr. Jose L, Dr. P. V. Joseph and the entire faculty, and their family members, classmates, prayer partners and other NTCians for their love, concern and encouragement.

I am profoundly thankful to Rev. Dr. M. Stephen for writing a valuable Foreword for my book.

Thanks to New Life Biblical Seminary family, especially to Rev. Dr. Johnson Daniel and Mr. Sam C. Daniel, my colleagues and my dear students of NLBS, COTRTS, and MITS. Special thanks to Rev. Dr. N. S. Simon, Director of Zion Sangam and Benny Simon for their contributions to this research in various capacities. Also Br. Jerome for proof reading the work.

I am indebted to my mother Mrs. Beulah Gnana Bai, wife Ross Mary, mother-in-law Yanimis and also to my brothers Mathew Raj, Rajan Mathew, Jose Raj, brother-in-law Paul Yani Jayaraj and their family members for unceasing prayer support and encouragement. Our home buds Kevin, Kalvin, Teslin, Paulina, Jeevan, Nevin and others who gave wonderful time to make me aware that I am a responsible son, brother, uncle, husband and finally a father.

A word of appreciation to Sudhanshu Kanda, and the entire editorial team of Christian World Imprints for showing their interest in publishing this work.

When I concluded my research work at Seminary, I came to know the sad demise of Dr. James Massey, one of the stalwarts of Dalit theology. I pay tribute to him with this research.

Josfin Raj
Thiruvananthapuram
February 2018
josfinraj@gmail.com

Introduction

This book brings you a new perspective to look at Christ in one's dalit situation. What is dalit situation? Perhaps, normal and immediate answer would be wretched face of the caste system. Let's ponder deep into dalit life situation – don't you see another blessed side of being a dalit? Dalits who are privileged to be in the margins and resist the process of marginalization with all their efforts. I feel, the dalit experience is also similar with the broken experience of the first century early Christian community. The etymological meaning of the word 'dalit' represents "Brokenness" and "Wholeness", which gives us new way to look Jesus from an 'inclusive' term and people as 'broken' ones. By definition, dalit is an 'inclusive' term, which is able to accommodate 'all' those who experience the condition of brokenness and strive for wholeness.

Christ is inclusive. This book develops an inclusive dalit interpretation of Jesus Christ. It should be faithful to the early church faith confession as well as to the meaning of the term 'dalit'. Contemporary dalit theology uses caste or class interpretation on Christ, whereas the term 'dalit' accommodates all castes. It does not project a caste meaning. Therefore, the term dalit is used in an inclusive sense. It discards any caste and class connotation. Any interpretation on Christ based on caste, limits the Christological effect into a particular sect/caste in the society. But Christ was not a possession of a particular community. He is 'inclusive'! The early communities of faith and their approach towards Jesus Christ (faith confession) serves as a best paradigm to interpret Jesus, the Christ. Jesus Christ is the source of early church's existence and identity in their 'dalit' struggle.

Christ is not exclusive. The community who possess Christ cannot be exclusive. Let's look into early church once again. The early faith community was characterized with two things; its solidarity and integration to the weaker sections of the society, and they were the 'dalit' community itself. In addition, the community's faith confession gave them an identity of full humanness and became a parallel tradition in the dominant structures such as of Greco-Roman and Jewish of that time. Their methods of critical suspicion and healthy dialogue, i.e., *samvad* with then dominant traditions are taken as an inevitable tool in doing dalit theology in any 'dalit' context. The complete content of the faith confession helps the early community to be an 'inclusive' community altogether. But, today it is not the situation. Christ is presented as exclusive and the more extreme is that the holders of Christ are also exclusive. It is vivid in the contemporary dalit faith confession. What is the remedy for this?

This book would provide a thriving experience to explore newfound meanings and definition for the Christian faith in dalit terms. Dalit Christology proposed here is not an another attempt to present *casteised* Christ or a local dalit deity, rather to present an inclusive 'dalit' Christ, who would able to reach out oppressed and oppressors equally in their condition of brokenness and wholeness – *Inclusive Christ to Broken People.*

Major Hypothesis and Other Premises

By the emergence of dalit theology, dalit theologians claim that a real Indian Christian theology has been emerged. In wider sense, dalits, as weaker section of the society constitutes the majority of Indian people such as Scheduled Castes, Scheduled Tribes, women, children, Dravidians and so on. But, it is a categorization based on caste, gender, region, community or religion. Dalit theology emerged in this context and retain such bifurcation based on the above criteria. These criteria to interpret dait is a fallacy. If caste, region or community are not the criteria to determine dalit, then what is the criteria to interpret a person as dalit? This study reframes dalits from its etymological meaning, that is, the criterion for dalit is one's *dalitness*, not caste. This vision on dalit could embrace 'all' people irrespective of their caste or class in the society. Looking from this perspective, the present dalit Christology is not an inclusive dalit Christology in the wider sense of the term "dalit". That means, the emergence of dalit Christology not only fails to solve the caste issues but also promotes caste conflicts in India. For example, the historical dalit consciousness turns out to be dalit *deshiyata* or *dalitvad*, means dalit nationalism. It sounds similar to the *hindutva* nationalism,[1] which poses a threat to the integrity of the nation India. Again, the Christology emerged out of caste context poses Christ of *Dravidian* culture or religion, who always conflict with non-Dravidians in strict sense. Therefore, a common ground for Indian Christology is to be sought on the basis of 'dalits' in its wider sense of the

[1] Even though there is no direct relation between dalit and Hindu nationalism, but ideologically both shares same aspirations. Dalit *deshiyata* is used to refer dalit nationalism that works for the upliftment and unity of *dalitstan*, the land of dalits. The term *Hindutva* is understood normally as Hinduness. Hindu *rashtra* (nation) is also constitute the same meaning to embrace all that is Hindu, that is, race, religion, land and language. However, present day these ideologies go extremity leading to fundamentalism that tries to separate the nation India on the basis of it. Hindutva ideology propagates that India is for Hindus, and Hindus alone are the people of the land. Relation to such dominant struggle, similarly, dalit fundamentalists bring the idea of *dalitstan*, where the land belongs only for the dalits. In this manner dalit *deshiyata* became a threat for the solidarity of nation India.

meaning, which will enable, on the one hand, to solve caste conflicts and on the other hand to work for the integration of nation India.

The early Christian community represented the 'dalits' of that time who were oppressed by the powers of religious, political, and intellectual world. The context of Jewish, Roman, and Hellenistic oppression and persecution caused the dalitness of the early church. Albeit the early church represented different communities of faith in the Palestine and beyond from the first century to the fourth century C.E., this work limited to the communities' common struggle for identity in its strange context. The response of the early Church to their weird context was not with communal nationalism or establishing "Christendom" by annihilating existing socio-political power. But rather they were in the process of emancipation and solidarity with the existing structures, not as subjugators, but as having a dignified identity. It reflected in their Christological expressions as they addressed Jesus as "the Christ" or "the Lord" or "the Logos" in the strange context. Such Christological expressions bestowed them a positive identity in Christ that eventually helped them to aspire and work for socio-economic and cultural emancipation that went along with national integration. They presented Jesus as superior to the existing dominant traditions of that time with a high consciousness of equality with them in midst of their dalitness.

The dalitness of Jesus of Nazareth in/of the New Testament texts is much emphasized. Jesus of Nazareth of/in the 'text', who is both dalit and liberator, has been the icon for contemporary dalit Christological discourses. Contemporary dalit theologians argue that Christ of faith, who was the object of the early church community's faith confession (icon) does not have any access to the concrete realities of dalits. It became a fashion to ignore Christ of faith and depend only on historical Jesus in doing dalit Christology. Don't you feel here a suspicion? We should not bypass any such Christological reduction. But, from a dalit point of view 'the text' always carry a connotation of oppression. Dalits were the subjects to 'the text' as tool for oppressors throughout century. Reading or re-reading the 'text' is a partial acceptance of the oppression. Then, one needs to depend on the early church's tradition(s) to articulate dalit theology. The early faith community's tradition(s), in the early centuries, was the marginalized 'dalit' tradition of that time. Perhaps the tradition of the early church carried forth Christ of faith than the Jesus of Nazareth. Then, Jesus Christ in/of New Testament must be viewed as the faith affirmation of the early Christian community in the midst of their 'dalitness'. That means, the term dalit does not merely constitute a particular group of people of a particular place. Dalit includes the person/s going through *dalitness*. In this wider inclusive spectrum, researcher envisions an authentic 'Indian' and 'dalit' Christology. The suitable paradigm can render from the early Church. They proclaimed Jesus as the Christ, the Logos, and the Lord over their dalitness. The main content of their faith confession, we find, emphasize both historical particularity of Jesus of Nazareth, one who they now consider as their

Christ of faith. Such Christological affirmation gave them new identity in Jesus at the same time solidarity with national pathos. It leads us to reconsider the present dalit Christology which is lopsided with historical Jesus derived from the text alone, which promotes caste conflicts and social disintegration. The 'con'textual Jesus of the early Church's expression is more concrete and appropriate to the dalit consciousness.

Major questions arise in this juncture are following: How a Christology can be constructed inclusively relevant for dalits in India in the light of the early faith confession on Jesus the Christ? What are the limitations of present dalit Christology to solve caste issues and conflicts that threaten national integrity of India? How far the 'dalitness' of the early Church has contributed to the formulation of early Christology? How one can identify the commonalities of the early Church situation with present dalits? How far "Jesus, the Christ of the early Church" is relevant for the emancipation of dalits and integration of Indian subcontinent?

The research work is important in different ways. It supplements the existing dalit Christology from the life experience of the early Church instead of 'the text'. It considers that the historical Jesus and Christ of faith is equally important in doing dalit Christology, and at times Christ of faith needs to be emphasized much since it is the expression of the early church's dalit experiences. It helps 'all' dalits to accept a dignified Jesus in their dalitness. Socio-politically, the research seeks for national integration, social harmony and emancipation of the dalits of all strata of society. It would be a correction and re-construction to the present consciousness of dalit *deshiyata*. Missiologically, the re-constructed Christology would play a vital role to reach a wider community since it accommodates common dalitness of India.

An integrative approach is maintained throughout this book. Historical and socio-political tools are employed to analyze dalits as 'broken people', their 'dalit' consciousness, and the emergence of dalit *deshiyata*. The same tool will be employed to understand the dalitness of the early faith community.

This book has four parts. First part frames the (ab)use of the term 'dalit' in various ways throughout history and recommends a working definition based mainly on etymological study. It also analyses the Christian theological reflections on 'dalit.' Second part analyses the faith confession of the early church community in their context of dalitness. Third part re-views the contemporary dalit Christology in the light of the early faith confession. In the final part, an attempt is made to propose an 'inclusive dalit Christology' to solve issues in the caste-conflicted society like India. Hence, this book proposes a Christology relevant for 'dalits' in India in the light of the early faith confession on Christ.

1

'Dalit' in Dalit Movements and Contemporary Dalit Theological Discourses: A Re-Consideration

Introduction

The term 'dalit' is commonly used in relation to untouchability and caste oppression experienced by a particular (out)caste group in Indian situation. Further, the dalit community is defined as a community in relation to caste (either inside of caste system or outside of it). This chapter reconsiders such traditional usages of 'dalit' and argues that caste or class mode of interpretation is against the real meaning of the a-caste term 'dalit'.

Contemporary Indian society carries forward, other than indigenous tribal traditions, three unique traditions/streams in its national discourses; they are brahmanic, dalit and Marxist discourses. When caste or class becomes the criteria for determining who dalit is, dalits become part and parcel of brahmanical or communist (Marxist) traditions. Hence, here, the researcher questions the legitimacy of categorizing dalits as a 'caste/class community' and tries to re-formulate the meaning of dalits as the people who experience *dalitness*. Thus, an in-depth study is rendered to explore complete etymological meaning of the term 'dalit' that would permit us to argue that *dalitness* is the base for dalits, not necessarily caste or class. This realistic interpretation of the term 'dalit' would supersede popular conceptions or misconceptions *per se* which limit the experience of dalit in relation to the caste system and its aftermath.

Further, it precedes with a historical analysis of the dalit movements and their philosophical strands that would help us to produce epistemological premise of dalits, that is, *dalitism*.[1] In addition, the study allows to critic the present (mis)use of the term dalit in both secular movements and in the Indian Christian

[1] *Dalitism* can be defined as philosophy ('ism') of dalits.

theological thinking that even can affect the integrity of the nation India. This critical approach would help us to construct an alternative dalit theology, purely in dalit terms with dalit natures. Thus, the attempt here is to interpret critically the concept of 'dalit' etymologically, historically and theologically. It would serve as a rapport between early faith community and their faith confession and contemporary dalits and their Christology.

1.1 Quest for the Term 'Dalit' in Indian Context

As already indicated, the term "dalit" has been interpreted mainly in two ways, such as: class and caste based interpretation. Class interpretation subsumes dalits within class or occupational categories, for instance, peasants, agricultural labour, factory workers, students and the like.[2] Caste based communal analysis provides the idea that the dalits are the people within Hindu fold who belong to those castes which Hindu religion considers to be polluted by virtue of hereditary occupation, i.e., *kula dharma* (caste duty).[3] These two interpretations *misrepresent* the meaning of the term dalit. On contrary the term dalit disowns or disregards any caste or class interpretation.[4] The argument here is that the criteria of defining dalit is the condition of *dalitness,* neither caste nor class. Therefore, an attempt is made to propose the *adi* (prime) usage of the term dalit in order to excavate 'the dalit meaning of the term dalit.' For that the word's etymology, historical usage and contemporary adoption in mainstream discourses is discussed in this particular section.

1.1.1 Etymology of the term 'Dalit'

Contemporary usage of the term dalit as 'low caste' will be discarded, when one finds the etymological meaning of the term. In Sanskrit, the term dalit is a

---

[2] Marxist interpretations on dalit can be seen in most of the subaltern studies including Dalit Panther manifesto – says Saral K. Chatterji in "Why Dalit Theology?," in *Indigenous People: Dalits, Dalit Issues in Today's Theological Debate* 1994, edited by James Massey (Delhi: ISPCK, 2006), 180.

[3] See J. R. Kamble, *Rise and Awakening of Depressed Classes in India* (New Delhi: National Publishing House, 1979). Also Atul Chandra Pradhan, *The Emergence of the Depressed Classes* (Bhubaneshwar: Bookland International, 1986). Also S.K. Gupta, *The Schedule Caste in Modern Indian Politics: Their Emergence as a Political Power* (Delhi: Munshiram Manoharlal, 1989). Also Trilok Nath, *Politics of the Depressed Classes* (Delhi: Deputy Publications, 1987).

[4] Deenbandhu Manchala proposes that the term dalit can include all those who oppose, reject, and strive to eradicate caste and class. Deenbandhu Manchala, "Expanding the Ambit: Dalit Theological Contribution to Ecumenical Social Thought," in Santhinathan Clarke, Manchela Deenabandhu and Vinod Philip Peacock, eds., *Dalit Theology in the Twenty First Century: Discordant Voices, Discerning Pathways* (New Delhi: OUP, 2010), 52. See also Paul Chirakkarode, "The Dalits and the Left in Kerala," *The Dalit Desiyata: The Kerala Experience in Development and Class Struggle,* edited by A. M. Abraham Ayrookuzhiel (Delhi: ISPCK, published for Bangalore: CISRS, 1990), 52-71.

passive participle of the verb *dal* which means to oppress, crack, tear, break etc.[5] When used as a noun or adjective, it means burst, split, broken or torn asunder, downtrodden, scattered, crushed, destroyed, etc.[6] As a noun, dalit can be used for all three genders, masculine, feminine and neuter. There are other possible words constitute with dalit such as *Dalana,* means tearing or causing to burst, *Dalita,* means split, broken, destroyed, scattered, torn asunder. The noun *dala*, besides the meaning of splitting, has also a *positive connotation. Dala* means 'unfolding itself' (*dala-komala,* a lotus *dala kosal* a jasmine, an imagery taken from the writings of Brahmabandhav Upadhaya).[7] Theoretically, it is an act happens within to become a complete being. This is a positive affirmation of the term dalit. Thus, Indian tradition possess double meaning of the term 'dalit'; on the one hand it is the condition of brokenness and on the other hand it is the strive for wholeness.

However, the term *dalit* can trace its origin back to pre-biblical and pre-classical Sanskrit era that goes beyond the contemporary meaning of 'low caste.'[8] In Old Assyrian noun *dullu* means trouble, toil, misery. Probably, it is a derivative of a verb *dalālu*, which means "to be miserable." Late Babylonian has the causative *dullulu*, "to oppress," "oppressed," "oppression."[9] There are two possible derivations such from Sumerian *dul*, "overcome," "to cover," and *dul* "depth," "sinking depression."[10] In Akkadian the verbal root *dalālu* has the basic meaning "to be miserable, poor," and in causative stem "to oppress."[11] In addition,

[5] A. P. Nirmal, "Doing Theology from a Dalit Perspective," in *A Reader in Dalit Theology*, edited by Arvind P. Nirmal (Chennai: Gurukul Lutheran Theological College & Research Institute, np, reprint 2007), 139. Also James Massey, "History and Dalit Identity," in *Dalit Solidarity,* edited by Bhagavan Das & James Massey (Delhi: ISPCK, 1995), 9. Also Anupama Rao, *The Caste Question: Dalits and the Politics of Modern India* (Ranikhet: Permanent Black, 2009), 1. Also Himansu Charan Sadangi, *Dalits: The Downtrodden India* (Delhi: ISHA Books, 2008), 60. Also Arun Dangle, "Dalit Literature: Past, Present and Future," translated by Avinash S. Pandit and Daya Agarwal in *Poisoned Bread: Translations from Modern Marathi Dalit Literature*, edited by Arjun Dangle (Hyderabad: Orient Longman, 1992, reprinted 1994), 264.

[6] Arvind P. Nirmal, *Heuristic Explorations* (Madras: The Christian Literature Service for the Gurukul Lutheran Theological College and Research Institute, 1990), 139. Also James Massey, *Roots: A Concise History of Dalits*, 2nd rev. 1991 (Published for CISRS, Bangalore by Delhi: ISPCK, 1994), 6. Also Kancha Ilaiah, *Why I am Not a Hindu: A Sudhra Critique of Hindutva Philosophy, Culture, and Political Economy*. 2nd edition (Calcutta: Samy, 2005), viii.

[7] I. Prasad, "Gems from India: Dalit," *VJTR* 65/4 (April, 2001): 320.

[8] Ancient form of the term dalit can be seen in Semitic languages. Semitic language refers to a group of ancient Akkadian (Babylonian) languages. Bonn Fabry, "דל," in *Theological Dictionary of Old Testament,* Vol. III, 1978, edited by G. Johannes Botterweck and Helmer Ringgren (Grand Rapid, Michigan: William B. Eerdmans Publishing Company, reprint 1988), 208.

[9] Bonn Fabry, "דַּל," 209.

[10] Bonn Fabry, "דַּל," 209.

[11] M. Daniel Carroll, "דַּלל," in *New International Dictionary of Old Testament Theology and Exegesis*, Vol. 1, edited by Williem A. Van Germeren (Michigan: Zondervan Publishing House, 1997), 951.

dullum means "trouble, oppression, distress, which penetrates to the heart, causes grief, and makes the heart burn."[12] In Ugaritic the root means "to make poor," or "oppress."[13] Semitic tradition also witnesses the double meaning of the term 'dalit' as oppress and overcome.

The parallel of the term dalit can also see in Hebraic tradition. In Hebrew language, the word *dall* can be identified as the root word.[14] It has various connotations as far as the Hebrew scripture is concerned – argues J. David Plenis. In the prophetical writings *dal* is an object of exploitation.[15] *Dal* can also further connote as (1) unfair treatment in legal cases (Isa. 10:2; 11:4); (2) unfair grain taxes paid to the large landowners (Amos 5:11); (3) Abuses in the debt slavery system (Amos 8:6); and (4) a lack of grazing land (Isa. 14:30).[16] The word *dal* is also used to indicate the political weakness of one group in relation to another (Judges 6:15; 2 Sam 3:1) and physically worn out (2 Sam. 13:4).[17] The expression can refer to physical weakness, but more often it refers to those who are *powerless due to low social status* (Italic is mine).[18] Further, the term refers to the *psychosomatic weakness* (2 Sam. 13:2).[19] It is also a *social concept*, especially in the book of Covenant and Priestly Code. As a social concept, *dal* is not adequately understood as a "proletarian who has no property" or as "one who has no property." Instead, *dal* pictures him/her as a free and full citizen, whose "property is small," who is perpetually caught up in the struggle to make a daily living by hard work, who in this constant grind has to give up his independence to large extent, and who is thus a "little man" and "helpless," particularly in court, where he needs special protection. In addition, *dal* also constitutes, one is that his possessions are withheld from him (Prov. 14:31) by naked forces (Prov. 22:22).[20] Perhaps the term also can refer to poor peasant farmers.[21] Their poverty and lack of status leaves them

---

[12] Bonn Fabry, "דַל," 213.

[13] The nominative form appears in an oft-cited passage in the Epic of Keret. King Keret is criticised by Yassib for allowing the poor to suffer affliction, thus failing to fulfil his royal duty towards the needy. M. Daniel Carroll, "דלל," 951.

[14] Francis Brown, *A Hebrew and English Lexicon of the Old Testament*, 1907, translated by Edward Robinson (Oxford: Clarendon Press, 1974), 195.

[15] J. David Plenis, "Poor, Poverty," in *The Anchor Bible Dictionary*, Vol. 5, edited by David Noel Freedman (New York: Doubleday, 1992), 403.

[16] J. David Plenis, "Poor, Poverty," 403.

[17] J. David Plenis, "Poor, Poverty," 405.

[18] D. E. Holwerda, "Poor," in *The International Standard Bible Encyclopaedia,* Vol. 3, rev. 1915, edited by Geoffrey W. Bromiley (Grandrapids, Michigan: William B. Eerdmans Publishing Company, 1986), 905.

[19] C.U. Wolf, "Poor," in *The Interpreter's Dictionary of the Bible: An Illustrated Encyclopaedia,* Vol. 3, 1962, edited by George Arthur Buttrick (Nashville: Abingdon Press, 15th printing 1985), 843. Also Bonn Fabry, "דל," 218.

[20] Bonn Fabry, "דל," 218-219.

[21] See M. Daniel Carroll, "דלל," 951.

exposed to injustice and thus helpless before cruel oppression within society.[22] In short, the term *dal* in the Hebrew language depicts the socially, politically, economically and psychologically marginalized elements of society and refers to 'complete brokenness.'[23] In the Hebrew language, *dal* is related semantically to the description of a quality and not to numerical quantity.[24]

In nutshell, etymological study provides the meaning of dalit as a condition of being broken and at the same time a quality of being whole. On the one side, the term becomes an umbrella for socially less recognized, economically underprivileged, politically facing injustice, physically abused, psychologically feeling lowest, culturally impaired, religiously polluted and so on. It reveals the vulnerability of human condition as 'dalit.' It is a condition of exploitation and oppression of an *undefined character*.[25] That means, dalit is a condition – condition of brokenness. On the other side, the term dalit is a status of 'overcoming' and 'unfolding.'[26] It stands in contrast to society's elites, having the energy to unfold and overcome itself. Thus, 'dalit' means people's positive striving for wholeness in a broken human condition.[27] These two dimensions needs to be taken in account as a basic definition of the term dalit.

1.1.2 Historical Usage of the term 'Dalit'

The usage of the term 'dalit' in public discourses is a recent phenomenon. Because, historically, the dominant brahmanical tradition regularly engaged in activities of naming other miniature traditions such as of dalit tradition as *Asura* (a divine being disfigured and hostile to brahmanic gods), *Rakshas* (demon or sub-human beings), *Mlecha* (degraded one), *Avarna* (caste less or without color), *Dasa/Dasyu* (servant or slave), *Chandala* (the most degraded of all mortals), *Panchama* (fifth caste), *Shvapaka* (one who eats dog's meat or dead animal's meat), *Varishals*, and so on.[28] Naming dalits as *Harijan* (Hari's Children) is also considered as a derogative term.[29] This naming activity had affected the very being, personhood, self-image

[22] M. Daniel Carroll, "דלל," 951.

[23] J. David Plenis, "Poor, Poverty," 405.

[24] Bonn Fabry, "דל," 218.

[25] J. David Plenis, "Poor, Poverty," 403.

[26] L. Prasad says, "The present struggle and self-assertion of the dalits can be linked with the positive connotation of *dala*: it is the dalits' unfolding their creative energies to establish a new society without oppressed and oppressors." L. Prasad, "Dalit," 320.

[27] Cf. Dionysius Rasquinha, "A Critical Reflection on the Meaning of Dalit Christian Theology," *VJTR* 66/4 (April, 2002): 252.

[28] Dionysius Rasquinha, *Towards Wholeness from Brokenness-The Dalit Quest: A Historical Analysis and Theological Response* (Delhi: ISPCK, 2013), 83.

[29] Gandhi's usage of *Harijans* is also perceived as derogatory and oppressive term today, since *Harijan* was originally used to denote the children of temple prostitutes because of the anonymity of their paternity. In addition, the term *Harijan* has been widely used by caste Hindus as a substitute for *achchuta*, i.e., untouchable. Gandhi borrowed the name from Narsinh Mehta, a Bhakti saint of

and identity of the 'named' dalit.[30] Therefore, historically, dalit conceptions had been (mis)carried with negative titles. Moreover, these terminologies are misrepresentation of the actual dalit traditions in India. In this particular context, it is a significant matter to deliberately choose their title as 'dalit' by themselves, because, it is this occasion that they enjoyed the privilege of naming themselves.[31] It asserts their identity, rights and self–respect.

During 1960s and following years witnessed a popular usage of the term dalit, especially because of the Dalit Panther Movement (henceforth DPM).[32] DPM traced back its origin from Jotirao Phule (1827 – 1890 Common Era, hence forth C. E.) and Ambedkar (1891 – 1956 C. E.), though the term dalit was used in Hindi and Marathi translation for 'Depressed Classes' during 1930s only.[33] Jotirao Phule, known as Mahatma,[34] consciously used this term to describe the untouchables and the oppressed victims of Hindu society.[35]

---

the 17th century C. E. See Santhinathan Clark, Manchela Deenabandhu and Vinod Philip Peacock, eds., "Introduction," to *Dalit Theology in the Twenty First Century: Discordant Voices, Discerning Pathways* (New Delhi: OUP, 2010), 8. Also L. Prasad, "Dalit," 320.

[30] Harry Emmanuel, "Violence Against Dalits: An Indian Christian Response," *Violence and Its Victims: A Challenge to Philosophising in the Indian Context*, edited by Ivo Coelho (Bangalore: ATC, 2010), 318.

[31] Other terms used instead of dalit to designate depressed peoples in India, but insufficient in many ways Identifying untouchables as 'dalit' has its own significance according to P. Mohan Larbeer, "1. It is a title chosen by ourselves. 2. It explains our own situation of suffering. 3. It is a political term which inspires us to revolt. 4. It is an all inclusive word which can bring many others into its fold in the process of change." P. Mohan Larbeer, "Dalit Identity- A Theological Reflection," 381. Also L. Prasad, "Dalit," 320. Also Ghanshyam Shah, "Introduction: Dalit Politics," in *Dalit Identity and Politics: Cultural Subordination and the Dalit Challenge*, Vol. 2, edited by Ghanshyam Shah (New Delhi: Sage Publications, 2001), 20-21. Also James Massey, "Christian Dalits: A Historical Perspective," in *Journal of Dharma* 1/1 (Jan.-March, 1991): 44-45. Also "A Vision of a Dalit" in *NCCR* CXII/7 (Aug., 1994): 573.

[32] See 1.2.3 Contemporary Dalit Movements.

[33] In 1930 C. E. there was a Depressed Classes newspaper published in Pune called *Dalit Bandu* (Friend of Dalits). John C. B. Webster, "Who is a Dalit?," 68. Also Atul Chandra Pradhan, *The Emergence of the Depressed Classes*, 125. Also Arvind Sharma, *Reservation and Affirmative Action: Models of Social Integration in India* (New Delhi: Sage Publication, 2005), 151.

[34] The title of 'Mahatma,' in India is designated only to two persons. Primarily to Mohandas Karamchand Gandhi is designated as 'mahatma.' It is historical at the same to less known truth that the title 'Mahatma' is designed to Jotirao Phule, a social reformer from the backward community of Maharashtra by Gandhi himself. Dhanjay Keer, *Mahatma Jotirao Phooley: Father of Indian Social Revolution*. Reprint 2002 (Bombay: Popular Prakashan, 1964), ix, 29 and 241.

[35] Jotirao Govindraw Pule, *Slavery in the Civilized British Government under the Cloak of Brahmanism* (Np: Pune City Press, 1873), 127. Also James Massey, *Roots*, 6. Also *Down Trodden: The Struggle of India's Dalits for Identity, Solidarity and Liberation* (Geneva: WCC Publication, 1997), 11-22. Also Eleanor Zelliot, *From Untouchable to Dalit* (New Delhi, 1992), 271.

Ambedkar chose the term 'broken men' [*sic*], an English translation of 'dalit.'[36] Consequently, DPM promoted the term in a wider sense including "members of the Scheduled Castes and Tribes, neo-Buddhists, the working people, the landless, poor peasants, women and all those who were being exploited politically, economically, and in the name of religion."[37] By using the term 'dalit,' DPM denotes the idea of a particular segregated communities in India who have been confronting oppression, and their condition of being deprived, oppressed people and their proud struggle for liberation from the inter-connected oppression of caste and class.[38] Thus, the DPM's concept of 'dalit' goes beyond the caste to class-and-caste as inter-related.[39] Further, the term dalit also connotes an ideology for fundamental change in the social structure and relationships.[40] In the words of James Massey, "The basic meaning of the term 'dalit' is not "poor" (economically) or "caste", it really denotes the state to which a certain section of people of a particular society have been reduced through a systematic historical-religious process of trampling them down. It refers to the broken or trodden-down state of people." In that sense, dalitness is a situation or experience of becoming an object of systematic oppression in subjugation. And dalit is a person who undergoes the dalitness.

Albeit the wider meaning is prevalent, there are obscure usages rampant among 'particular' people groups to make dalit as people of caste only.[41] Indian constitution uses Scheduled 'Caste' to refer dalits instead of Depressed 'Class' that had been used by British Government that generally referred to the deprived condition of common majority people of India.[42] The replacement of the term

---

[36] Though, B. R. Ambedkar did not popularize the word 'dalit' for untouchables, but his philosophy has remained a key source in its emergence and popularity. He had often described the outcastes as untouchable broken people, although he does not seem to have explicitly used the term dalit. John C. B. Webster, "Who is a Dalit?," 68. Also Ghanshyam Shah, "Introduction: Dalit Politics," 22.

[37] M. E. Prabhakar, "The Search for a Dalit Theology," in *Indigenous People: Dalits, Dalit Issues in Today's Theological Debate* 1994, edited by James Massey (Delhi: ISPCK, 2006), 36.

[38] See M. E. Prabhakar, "Dalit Concerns in the Context of Religious Fundamentalism in India," in *Religious Fundamentalism: An Asian Perspective*, edited by J. Augustine (Bangalore: SATHRI, CCA/WARC, 1993), 84.

[39] Gail Omvedt, *Dalits Visions: The Anti-Caste Movement and the Construction of an Indian Identity* (Hyderabad: Orient Longman, 1995), 72.

[40] Ghanshyam Shah, "Introduction: Dalit Politics," 22. Also Sanjay Parwan and Paramanshi Jaideva, eds., "Introduction," to *Encyclopaedia of Dalits in India: Leaders*, Vol. 4 (Delhi: Kalpaz Publications, 2002), 11.

[41] Namdevo Desal, pioneer of DPM, found the trend of misusing 'dalit' in castiestic gain and appeal for wider usage of the term. Later, this obscure use of the title dalit in caste terms for particular communities caused him to quit DPM. Lyla Bavadam, "Obituary: Voice of the Oppressed," *Frontline* 31/2 (Feb 7, 2014): 116.

[42] The Government of India Act of 1935 replaced 'Scheduled Class' by what is now called 'Scheduled Castes.' Change of title also a kind of brahmanical act arguing for the reservation only

'caste' over 'class' can be seen as a transition from 'class interpretation' of dalits into 'caste interpretation' of the depressed people in India. It is a narrow or parochial view of the term, in which caste or class becomes the sole criterion to determine who is a dalit.[43] Dalits do not subscribe to any caste interpretation that keeps them 'low.' For example, according to the 1891 Madras Census Commissioner noted Nadars (Shanars is original title) in South India belongs to polluting caste, where Nadars objected violently claiming the position of Kshetriyas.[44] Nor they adopt class as their definition. The dalitness is neither limited to brahmanical/caste oppression alone, nor class oppression. But rather it must be a broader terminology that encompasses all those considered to be broken in every respect.[45] 'Dalit' represents 'holistic pathos' which integrates caste and class issues along with other components that contribute for the common *dalitness*.[46]

In nutshell, the term 'dalit' has *no* caste or class connotation in strict sense. Casteism is a contemporary ascription to the term. The term Dalit goes beyond caste and class interpretation and its implications. Then one has to remove such particularistic nature of the term and the fallacies attached to it in the present dalit discourses. Then the question is, who is dalits? Arvind P. Nirmal describes dalits in six senses that is in line with etymology; "(1) the broken, the torn, the rent, the burst, the split; (2) the opened, the expanded; (3) the bisected; (4) the driven asunder, the dispelled, the scattered; (5) the downtrodden, the crushed,

---

people belongs to Hindu religious fold according to the Presidential Order 1950. The Scheduled Castes (dalits) were divested of their minority status during the constitution debates of 1947 and given safeguards, by the manipulations of Sri. K. M. Munshi, saying, "*Harijans* are part and parcel of Hindu community. Safeguards are given to them till they are absorbed in the Hindu community." M. E. Prabhakar establishes, Munshi's untruth won the day. Ambedkar warned against the conclusion that the Hindu and untouchables have a common religion. The after effect of this situation was that the converts from scheduled caste origins lost their status of SC status although s/he "remains economically, educationally, socially and politically backward as much as before conversion." It also noted that usage of the term 'dalit' is unconstitutional. M. John, "The Church in the Service of Dalits: Statistics and Policy," 122-123. Also M. E. Prabhakar, "The Search for a Dalit Theology," 43. Also Ch. Vasantha Rao, "Dalit Christians' Struggle for Justice in the Indian Sub-continent," in *Towards Theology of Justice for Life in Peace: Minjung-Dalit Theological Dialogue*, edited by kwon Jinkwan and P. Mohan Larbeer (Bangalore: BTESSC, 2012), 63. Also Madhu Chandra, "Dalit Christian Reservation – Then and Now," *Religion and Society* 55/4 (Dec., 2010): 65. Also Subash C. Kashyap, *Our Constitution: An Introduction to Indian's Constitution and Constitutional Law*, 1994, 2nd edition (New Delhi: National Book Trust, reprint 2000), 272-273. Also P. M. Bakshi, *The Constitution of India with Comments and Subject Index*, 1st edition, 1991, 3rd edition 1996 (Delhi: Universal Book Traders, reprint 1999), 261-269. Also M. V. Pylee, *An Introduction to the Constitution of India*. 5th edition (New Delhi: Vikas Publishing House, 2007).

[43] John C. B. Webster, "Who is a Dalit?," 68.

[44] See Nicholas B. Dirks, *Castes of Mind: Colonialism and the Making of Modern India* (Delhi: Permanent Black, 2001), 239.

[45] John C. B. Webster, "Who is a Dalit?," *Dalits in Modern India: Vision and Values*, edited by S. M. Michael (New Delhi: Vistaar Publications, 1999), 68.

[46] John C. B. Webster, "Who is a Dalit?," 68.

the destroyed; (6) the manifested, the displayed."[47] In short, dalits are people who experience the condition of brokenness and strive for wholeness.

Thus, above analysis rejects any implication of the term dalit for any particular communities which are based on caste or class. When caste or class 'names' a community, the nature of the community become caste/class exclusive. That means, from a caste or a class point of view, the term dalit is exclusive that denies the nature of 'dalit' which embraces 'any' or 'all' who experience dalitness. More clearly, when the condition of *dalitness* is applied to people group of a particular caste, dalit becomes caste community. This is not acceptable. Because, dalits are not necessarily 'dalit' because of their low-caste status, but only because of the experience or the condition of *dalitness*. That means, the naming of a particular people as dalits must be based on the experience of *dalitness*, not on caste or class.

Briefly, the 'term' dalit does not attempt to signify another caste identity, but rather names the aspirations and the dynamism to forge a collective movement, as recent dalit theologians argue. This inclusive nature allows dalits to encompass other subjugated identities to establish a new humanity and creation. Thus, the term dalit signifies an identity that is *dynamic and open* because this will be more effective to mobilize and heal broken and crushed identities, as Clarke, Manchela and Vinod proposes in their ground breaking work on dalit theology.[48] In this alternative framework, 'dalit' is *inclusive* in nature, *holistic* in approach and '*undefined dalitness*' is the criterion. Then the term dalit would be a celebration for all weaker sections of the Indian society. This would be more authentic expression of 'dalit' in Indian context of diversified pathos.

1.2 Dalit Movements and their 'Dalit' Discourses in India

The term movement refers to a group of people who share the same aim and work together to achieve it. It also means that change leading towards improving situation or solving a problem. Then, dalit movements are movements lead by the people group who experienced dalitness by aiming at improving of human situation in their dalitness.[49] It is a process of people having an aim to solve or improve the 'dalit' situation and leads to emancipation.[50] These movements are difficulty to identify, because of its caste-class reading.[51] Thus, this section

[47] A. P. Nirmal, *Heuristic Explorations*, 139.

[48] Clarke, Manchela, and Vinod, eds., "Introduction," to *Dalit Theology...*, 5-6, 13.

[49] Cf. R. K. Kshirsagar, *Dalit Movements in India and Its Leaders* (New Delhi: M.D. Publications, 1994), 4-5.

[50] T. K. John, "Method of Collaboration in Theological Journey," in *Dalit-Tribal Theological Interface: Current Trends in Subaltern Theologies*, edited by James Massey and Shimreingam Shimray (Jorhat and New Delhi: TSC/WSC and CDS, 2007), 248.

[51] Dalit scholars opines that there has not been a single, unified dalit movement in the country. Notwithstanding the difficulty of identifying dalit movements, Ghanshyam Shah classifies them

would analyze the movements and attempts made to change brokenness of the humanity into wholeness in the Indian history from dalit point of view.[52] Further, this historical analysis would give importance to the emergence and development of dalit epistemology/discourses that nurtured and sustained of the weaker sections of the Indian society throughout centuries along with their movements. That means, dalit movements are coxswain with dalit epistemology/discourses, which may overlap its expression in different periods.[53] Therefore, mainly, in this historical analysis one could find emergence of an alternative Indian stream, i.e., dalit, strongly in opposition to dominant traditions of the society, especially, of brahamanic tradition.

1.2.1 Ancient Movements

Recurrently the Indic philosophy is defined in terms of the discourse between elitism[54] and *bahujan*.[55] Origination of dalit movements, as etiquette in dalit studies, traces back to the struggle of *Charvakas* against Aryan domination whom usually are recognized as the propagators of caste ideology for the purpose

---

into (a) reformative and (b) alternative movements. The Dalit Reformative Movements try to reform the caste system to solve the problem of untouchablity and the Dalit Alternative Movements attempt to create an alternative socio-cultural structure by conversion to other religions or by acquiring education, economic status and political power. The reformative movements further divided into Bhakti movement, neo-vedantic movement, and sanskritisation movement. The alternative movement are divided into conversion movement and religious or secular movements. Ghanshyam Shah, "Dalit Movements and the Search for Identity," *Dalit Identity and Politics: Cultural Subordination and the Dalit Challenge,* Vol. 2, edited by Ghanshyam Shah (New Delhi: Sage Publications, 2001), 195. Also see Ghanshyam Shah, "Anti-Untouchability Movements," in *Caste, Caste-Conflict and Reservations* (New Delhi: Ajanta, 1985).

[52] R. S. Sharma, *Rethinking India's Past* (New Delhi: Oxford University Press, 2009), 291-292. Also A. Bardhan, "Caste-Class Situation in India," in *Caste and Class in India*, edited by K. L. Sharma (Jaipur & New Delhi: Rawat Publications, 1994), 408.

[53] The overlapping of dalit movement exemplified in ancient Buddhism and contemporary neo-Buddhism, medieval Bhakti cult and influence on Phule, Ambedkar and Periyar. Buddhist influence on Bhkati movements and so on. These alternative movements are both continuation of past and persisting in present in Indian society. Katti Padma Rao, *Caste and Alternative Culture*, 60, 113.

[54] Elitism can, perhaps, compare with Brahmanism and other ideology that works for the benefits of high class/caste minority of Indian society.

[55] The term *bahujan*, means majority Indian ordinary people, represents an alternative term for dalits. The bahujan ideology stands opposite to the elite section of the community. It is a confrontation of ordinary as opposed to oligarchy. This philosophical strand most lean towards the upliftment and express common people of the society. Gopal Guru writes, "use of the dalit category based on the ontological category is class, hence it is undesirable.... In recent years, some politicians discarded the Dalit category as a socially reactionary, negative one and sought to replace it with the 'Bahujan' category." Gopal Guru, "The Language of Dalit-Bahujan Political Discourse," in *Dalit Identity and Politics*, Cultural Subordination and the Dalit Challenge, Vol. 2, edited by Ghanshyam Shah (New Delhi: Sage Publications, 2001), 98.

of exploiting the indigenous people.[56] Next to the *Charvakas*, *Tantriks* put up a severe fight against the domination of caste and *varna*.[57] Dalit thinkers called both of these strands as *Lokayatas* or *Lokayatikas*, who were "pro-people and proto-materialist" aiming at welfare of the 'whole' society.[58] Further, the counter tradition of egalitarianism against Vedic Brahmanism represented by a differentiated heterodoxy is called as *Shramanism*.[59] Braj Ranjan Mani argues that a Shraman can be identified as the practitioners of Buddhism and Jainism as well as all those opposed to the Vedic religion.[60]

It is argued that Buddhism emerged as a reaction to the so-called brahmanic orthodoxy. Buddha not only emphasized the *Lokayata* view but strengthened it by dialectising it more.[61] Buddhism became a popular movement because of its concern over the social questions of the day.[62] At time when Brahmanism made '*Braman hitya brahman sukhaya*' (the pleasures and prosperity of Brahmans is most important) as their main slogan, Buddha believes in *Bahujana hitya Bahujana sukhya* (The prosperity and pleasure of majority of people is the most important

[56] *Charvakas* are misrepresented in the Vedic religious texts as *asura* or demons. See Katti Padma Rao, *Caste and Alternative Culture* (Madras: The Gurukul Lutheran Theological College and Research Institute/Centre for Research on New International Economic Order, 1995), 59, 144. Also see 1.1.2. Historical Usage of the Term 'Dalit'- for details on the titles used by brahamanical tradition to denote non-brahamnical traditions from ancient time onwards.

[57] *Tantriks* were followed a matriarchal system, rejected Aryan's socio-religious systems. Katti Padma Rao, *Caste and Alternative Culture*, 60.

[58] *Lokayatas*, also known as *Barhaspatya*, were the earliest Dalit-Bahujans who fought against the Aryan invaders who gradually established the Brahminical socio-political and economical system in India. Lokayats were materialists and rejected karma, *punarjanma* (rebirth) and *moksha* (salvation). It was called *lokayat*, since the ideology was prevalent (*lokesu*) amongst people. Brhaspati (Ca. 7th century – 6th century B. C. E) is believed to be the founder of *Charvaka-Lokaytika* school. Ghanshyam Shah, "Introduction: Dalit Politics," 23. Also Kancha Ilaiah, "Dalitism vs Brahmanism: The Epistemological Conflict in History," *Dalit Identity and Politics: Cultural Subordination and the Dalit Challenge*, Vol. 2, edited by Ghanshyam Shah (New Delhi: Sage Publications, 2001), 113, 127. Also Braj Ranjan Mani, *Debrahmanising History: Dominance and Resistance in Indian Society* (New Delhi: Manohar, 2005), 74. Also Ram Puniyani, *Religion and Politics: Essays on Contemporary Issues* (Thiruvananthapuram: Mythri Books, 2009), 97.

[59] Shramanic tradition is a tradition of resistance and equality propounded by Shramans, who were non-vedic and antagonistic to the brahmanical religion and politics. Braj Ranjan Mani, *Debrahmanising History*, 41, 45-84.

[60] Braj Ranjan Mani, *Debrahmanising History*, 417.

[61] Kancha Ilaiah argues that, "Buddha had nailed Brahmanism when he declared 'where name and form is, there is cognition.' He realized that name is only an expression of forms. To attack brahmanical notion of God being all-pervasive, 'unseen and untouched', Buddhist said, 'where becoming is absent birth is absent, feeling is absent, when contact ceases feeling ceases. By saying so he made it very clear that 'unseable and untouchable god is unreal.'" Kancha Ilaiah, "Dalitism vs Brahmanism: The Epistemological Conflict in History," 117.

[62] Refer W. K Vijayakumar, "A Historical Study of Buddhism in India," in *Ambedkar and the Neo-Buddhist Movement*, edited by Wilkinson and Thomas (Bangalore: CISRS/CLS, 1972), 7.

task).[63] Therefore, the emergence of the Buddhist literature became a challenge to the Vedic brahmanical tradition.

The ancient *bahujan* trend is represented in *Lokayata* stream over against Aryan tradition and caste-*varna* ideology. This can be considered as ancient dalit school of thought, since *lokayata* represents a *bahujan* philosophy and way of life. It honors *jeeva* (life) and *prakuriti* (nature).[64] Dalits interact with *prakruthi* to both produce and reproduce nature and their own beings. In the process, their consciousness produces its own world-view. It is more of a materialistic in nature. Dalit School responded to brahmanic exploitative *paralokadhyana* (consciousness of the other world) with an approach of extreme non-violence, which is founded on protecting every *jeeva* as its prime concern.[65] Therefore, it is more of agriculture in its root, and suitable to any eco-system. The *vitanda vada-Satha* (science of dialectical discourses) that the *Lokayatas* developed was in the context of agriculture work.[66] The major characteristic of dalitism of that time was its humanistic outlook.[67] It was more social than philosophical.[68] It was against any caste ideology and anti-brahmanic in nature. So it was drawn upon the dialectical materialistic discourses that started in a proto-materialist form from Indus-based *Lokayatas* or *Charvakas* and continued to operate all through history.[69]

Arvind P. Nirmal explains the philosophy of early *Lokayatas*. For *Lokayata*, perception (*pratyaksha*) was the primary source of knowledge and that they regarded inference (*anumana*) as a secondary source, the validity of which was dependent upon perception. Perhaps the real reasons for the *Lokayata's* rejection of the validity of inference as a source of knowledge of the transcendent realm were socio-political in nature.[70] *Lokayata* is the only school of Indian philosophy which does not subscribe to *karma samsara*.[71] It does not deny the self, because self for *Lokayata* is *deha* (body). *Lokayata* understands *consciousness* in terms of the

---

[63] Kancha Ilaiah, "Dalitism vs Brahmanism: The Epistemological Conflict in History," 118.

[64] Kancha Ilaiah, "Dalitism vs Brahmanism: The Epistemological Conflict in History," 117.

[65] Kancha Ilaiah, "Dalitism vs Brahmanism: The Epistemological Conflict in History," 117.

[66] According to Chattopadhyaya, *Lokayata* was the philosophy of people, philosophy of this worldiness or instinctive materaslism. Budhaghisha described *Lokayata* as *vitanda-vada-satha*. The word *Satha* in Pali means science. *Vtanda vedam* means uneding argument to prove a point. Kancha Ilaiah, "Dalitism vs Brahmanism: The Epistemological Conflict in History," 113, 127. Refer more about this forgotten philosophical tradition of dalits and *Lokayata* from A. P. Nirmal, *Heuristic Explorations*, 102-119.

[67] Sanjay Parwan and Paramanshi Jaideva, eds., "Introduction" to *Encyclopaedia of Dalits in India*, 11.

[68] Braj Ranjan Mani, *Debrahmanising History*, 75.

[69] Indus valley civilization is an early urban culture in the Indus river basin around 2300-1750 B. C. E. It is believed that the history and culture of the dalits and tribal began with this civilization. Jojo Varavukala, "Dalitharenna Daivajanam (Mal)," *Jeevadhara* XXXV/ 206 (April, 2005): 117.

[70] A. P. Nirmal, *Heuristic Explorations*, 109.

[71] A. P. Nirmal, *Heuristic Explorations*, 111.

combination of different elements in particular way. The fact of 'integration' (*yoga*) is very important than the elements.[72] Ironically, the dalitism and Brahmanism was always in philosophical and cultural conflict. It is reflected even in the naming of the mass or the *bahujans* such as *Dehavadi*, *Nisada*, *Prakritian* (those who speak Prakrit language and also those who argue about the all-powerfulness of nature), *Nastikavadi* (agnostic) etc.[73] It is, therefore, clear that dalit-*bahujan* epistemology is constructed around materialism.[74] Then, dalitism is opposite to the philosophical and cultural consciousness of Brahmanism, which is of so-called elites.[75] Dalitism stands as an ideology with common and ordinary masses to protect and save human-cosmos relationship. The epistemology of these two schools or two societies such as of dalitism and Brahmanism maintained parallel position the society dialoguing with each other.

The above said dalit philosophical and religious movements like of Buddhism, *Lokayatas*, etc., synthesized different ethno-cultural streams altogether into one fold.[76] That shows the openness or inclusiveness of dalit movements of ancient time. For instance, Buddha opened the gates of his *Sangha* to all without discriminating anyone on the race, caste, sex or place of birth. All could follow the path of *Nirvana* by coming to his *Sangha*.[77] In the context of fourfold *varna* and multi-caste system, Buddhist school built a theory that society should be 'an ocean where streams consisting of waters of different colours meet to fuse into a colourless ocean' (*varna*-less and casteless society).[78] Thus, these ancient movements were aimed at "all" for holistic upliftment and resisted oppression and subjugation, but failed in many respects because of hegemonic brahmanic oppression.

1.2.2 Medieval Movements

The Medieval period mostly revolved around the bhakti movements that emerged within Hindu and Muslim societies and opposed caste and sought greater

[72] A. P. Nirmal, *Heuristic Explorations*, 111.

[73] It is in this context that one has to understand the naming of 'dalit' is historically important for *bahujans* who named themselves as dalit. See 1.1.2. Historical Use of the Term 'Dalit.' Also Kancha Ilaiah, "Dalitism vs Brahmanism: The Epistemological Conflict in History," 113.

[74] Kancha Ilaiah, "Dalitism vs Brahmanism: The Epistemological Conflict in History," 110-111.

[75] This philosophy was spread with social institutions such as *sabha*, *samiti*, *gana* and *janapada*, which evolved out of tribal and *Lokayata* democratic republicanism, were brahmanised by prohibiting the entry of tribals, Shudras and Chandalas. Those who created these institutions got alienated from them – arguing Kancha Ilaiah in "Dalitism vs Brahmanism: The Epistemological Conflict in History," 116.

[76] Shrirama, "Untouchability and Stratification in Indian Civilization," in *Dalits in Modern India: Vision and Values*, edited by S. M. Michael (New Delhi: Vistaar Publications, 1999), 60.

[77] "Introduction," in *Encyclopaedia of Dalits in India*, Vol. 1: General Studies, edited by Sanjay Parwan and Paramanshi Jaideva (Delhi: Kalpaz Publication, 2002), 11.

[78] Kancha Ilaiah, "Dalitism vs Brahmanism: The Epistemological Conflict in History," 118.

equality.[79] It was the context of Muslim rulers invading towards India and took initiation to syncretize with Indian tradition.[80] The period witnessed the religious revolt of the untouchables against socio-religious hierarchical values. With Bhakti movement, the untouchable saints and poets lead a radical movement ridiculing religious and social hypocrisy of the orthodox. It emphasized an individualistic relationship with a personal deity rather than rule-bound structures of Vedic Hinduism. They opposed caste distinctions and asserted equality before God. The *bhakti* songs taught low castes and *achchutas* the doctrine of spiritual salvation through bhakti.[81] They proposed ideal of humanism.[82] The Bhakti Movement became popular among the *Shudras* and *Ati-Shudras*.[83] This paved the way for the movements that is non-conformity to dominant structures in nature and revolt against such structural evil in the modern dalit movement undertaken by educated and enlightened dalits.

Some saw medieval movement as a liberative period of dalits, but some object by stating that it was a subtle way to propagate caste Hinduism.[84] However,

---

[79] The development of bhakti movement took place in Tamil Nadu between 7th and 12th centuries C. E. It was reflected in the poems of Nayanars (devotees of Shiva) and Alvars (devotees of Vishnu). Between the 10th and 13th centuries C. E., the Bhakti Movement spread all over the continent to popularize Hinduism. Ramanand and Raidas in the north; Chaitanya and Chandidasa in the east; Zeknath, Chikha Mela, Tukaram and Basava in south India were among of the important Hindu dalit saints. Sufism, a reform movement in Islam, and individuals within popular Hindu tradition continued the saga against social oppression and religious superstitions. Katti Padma Rao, *Caste and Alternative Culture*, 105-110. Also Ghanshyam Shah, "Dalit Movements and the Search for Identity," 198. Also Rudolf C. Heredia, "Search for Identity, Quest for Dignity: The Dalit's Long March," *VJTR* 74/10 (Oct., 2010): 756. Also Chinna Rao Yagati, *Dalits' Struggle for Identity: Andhra and Hyderabad, 1900-1950* (New Delhi: Kanishka Publication, 2003), 28. Also Mohua Dutta, "Bhakti Movements: A Socio-Religious Struggle of the Marginalized Society," *Indian Journal of Applied Research* 4/8 (Aug., 2014): 685-687.

[80] Asaf A. A. Fyzee, "Islamic Law and Theology in India – Proposals for a Fresh Approach," in *Cultural and Religious Heritage of India: Islam*, edited by Suresh K. Sharma and Usha Sharma (New Delhi: Mittal Publications, 2004), 144. Also J. L. Mehta, *Advanced Study in the History of Medieval India*, Vol. 1 (1000-1526) (New Delhi: Sterling Publishers, 1979), 300.

[81] The poetry of Dnyaneshwar, Namdev and Tukaram were some of the examples of Bhakti poets who influenced low caste people to seek spirituality. J. C. Winslow, *Narayan Vaman Tilak: The Christian Poet of Maharashtra* (Calcutta: Association Press, 1923), 59, 71.

[82] Comparing to preceding philosophy, medieval period witnessed an ideal humanism in which human being become the center of philosophical and religious reflection. Cf. *Vedartha-Sangraha of Sri Ramanujacarya,* translated by S. S. Raghavachar (Mysore: Sri Ramakrishna Ashram, 1978), 188.

[83] Shudras are considered as backward-castes where Ati-Shudras are untouchables. Cf. Neeladri Bhattacharya, "Editorial Preface," in *Dalit Vision,* Tracts for the Times 8, third revised edition 2006 (Hyderabad: Orient Longman, 1995), xi. Also Ghanshyam Shah, "Dalit Movements and the Search for Identity," 198.

[84] It is argued that Bhakti movement caused for extinguishing of last flicker of Buddhism. Eventually the movement also encapsulated as religious seats and given their own niche in the caste hierarchy, becoming in the process sub-castes in their turn. Chinna Rao Yagati, *Dalits' Struggle for*

this period also witnessed two parallel traditions, one of the *bahujan*-masses, other of elite brahmins. One of the medieval dalit discourses were, according to Ilaiah, the becoming of *shakaharis* (vegetarians) by brahmanism and remaining *mansaharis* (meat eaters) by dalits. It created explicit cultural gap between weaker sections of the people (dalits) and the elites Brahmanical forces.[85] Though, the Brahmanism of that period was divided into *Vaishnavite* and *Shaivite* sects,[86] the common ground on which they were united was on the question of maintenance of *Varnavyavastha* and the exclusion of productive Shudras and Ati-Shudras from the state and civil affairs.[87] In this way one can view Bhakti cult as a process of Sanskrtization that negatively impacted upon dalit-*bahujan* ideology.

1.2.3 Contemporary Dalit Movements

Contemporary dalit movements are continuation of the early movements. Mainly, Jotirao Phule, B. R. Ambedkar and E. V. Ramasamy Naicker (also known as Periyar) laid foundation of contemporary dalit movements, and later followed up by Dalit Sahitya Movement, Dalit Panthers Movement and Contemporary Dalit-*Bahujan* Political Movements. Its epistemology is more or less political in nature, since the modern period witnessed a transition of British colonial administration to an Indian democratic government. In this transition period, dalit discourses played a vital role. As elsewhere mentioned, dalit is one of the Indian discourses along with the socialist and brahmanical streams, but got less recognition in contemporary national discourses. Analysis of contemporary dalit movements would reveal the reasons and process of dalit becoming an alternate and strong Indian identity. For a lucid understanding, we may divide the contemporary movements into pre-independent and post-independent movements.

1.2.3.1 Dalit Movements in Pre-Independent India

Jotirao Phule – B. R. Ambedkar – Periyar trio represent the dalit voice in the Indian freedom struggle discourses.[88] In the Dalit-*Bahujan* nationalist epistemology,

Identity, 28. Also Rudolf C. Heredia, "Search for Identity, Quest for Dignity: The Dalit's Long March," 756.

[85] The principal theoretician of the mediaeval Brahmanism- Sankara, Madhava and Ramanuja- operated in 'Dwaita and Advaita' paradigms with a fundamental aim to establish a philosophical and material hegemony over the Dalit-*bahujan* masses in order to build an unshakable 'consent' system, argues Kancha Ilaiah, "Dalitism vs Brahmanism: The Epistemological Conflict in History," 121-122.

[86] Vaishnavite and Shaivite are the names of Hindu medieval sects named after the names of deity that they worship. For Vaishnavite Vishnu is the god and for Shaivite, Shiva is the deity.

[87] Kancha Ilaiah, "Dalitism vs Brahmanism: The Epistemological Conflict in History," 122.

[88] This trio influenced each other in different ways. For instance, Ambedkar recognised the work of Periyar in relation to the Vaikom Satygraha. It also noted that Periyar translated Ambedkar's *Annihilation of Caste* widely publicised in Tamil language. Katti Padma Rao, *Caste and Alternative Culture*, 126.

Jotirao Phule saw the historical limitations of the Brahmanical nationalist paradigms of R. M. Roy (Brahamo Samaj) and Dayananda Saraswati (Arya Samaj), which aimed at modernizing the Brahmnical castes/classes.[89] Hence, he decided to start a secular anti-caste (not anti-Brahmin) Satyashodhak Movement (movement for discovering the truth).[90] Phule examined dalit traditions such as the Shudra, Ati-Shudra, Buddhist, *Charvaka* and bhakti traditions, and envisioned 'Bali Rajya' instead of Rama Rajya.[91] He located his enemy in the twin structure – colonialism and Brahmanism.[92] Hence, nationalism for him meant overthrowing the hegemony of "British, Bhatji and Shetji" exploitation.[93] Since, Indian Brahmanism were hand-in-glove with colonialism, Phule argued that, both feudalism and capitalism were fused into caste and class mode of Brahmanism. Therefore, without fighting Brahmanism talking about anti-colonial nationalism was going to serve the interests of Brahmanism.

Further B. R. Ambedkar continued dalit discourse on nationalism by building a dalit ideological alternative to the Congress, "in seeking an alliance with non-Brahmans (a Dalit-bahujan or Shudra-Atishudra alliance), in seeking to organize peasants and workers, and in fight for the destruction of the caste system

---

[89] It is considered that Phule is the pioneer in the religious and social awakening of the non-Brahmin classes. In the opinion of Gail Omvedt, "Phule's was the first historical materialist theory of caste, and it heralded major themes of the dalit and non-brahmin movements that were to develop in the twentieth century." Gail Omvedt, *Dalits and the Democratic Revolution: Dr. Ambedkar and the Dalit Movement in Colonial India* (New Delhi, London: Sage Publications, 1994), 23. Also Sanjay Parwan and Paramanshi Jaideva, eds., "Introduction," 14.

[90] Satyashodhak Samaj's ideology sought to arouse the Shudras or *bahujan samaj* with a universalistic, equalitarian, and rationalistic outlook against the brahminical traditions. Gail Omvedt, *Dalits and the Democratic Revolution*, 149, 242. Also Braj Ranjan Mani, *Debrahmanising History*, 251-290.

[91] Instead of Rama Rajya, Phule emphasized king Bali to envision a Bali Rajya. This symbol was in a sense his reply to the elite's use of Ram, Ganapati or Kali, at the same time it was a symbol that united the Maharashtrian peasant masses with the tales of Aryan invasions. Bali is an ancient and valued symbol for the peasant and at the same time represents a sort of golden age, expressed in the Marathi saying, "let sorrow and unhappiness go, let the kingdom of Bali come!" This slogan infiltrates a negative connotation to Rama, who murdered king Bali by cheating. This tradition was nurtured in the Buddhist and Jainist version of *Ramayana*. In this tradition Ravana, a demon king, enemy to Rama in Valmiki's *Ramayana* texts appeared to be pious and a sage. For detail on contemporary usage of 'Bali Rajya' see, Gail Omvedt, *Dalit Vision*, 85. Also *Jotirao Phule and the Ideology of Social Revolution in India* (New Delhi: Critical Quest, 2004), 16-17. Also Kancha Ilaiah, "Dalitism vs Brahmanism: The Epistemological Conflict in History," 124. Also Ram Puniyani, *God Politics* (New Delhi: Vitasta, 2012), 219-220.

[92] The title of his book – *Slavery in the Civilized British Government under the Cloak of Brahmanism* – itself shows his thought on Indian freedom means, freedom both from brahmanism and British colonialism.

[93] Jotirao Govindraw Pule, *Slavery in the Civilized British Government under the Cloak of Brahmanism*. Cf. Kancha Ilaiah, "Dalitism vs Brahmanism: The Epistemological Conflict in History," 124-125.

and the 'abolition of untouchability.'"[94] He wrote extensively to construct dalit perspective of nationalism and built an anti-Hindu and anti-Gandhian discourse for liberation of the *bahujan* masses.[95] Colonialism was a common enemy to both Ambedkar and Gandhi, but their approach was different. On the one side, Ambedkar worked for Dalit-*Bahujan* nationalism from a position of disadvantage and on the other side Gandhi for brahmanical nationalism from a position of advantage. Ambedkar laboriously built a Dalit-*Bahujan* ideology and positioned parallel to the ideology and structures of Gandhi.

In developing dalit nationalistic ideology in India, Ambedkar's two historical steps for the advancement of the weaker section also be noted; such as his attempt to conversion to Buddhism and dalit ideological concentization. By conversion from Hinduism to Buddhism, it can be argued that, Ambedkar took an extra step towards creating a dalit-*bahujan* secular nationalism.[96] In choosing to convert to Buddhism, in the opinion of Omvedt, "Ambedkar achieved making a conscious non-Hindu identity a collective material and radicalizing force in India, which Phule and Periyar failed to achieve."[97] Republican Party, which claimed to be in the tradition of Ambedkar's ideology, argue that Ambedkar worked out a political programme to bring about the dalit democratic revolution based on the principle of liberty, equality and fraternity.[98] However, contemporary dalit political parties are carried away with matter of receiving reservation from center and increasing the quota for dalits in mainstream of society than following Ambedkar's vision of dalit-bahujan secular nationalism.

In addition, Periyar fought mainly for the recovery of the self-respect lost by the dalits and the weaker sections of the Indian society by brahamanic culture.

---

[94] Gail Omvedt, *Dalits and the Democratic Revolution*, 166.

[95] Ambedkar's works such as *Annihilation of Caste with a Reply to Mahatma Gandhi* and *What Congress and Gandhi have done to the Untouchables* show the sheer criticism towards Gandhi and Congress ideology of that time. See in *Dr. Babasaheb Ambedkar Writings and Speeches,* Vol. 1 & 9, compiled by Vasant Moon (Maharashtra: Education Department, 1989 & 1991). Cf. V. R. Krishna Iyer, *Dr. Ambedkar and the Dalit Future* (Delhi: B. R. Publishing Corporation, 1990).

[96] For Ambedkar, conversion is the method of dalit emancipation from their dalitness of historical past. Arvind P. Nirmal, "A Dialogue with Dalit Literature," in *Towards a Dalit Theology,* edited by M. E. Prabhakar (Delhi: ISPCK, 1989), 68.

[97] Gail Omvedt, *Dalits and the Democratic Revolution*, 249.

[98] Ambedkar's party-building, according to Christopher Jaffrelot, had two stages. Primarily, the Independent Labour Party (1935) aimed at rural and urban workers, then to launching Scheduled Castes Federation (1942) aiming to dalits. Finally, he reverted to a mixed approach that was intended to all the depressed categories of the lower castes by initiating the Republic Party of India (1956), which came to existence after Ambedkar's death. "The BSP in Uttar Pradesh: Whose Party is It?," in *Dalits in Modern India: Vision and Values*, edited by S. M. Michael, 2nd edition (New Delhi: Sage Publications, 1999, 2007), 260. Gail Omvedt, "Ambedkar and After: The Dalit Movements in India," in *Social Movements and the State*, Readings in Indian Government and Politics – 4, edited by Ghanshyam Shah (New Delhi: Sage Publications, 2002), 299.

He helped to revive the self-confidence and spirit of rationalism.[99] Treating God, caste and Brahmanism, as a triple chain of bondage, he fought relentlessly to cut it asunder. He started the 'Self – Respect Movement.'[100] His establishment of Self-Respect League in 1925 oppose to Congress, had three main objectives. They are: (1) creating self-respect among the dalits; (2) eradication of superstitions; and (3) liberation of women.[101]

Along with Phule-Ambedkar-Periyar trio-dalit movements, there were number of pre-independent dalit movements under the leadership of dalit personalities in different regions of India.[102] One of the noted places of this upsurgence was Kerala. In between 19th and 20th centuries, Kerala witnessed the beginning of dalit social reform movements waged by enlightened reformers like Vaikunda Swamigal,[103] Sri. Narayana Guru,[104]

---

[99] E. V. Ramasami Naicker, *The Words of Freedom: Ideas of a Nation* (New Delhi: Penguin Books, 2010), 4. Cf. Katti Padma Rao, *Caste and Alternative Culture*, 124.

[100] Katti Padma Rao, *Caste and Alternative Culture*, 123.

[101] Katti Padma Rao, *Caste and Alternative Culture*, 126.

[102] Region wise the dalit movements and personalities can be listed as follows: Sri Narayana Guru, Poyykayil Appachen, Subbanandha Swami, Ayyankali, P. K. Karuppan in Kerala; Subramania Bharati, Ramalinga Swami, Ramasami Naickar, C. A. Ayyamuthu, Bharati Dasan, Muthu Kutti Ayya in Tamil Nadu, Yogi Pothuluri Vira Brahman, Joshua in Andhra Pradesh, Shyam Sunder and Bhimsena movement in Hyderabad-Karnataka, the movement under Phule and Ambedkar in Maharashtra; Adi-Dharm Movement in Punjab, the Namashudra movement in Bengal; the Messianic Movement among the Pankas of Rajpur district, the Satnami uprising of the Chamars in Chattisgarh District, Achchutananda and Jigvasu in Lucknow-Kanpur region are some of the most important cultural forces which paved the way for dalit entry into the religio-cultural life of the country. Adopted from A. M. Abraham Ayrookuzhiel, "Dalit Theology: A Movement of Counter-Culture," in *Towards a Dalit Theology*, edited by M. E. Prabhakar (Delhi: ISPCK, 1989), 101-102. Also Chinna Rao Yagati, *Dalits' Struggle for Identity*, 28.

[103] Vaikunda Swamigal (Ca. 1808 - 1852 C. E.), a Nadar by birth inspired by Thirukkural, a text of bhakti tradition become a social reformer in Kerala. He called Travancore king Swathi Tirunal as *Ananthapuri Neechan* because of his policy towards poor people and cursed Brahmins as *Karineechanmar* (Black cheater). He condemned British people as *Venneechan* (White cheater). His idea of the reign of *Dharma Yuga* made him a great humanist. His principles of casteless society and unity of all people were radical thought of that time which motivated the weaker sections of the society. I. Esthak, *Mathru Bhoomi Weekly* (February 12, 2006).

[104] Narayana Guru (1854 – 1928 C. E.) (early name was Nanu Guru) was a reformer from the weaker section of the Kerala society. Emphasizing the fundamental oneness and equality of humankind he declared. 'One Caste, one Religion, one God for human'. He professed the brotherhood of human and equality of all before God. Caste is the greatest evil affecting whole of India. In 1888 C. E., he consecrated an idol of Lord Shiva at Aruvipuram, a village in South Travancore, a bold movement of a low caste to perform religious activity, which was only meant for brahmins. He opposed inequalities in religion and society. He was concerned about people, rather than religion: His conviction was that religion is for human and not human for religion. One of his famous statements runs as follows: 'Whatever be the religion it is enough if the human is improved'. The Sree Narayana Dharma Paripalana Yogam (S. N. D. P.) is a later organization formed in the name of Sri Narayan Guru. Chandra Mohan P, *Popular Culture and Socio-Religious*

Chatambi Swamigal,[105] Ayyan Kali,[106] Viakkom Maulavi[107] and others. They devoted their life for the propaganda against social evils, Brahminic ascendancy and campaigned for the mitigation of caste.

Thus, dalit nationalism and social discourses in pre-independent period of India aimed at a future Indian society constructed from the energy of the Shudra and Ati-Shudra masses and not from the false 'nationalism' of Brahmanic elite.[108] Some of the dalit noted epistemological framework that are outlined here proved it. For instance, Phule's concept of 'Bali Rajya,' and Satyashodak,[109] or Periyar's notions of 'Dravida Rajya' or 'Ravana Rajya'[110] or Ambedkar's notion of 'Same Sangha Nirmana' (state socialism), all were built in opposition to the Hindu Brahmanical ideology of nation such as 'Akhanda Hindu Rajya/Rashtra', or 'Rama Rajaya'.[111] The emergence of the dalit *desiyatha*, in *contra to* the oppressive nature of Hindu nationalism, maintained solidarity with the broken one in the

---

Reform: Narayana Guru and the Ezhavas of Travancore, Studies in History, Vol. 3 (New Delhi: np., 1987), 57.

[105] Chatambi Swamigal (1853 – 1924 C. E.) was a social reformer in Kerala. He proposed an original casteless society as of ancient Kerala and condemned *Chaturvarnya*. He believed in *Ahimsa*, non-violence.

[106] In 1907, Ayyan Kali (1863 – 1941 C. E.) formed an organization by name 'Sadhu Paripalana Sangham' which aimed at the socio-economic emancipation of the Pulayas, a low caste community of Kerala. His main concerns were providing education, employment and land. R. K. Kshirsagar, *Dalit Movements in India and Its Leaders*, 170.

[107] M. Muhammad Abdul Qadir, who later became famous as Vaikkom Maulavi constituted 'Islamika Paripalana Yogam' for removing sectarian as well as other differences within the Muslim communities of Kerala. Islamika Dharma Paripalana Yogam looked forward for a universal brotherhood of Muslims. For him, the Muslims were simply a crowd (*Bahujanangal*), but to be a Muslim means one is supposed to be part of the Muslim community (Muslim Samudayam). To him 'community' means, they were supposed to possess the moral and religious essence of Islam. *Vakkom Moulaviyude Therenjeduthe Kruthikal* (Selected Writings of Vakkom Moulavi), edited by A Muhammad Abda (Vaikkom: Vaikkom Moulavi Publications, 1979), 13.

[108] Gail Omvedt, *Dalits and the Democratic Revolution*, 241.

[109] Dhanjay Keer writes, "The objects of [Satyashodak] Samaj were to redeem the Shudras and Atishudras from the influence of Brahmanical scriptures under which the Brahmin priests fleeced them, to make them conscious of their human rights, and to liberate them from mental and religious slavery." Dhanjay Keer, *Mahatma Jotirao Phooley*, 127. Cf. Ram Puniyani, *Religion and Politics*, 108.

[110] The dravida nationalism (mainly Periyar) was strongly rooted in Tamil linguistic, Dravida, non-Aryan cultural history. Periyar built a notion of Ravana Rajya as against Rama Rajya of Gandhi. He organized to publically denounce the Hindu gods, and many Hindu deities' statues were removed from the temples. As against the celebration for 'Ram Leela' festivals in the north India, the DK movement used to organize 'Ravana Leela' festivals. Ilaiah observes that, "of course, it built its discourses more as an anti-Brahman rather than anti-caste discourse." Kancha Ilaiah, "Dalitism vs Brahmanism: The Epistemological Conflict in History," 125.

[111] Kancha Ilaiah, "Dalitism vs Brahmanism: The Epistemological Conflict in History," 126. Cf Ram Puniyani, "Rashtriya Swayamsevak Sangh: Politics as 'Culture'," in *Communal Violence*

society. It also contributed for the development of dalit regionalism (*rajyas*).[112] Phule's emphasis on 'adi' ideology oppose to Aryan theory of race that argue for the Indian civilization as Aryan civilization[113] influenced the dalit movements to prescribe a regional and separatist consciousness. During 1920s a new set of self-conscious identities of dalits claimed that they were the original inhabitants of the land and the 'sons of the soil,' whereas Aryans are foreign invaders.[114] Chinna Rao Yagati tells that, "this culminated into an 'adi' (original) ideology that came to be prefixed to their regional identity."[115] Ambedkar's attempt of rejecting Hinduism and embracing Buddhism is also viewed as "a return to an 'original' and egalitarian Indian religion."[116] 'Adi' ideology as indigenous people, in some extend, demonstrates a kind of dalit nationalism in relation to their regional consciousness.[117] Such consciousness is expanded on the basis of languages and ethnic origins in post-independent India such as the emergence of Tamil

---

and Minorities: Gujarat Society in Ferment, edited by Lancy Lobo and Biswaroop Das (New Delhi: Rawat Publications, 2006), 169.

[112] Dalit nationalism has its root in the petty kingdoms of pre-independent India that gave birth to regionalism based on the geographical politics as well as it is a battle of diverse cultures. This regionalism started with the partition of India into Pakisthan, Bengladesh, and later the demands for *Pathiristhan* in North East India, a nation for Punjab in the North and *Dravidisthan* or Tamil nationalism is another emerging and visible sign for regional consciousness. Rajiv Malhotra and Aravindan Neelakandan, *Breaking India: Western Interventions in Dravidian and Dalit Faultlines* (New Delhi: Amaryllis, 2001), 92, 319-320.

[113] The ideology based on Aryan theory of race which was developed in the 1840s and 1850s by German philogists and popularized by Max Muller. Max Muller, *The Sacred Laws of the Aryas as thought in the Schools of Apastamba, Gautama, Vaishtha and Baudhayana*, Sacred Books of the East Series 2, translated by Geroge Buhler (Delhi: Motilal Banarsidass, reprint 1986, first published by Clarendon Press 1879), ix-xi.

[114] Phule's interpretation of the nine avatars of Vishnu was seen as different stages of the Aryan conquest. *Matsya* and *Kaccha* represented invasion by sea; *Varah* (the boar) was so-called because the original Aryans were seen as barbarians by the more civilized native kshatriyas. The story of *Narasinh* (th man-lion) and Prahlad represented conquest by treachery and propaganda, where the mind of a local prince was corrupted to the point where he was willing to kill his own father. Finally, *Waman* (the Brahman boy) represented a kind of culmination of the Aryan conquest of Maharashtra by cheating the great Bali out of his kingdom. Not much attention was given to the later avatars, Parashuram, Krishna, or Rama, but the approach was clear. The "dasyus" or non-Aryans and the demons of the Vedas and Puranas represented the indigenous population and were depicted as enlightened kings and warriors, the Aryans and their gods as treacherous invaders. Ambedkar also considered Vedas as a political document. Dhananjay Keer, *Mahatma Jotirao Phooley*, 131. According to Ambedkar, the caste system has been legitimized through the Shastras. It has religious sanction. Ghanshyam Shah, "Introduction: Dalit Politics," 18. Also Gail Omvedt, *Jotirao Phule and the Ideology of Social Revolution in India*, 16.

[115] Chinna Rao Yagati, *Dalits' Struggle for Identity*, 16. Ghanshyam Shah, "Introduction: Dalit Politics," 18. Also Gail Omvedt, *Jotirao Phule and the Ideology of Social Revolution in India*, 16.

[116] Bharat Patankar and Gail Omvedt, *The Dalit Liberation Movement in Colonial Period* (New Delhi: Critical Quest, 2004), 16.

[117] Saral K, Chatterji, "Why Dalit Theology?," 190-196.

nationalism based on Dravidian ethnicity and language.[118] The contemporary communal clashes also signs an aggressive mood of regionalism that may end up in division of the nation India based on these regionalism. Rajiv Malhotra and Aravindan Neelakandan argues such tendency that will result into the segregation of India in their work *Breaking India: Western Interventions in Dravidian and Dalit Faultlines.*[119]

1.2.3.2 Dalit Movements in Post-Independent India

The post-independent India inherited two epistemological discourses such as the dalit *Bahujan* nationalist discourses and the Hindu nationalist discourse.[120] The other forces, such as Marxism, appear to have been absorbed into these two contending political-ideological social forces- Dalitist and Brahmanical.[121] Thus, these two strong, contending social forces have divided the Indian society into two opposite camps. The Dalitist School represents an ideology of socio-political change and the Brahmanical school represents a kind of modernized (in the place of *Sanatan*) Hindu fundamentalist social base.[122] This opposite pole can be described as *hindutva* in conflict with *dalitva(d)* and vice versa.[123] This ideological standpoint of dalit, called *dalitvad*, acquired centrality in Indian discourse and is closely linked to the question of reshaping the Indian nationalism. Because they took, according to Gail Omvedt, "effort to construct an alternative identity of the people, based on non-north Indian and low-caste perspectives, critical not only of the oppressiveness of the dominant Hindu caste society but also of its claims

---

[118] Robert Caldwell, *A Comparative Grammar of the Dravidian Languages* (London, 1875) mentioned in Charles A. Ryerson, "Meaning and Modernisation in Tamil Nadu: Tamil Nationalism and Religious Culture," *Religion and Society* XVII/4 (Dec., 1970): 234.

[119] See Rajiv Malhotra and Aravindan Neelakandan, *Breaking India*, 319. In this book, writers argue that the India is divided into dalitsthan, dravidisthan, and mughalsthan.

[120] According to Kancha Ilaiah, the Indian nationalistic discourse can be categorized into three schools: (i) Hindu nationalism, (b) Dalit nationalism and (c) Communist secular socialist nationalism. Kancha Ilaiah, *The Weapon of the Other: Dalitbahujan Writings and the Remaking of Indian Nationalist Thought* (Delhi: Pearson, 2000), 2; Also "Dalitism vs Brahmanism: The Epistemological Conflict in History."

[121] As far as the dalit *bahujans* were concerned, the third school called the Marxist school emerged and remained in the hands of Brahmnical upper castes. They were in the task of 'abolition of class' with a 'caste-blind' scheme of 'revolution' or transformation of the Indian society into a 'secular, socialist and communist' society. This school is represented by M. N. Roy, R. P. Dutt, T. Nagi Reddy, E. M. S. Namboodiripad and others. Kancha Ilaiah, "Dalitism vs Brahmanism: The Epistemological Conflict in History," 109, 126.

[122] Kancha Ilaiah, "Dalitism vs Brahmanism: The Epistemological Conflict in History," 108.

[123] The *hindutva* ideology is a political category based on brahmanical stream of Hinduism, that is Hindu religious nationalism represented by Tilak, Golvalkar and Shyam Prasad Mookerjee. Whereas Dalit nationalism believed in restructuring the Indian society into a casteless, classless, egalitarian *sangha* represented by Phule, Ambedkar and Periyar. Ram Puniyani, *God Politics*, 31, 91. Cf. V. R. Krishna Iyer, *Dr. Ambedkar and the Dalit Future.*

to antiquity and to being the major Indian tradition."[124] It is expressed in various facets of dalit activities in the post-independent India.

The modern dalit national discourses provide mainly two characteristics such as of 'adi' ideology and 'anti' ideology. 'Adi-ideology' tells the glorious past heritage of dalit as original inhabitance of the land India and their historical oppression by other dominant traditions.[125] The 'anti-ideology' is counter-cultural dalit aggression that reflects in the socio-political and religious movements against other dominant traditions.

In post-independent India, Dalits have been organizing politically. Dalit political parties, like The Republican Party, Bahujan Samaj Party, Bahujan Republican Party of India, etc., are with a strong and aggressive pro-dalit strand try to fulfill Ambedkar's saying that "we must become a ruling community."[126] However, in post-Ambedkar era, besides reservations and a claim to equality, no broader agenda have developed by dalit political parties.[127] They challenge the aspects of oppression and exploitation, but fail to show the way to transformation as Ambedkar could do.

Ideologically, thus, the current Indian dalit discourses can be identified in relation to *dalitism*, *dalitness* and *dalitvad*. *Dalitism* represents the dignified stage of dalits, *dalitness* represents the historical pathos, and *dalitvad* represents aggression and revenge against their historical oppressors. With these three characteristics, from 1960s onwards new literary and philosophical dalit movements have emerged to assert dalit identity and emancipation as a continuation of pre-independent dalit movements. Historical oppression was one of the hectic issues for this dalit discourse which reflected in the literary publications and philosophical movements. They have stated the condition of dalits as the most degraded, downtrodden, exploited and the least educated in the Indian society is a historical act. This recognition of their historical exploitation, they have cherished an anti-caste vigor believing that the common reason for the dalitness is caste system, Brahmanism and Hindu culture.[128] 'Out-caste' is one of the expressions of their dalitness. It is a feeling of 'out' from the social system of caste. '*A-varna*' is also an expression of isolation and exclusion from the *varna* system of Brahmanism- dalitness is without a *varna*. They have been declared ritually unclean, hence *untouchable*; and pushed out for fear of pollution to live

---

[124] Cf. Gail Omvedt, *Dalits and the Democratic Revolution*, 244.

[125] See for the discussion on 'adi-ideology' 1.2.3.1. Dalit Movements in Pre-Independent India.

[126] A. M. Abraham Ayrookuzhiel, "Dalit Theology: A Movement of Counter-Culture," 95. Also Kancha Ilaiah, "Dalitism vs Brahmanism," 126. Also John C. B. Webster, *The Dalit Christians: A History* 1992, 4th edition. ISPCK Contextual Theological Education Series No: 4 (Delhi: ISPCK, 2009), 205.

[127] Gail Omvedt, "Ambedkar and After: The Dalit Movements in India," 306.

[128] Braj Ranjan Mani, *Debrahmanising History*, 17.

on the outskirts of villages, hence *segregated.*[129] The dalitness of people expressed in the terminology used by oppressors and preservers themselves; *Antya* (added last or at the end); *Bahya* (who lives or stays outside the village); *antyaja* (born at the end), *antyavasin* (those who live in the end).[130] *Mlecha* and *Chandala* used by Manu to refer polluted people group.[131] Such expressions really questioned the identity of the common people who are 'outside' of the caste and no longer a *varna* too. Dalitness, then, is also meant by being 'no' people in midst of some people. This consciousness, called as dalit historical consciousness, constitutes a rage against other dominant traditions like of brahmanic discourse. The result of this consciousness is the militant approach of dalits towards the 'historical enemy' Brahmins or high castes. These 'anti' and conflicting attitude reflected clearly in the contemporary dalit movements to mobilize a large mass of Dalits for collective action.[132]

Further, Dalit Sahitya Movement[133] paved a literary and philosophical background for subsequent dalit movements. Dalit literature was a protest on behalf of self-determination and for an end to social and religious subjugation.[134] Katti Padma Rao observes dalit literatures, in this period were having three principles such as of scientific, universal and revolutionary outlook.[135] These dalit movements accept the dalitism as a distinct stream of Indian tradition. However, Dalits have recently emphasized it on their literature to sustain the dalit aggressive

[129] M. E. Prabhakar, "The Search for a Dalit Theology," 40. Also N. Sudhakar Rao, "The Structure of South Indian Untouchable Castes: A View," in *Dalit Identity and Politics*, Cultural Subordination and the Dalit Challenge, Vol. 2, edited by Ghanshyam Shah (New Delhi: Sage Publications, 2001), 95.

[130] Chinna Rao Yagati, *Dalit's Struggles for Identity*, 16.

[131] *The Law of Manu*, in Sacred Books of the East Series: XXV, translated by G. Bühler (Delhi: Motilal Banarsidass, reprinted 1988, first published in 1886), 401-419.

[132] Ghanshyam Shah, "Dalit Movements and the Search for Identity,"197. Cf. Rudolf C. Heredia, *Changing Gods: Rethinking Conversion in India* (New Delhi: Penguin Books, 2007), 227-239.

[133] The term 'Dalit Sahitya' refers to the body of literature, which gives expression to the feelings, and experiences of the writers representing the people who are broken, downtrodden, crushed, etc. More narrowly, the term represents the body of literature produced by the writers and poets belonging to the so-called outcaste communities, the untouchables. Some have tried to trace the origins of the movement in Buddha, some in the Maharashtriyan saint-poet Chokha Mela, some in Phule and some others in the early dalit writer Kisan Bansode. But there is a near consensus that the real origin of the present movement lies in the writings, leadership and thoughts of B. R. Ambedkar. Arvind P. Nirmal, "A Dialogue with Dalit Literature," 67. Cf. Ram Puniyani, *God Politics*, 21.

[134] Arvind P. Nirmal, "A Dialogue with Dalit Literature," 73. Also J. H. Anand, "Dalit Literature is the Literature of Protest," in *Dalit Solidarity*, edited by Bhagavan Das and James Massey (Delhi: ISPCK: 1995), 177-184.

[135] Katti Padma Rao, *Caste and Alternative Culture*, 137.

consciousness of *dalitvad* than ever.[136] The Dalit Sahitya Movement caused for the emergence of Dalit Panthers Movement founded by Namdev Dhasal, Arjun Dangle and J. V. Pawar.[137] Dalit Panthers Movement shows such militant nature of dalit extremism.[138]

Summing up the historical development of dalit ideology along with dalit movements, one can draw these conclusions. Dominant dalit movements in different parts of the country at the local and regional level, both in the past and in the present, provide more or less similar ideology and framework. Dalit movement was a wide spread *social movement* aimed at fundamental change of a system seen as exploitative and oppressive. It was mainly a struggle against all that subjugates the identity and respect of a person or a group in society. But in contemporary scene, the term dalit is misrepresented within the caste hegemony. Dalit movements obsessed with the furious past pathos of their ancestors, which creates a deviation of dalitness into *dalitvad* and *dalitsthan* – envision of divisive nationalism. This, unintentionally, leaves out from the Indian national ethos, where dalit has a distinct or unique place to cherish their *dalitism*. Any attempt of dalit in deviating from Indian national ethos can be named as *dalitvad* over against dalitism. It is a 'false psyche of dalits.'[139] This extremity of dalitness leads to *dalitvad*, not necessarily the dalitism, the original philosophical or epistemology of the 'dalit-bahujans' in general, which is centred on *prakruti* and *jeeva*. The dalit should be inclusively read along with the wider Indian national discourses such as Marxist and Brahmanic traditions. Unless *dalitism* becomes the dominant note of their identity no movement or ideology can liberate them.[140]

1.3 Contemporary Indian Christian Theological Discourses on 'Dalit'

Albeit dalit discourses in Indian Christian theological arena are recent phenomena, Christians in general cherished a radical approach towards weaker sections

---

[136] For instance, *Dalit Mitra* in Gujarath, *Dalit Voice* from Bangalore, *Dalit Azhaham* from Madras, *Dalithakam* from Kozhikode, *Voice of the Weak* from Delhi, etc. Dalit literature has much influenced in the modern time to form dalit identity. S. P. Punalekar, "Dalit Literature and Dalit Identity," in *Dalit Identity and Politics: Cultural Subordination and the Dalit Challenge*, Vol. 2, edited by Ghanshyam Shah (New Delhi: Sage Publications, 2001), 214-241. Cf. Salauddin Khan, "Globalization, Dalits, Adivasis and Naxalite Movements," in *Dalits and Tribes of India*, edited by J. Cyril Kanmony (New Delhi: Mittal Publications, 2010), 75-83.

[137] Namdev Dhasal (15 Feb. 1949 – 15 Jan. 2014), who was a "dalit writer, reformist and activist, believed in the power of the written word to bring about social change." Lyla Bavadam, "Obituary: Voice of the Oppressed," 116. Also Arvind P. Nirmal, "A Dialogue with Dalit Literature," 73.

[138] Lyla Bavadam, "Obituary: Voice of the Oppressed," 116. Also Katti Padma Rao, *Caste and Alternative Culture*, 143-157.

[139] K. Wilson develops dalit theology based on the assumption that dalits got a "false psyche," when they were subjugated by caste or Aryan invaders. K. Wilson, "An Approach to Christian Dalit Theology," in *Towards a Dalit Theology*, edited by M. E. Prabhakar (Delhi: ISPCK, 1989), 48-49.

[140] A. M. Abraham Ayrookuzhiel, "Dalit Theology: A Movement of Counter-Culture," 95.

of the society.[141] Indian Christian theology have been growing its terrain from brahmanical tradition continued with secular or socialist approach and recently reached to the contextual theological expression from the margins.[142] The secular

---

[141] Recently, it is argued that Apostle Thomas visited and converted dalits than Brahmins. Further, the protestant missionaries tend to share good news and social transformation to the weaker section of the community. Early Pentecostal revivals in India stood along with dalits and tried to uplift them. However Christians from upper caste, in certain instances, practiced taboo towards the low strata of the society that even lead for division inside denominations. But generally, comparing to other religious traditions, Christianity gave dalits new aspiration and liberation that was visible in the mass conversion of the people towards Christian faith. But the theological articulation become visible through the thought proposed by A. P Nirmal, in 1981 at the valedictory address to the Carey Society of UTC, Bangalore – "Towards a Sudra Theology". Later the term 'Shudra' changed into 'dalit' as he found the similarity with Dalit Panther Movement and Dalit Sahitya Movement of that time in Maharashtra and Marathi literature. A. P. Nirmal, "A Dialogue with Dalit Literature," 66. Cf. Kancha Ilaiah, *Post-Hindu India: A Discourse on Dalit-Bahujan, Socio-Spiritual and Scientific Revolution* (New Delhi: Sage Publications, 2009), xvi.

[142] The development of Indian Christian theology was considered as having three stages of development – philosophical, political (social) and contextual theological reflection. Philosophical stream of Indian Christian theology is more depended on the brahmanical tradition as the only Indian tradition to be theologized. Indian Christian theology has failed to take account of the suffering and hopes of majority of Indian Christians who hail from dalit context. Its approach, primarily, was responding to the philosophical-theological conceptions of the dominant brahminical religion and culture which had not paid enough attention to dalit aspirations. For instance K. M. Banerjea's *Arian Witness* attempted for relating *Prajapathi* of Vedic scriptures to Christian faith and recently Raimando Panikkar's *Christophany* also represent such trend. K. M. Banerjea, *The Arian Witness* (Calcutta: Thacker, Spink & Co., 1875 in K. P. Aleaz, *From Exclusivism to Inclusivism: Theological Writings of Krishna Mohun Banerjea (1813-1885)* (Delhi: ISPCK, 1998), 514. The primary work of Robin Boyd, *Indian Christian Theology* and *Kristhavaadvaitha*, *Bhakti Marga* of Chenchiyya, and Vengal Chakkarai's Jesus the *Avatar*, *Vengal Chakkarai*, Vol. 1, edited by P. T. Thomas (Madras: CLS, 1981) are falls in this category. The Robert de Nobile's adoption of Indian culture as Brahminic culture is another historical example. All these show that Indian tradition means only brahmanical tradition. Second trend in Indian theological thought was, as a result of freedom struggle and nationalism, centred on the political or secular reality of India. Christian political and social thought concentrated on the socio-political realities of India brought forward by P. D. Devanadan, M. M. Thomas and the like that become a signpost for the emergence of contextual theologies particularly dalit theology. See P. D. Devanandan, *Preparation for Dialogue: A Collective Essays on Hinduism and Christianity in New India*, edited by Nalini Devanandan and M. M. Thomas (Bangalore: CISRS, 1964). Also M. M. Thomas, *Christian Social Thought and Action- A Necessary Tragedy*, in *M. M. Thomas Reader: Selected Texts on Theology, Religion and Society* (1943), edited by T. Jacob Thomas (Thiruvalla: CSS, 2002). Cf. Adrian Bird, *M. M. Thomas and Dalit Theology*. Recent and third trend is on the contextual issues picked up by liberation theologies, third world theology and other contextual theology such as dalit and tribal theologies. A. P. Nirmal, pioneer in dalit theology, acknowledges the insufficiency of Indian Christian Theology that gave little or even no space to the dalit tradition of India. It is the ignorance and avoidance of Indian Christian Theology towards dalit movements caused the emergence of an alternative theology known as dalit theology. A. P. Nirmal, *Heuristic Explorations*, 111. Also Franklyn J. Balasundaram, "Dalit Theology and Other Theologies," in *Frontiers of Dalit Theology*, edited by V. Devasahayam (New Delhi: ISPCK, 1997), 260. James Massey proposes, not rejecting of the known expressions or its usefulness, "We have to

dalit movements had far reaching effect in this paradigm shift of Indian Christian Theology to the aspirations of dalit struggle. Anthoniraj Thumma states, "dalit liberation theology is the product of dalit movements' struggle and reflections for their dignity and liberty."[143] Secular dalit movements opened up dalit-bahujan ideology, i.e., in one side Indian and on the other side opposing to the existing brahmanical dominance, rendered by new theological venture known as dalit theology. Then, dalit theology is a theological movement which tries to answer and response to existential questions which emerge from the historical and current life-situations of dalits.[144] Considering this historical development of Indian Christian theology, here the researcher critically looks at the imposition of dalit movements' ideology into theological articulation at the same time appreciates genuine 'dalit' attempt of theologizing. Since it is purely a 'dalit' attempt, this would discard any caste (i.e., brahmanical) interpretation and foster an inclusive outlook to the concept of 'dalit' in Christian theological articulation in India based on the etymological definition, and would re-capitulate foundation, structure and other basics of dalit theology.

Dalit theological expressions in India have three major dimensions that can be named as dalit cultural theology, dalit Christian theology and dalit biblical theology. The main concern of these dalit expressions is to address the dalitness and strive for wholeness in a dalit way, but differs in its subject and object of theologizing. For example, Dalit cultural theology is a wider umbrella that opens towards Dalit religious faith, culture and other ancestral customs seriously.[145] It embraces all dalits irrespective of faith traditions. Dalit cultural theology appreciates and encourages traditional dalit religious system as a subject to be used in order to formulate dalit theology. Whereas dalit Christian theology has a critique towards dalit cultural elements as subject but considers it as mere object for transformation or liberation. Dalit Christian theology is considered

---

work out another expression of Indian Christian theology which should be relevant to the living situation of the vast majority of people in their widely dissimilar regions." Thus, Indian Christian Theology is in a pilgrimage begun with philosophical discussions to socio-political context, now dwelling among the people in their particular contexts. James Massey, "Ingredients for a Dalit Theology," 59.

[143] Anthoniraj Thumma, *Dalit Liberation Theology: Ambedkarian Perspective* (Delhi: ISPCK, 2000), viii.

[144] Charles Singaram, *The Question of Method in Dalit Theology: In Search of Systematic Approach to the Practice of an Indian Liberation Theology* (Delhi: ISPCK, 2008), 48.

[145] Santhinathan Clarke, uses the dalit symbolic world to apprehend Jesus Christ. He creatively interprets the resistive and the constructive dimensions of dalit religion by analyzing two important symbols of dalit religion- the goddess *Elliaiyamman* and the dalit Drum. He also corrects the misconception that dalit religion is demonic by exposing the Christic presence in the religious tradition of dalits. By adopting an approach which affirms dalit culture and religion, Clarke's theological expositions are useful at various levels. This way of dalit theologizing can be categorized as dalit cultural theology. Santhinathan Clarke, *Dalits and Christianity: Subaltern Religion and Liberation Theology in India* (New Delhi: OUP, 1998), 12.

to be a comprehensive process of transform the cultural, social, economic and spiritual slavery of dalits.[146] Dalit Christian theology articulates dalit theology in a Christian way of having a dialogue with its object dalit culture, that is, a Christian theology from dalit perspective. Dalit Christian theology, expecting humanization, involves three vital steps, namely, (a) revelation in one's self (b) revolution in one's life situation and (c) revaluation of the value system to bring about a new culture, as K. Wilson argues.[147] Nevertheless, the main subject of dalit biblical theology is scripture. The primacy of scripture is emphasized than dalit culture or systematic presentation of Christian faith. Further, Dalit biblical theology constitutes of biblical interpretation from Dalit point of view.[148] There is no clear demarcation between these dalit-theologizing enterprises. Conversely, other characteristics make dalit theology as a single stream and various dalit issues addressed together.

For instance, dalit theology is considered as a *people's theology* or democratic theology, i.e., *of* the dalits, *by* the dalits, *for* the dalits.[149] Dalit theology is a *new theology* because it is from "below" and uses dalit languages and expressions, dalit stories and songs of suffering and triumphs, popular wisdom including dalit values, proverbs, folklore, myths and so on to interpret their history and culture, and to articulate a faith to live by and to act on.[150] M. E. Prabhakar says,

It is not only a *prophetic theology* for identification with the oppression of dalits and their struggles for equality and justice, but also a *political theology* for social action towards the transformation of unjust, undemocratic and oppressive structures. It is *doing theology* in community within the context of the sufferings and struggles of dalits through dialogue, critical reflection and committed action for building a new life-order.[151]

Thus, Dalit theology will represent a radical discontinuity with the traditional Indian Christian theology because, according to Nirmal, the dominant trend in Indian Christian theology is essentially brahmanic in character, not dalit.[152] This means that dalit theology will be a *counter theology*.[153] Dalit theology is a counter theology opposing the dominant theology which is at its core brahmanic in

[146] M. E. Prabhakar, "Caste-Class, Patriarchy and Doing Dalit Theology," in *Frontiers of Dalit Theology* (Delhi/Madras: ISPCK, Gurukul, 1997), 90.

[147] K. Wilson, "An Approach to Christian Dalit Theology."

[148] For instance, V. Devasahayam, "Bible Studies," in *Frontiers of Dalit Theology*, 3-75 reflects biblical interpretation from dalit point of view by Devasahayam.

[149] M. E. Prabhakar, "The Search for a Dalit Theology," 43.

[150] A. M. Abraham Ayrookuzhiel, "Dalit Theology: A Movement of Counter-Culture," 83-103. Also "The Search for a Dalit Theology," 44.

[151] M. E. Prabhakar, "The Search for a Dalit Theology," 44.

[152] A. P. Nirmal, *Heuristic Explorations*, 144.

[153] A. P. Nirmal, "A Dialogue with Dalit Literature," 76.

character. It counters brahmanical culture.[154] Dalit theology, as a counter-culture, is considered to be a *spiritual struggle*. In order to remain dalit theology as a counter theology, A. P. Nirmal argues, it is necessary that it must be exclusive in character. He writes, "[T]his exclusiveness is necessary because the tendency of all dominant traditions-cultural or theological- is to accommodate, include, assimilate and finally conquer others."[155] As a self-defense, dalit theology must be exclusive. Therefore, the methodology for doing dalit theology will be methodological exclusivism. Further, in dalit methodology, pathos is stressed more than praxis, unlike other liberation or people's theologies.[156] Then, methodologically the dalit Christian theology is an articulation of the *dalitnesss*, i.e., pathos. Thus, contemporary dalit theological trend revolve around the methodological exclusivism, dalitness and praxis as the foundation and structure of it. As these components are analyzed in some detail, along with it, an attempt to critically look at such trend and proposes an alternative definition for dalit theology and its configurations so that it would work as a ground in which dalit Christological articulation can be understood more decisively.

1.3.1 *Dalitness* in Dalit Theology

'Dalitness' is one of the characteristics of dalit theology. Dalit theology is grounded on dalits' pathos, thus dalits' pathos becomes the starting point for dalit theology. While brahmanism serves elite in their *sitz im leben*, *dalitism* serves the marginalized or the 'others' in the Indian society.[157]

The dalitness is expressed in many ways in different times in Indian history. 'The dalit condition' is that of destitution and dehumanization. Ambedkar recognized that the main problem of the depressed classes was that of misery (*dukha*). A. P. Nirmal says that the misery is operative on three levels: "on the first level is a physical misery, caused above all by poverty, on the second level is mental misery, caused by the disregard of human dignity; on the third level is spiritual misery, caused by guilt and sin."[158] These three constitutes the 'wounded psyche of dalits'. This reciprocal relationship between theology and context is observable in the dalit articulation of theology. Nirmal's concept of God as 'Servant God' is also relevant to this context. He writes,

[B]ut the God whom Jesus Christ revealed and about whom the prophets of the Old Testament spoke is a dalit God. He is a servant God – a God who serves. Service to others have always been the privilege of dalit communities in India.

[154] A. M. Abraham Ayrookuzhiel, "Dalit Theology: A Movement of Counter – Culture."

[155] A. P. Nirmal, *Heuristic Explorations*, 144.

[156] Anthoniraj Thumma, *Voices of the Victims: Movements and Models of People's Theology* (Delhi: ISPCK, 1999), 38.

[157] V. Devasahayam, "Introduction," to *Frontiers of Dalit Theology*, edited by Devasahayam (Delhi/Madras: ISPCK/Gurukul, 1997), xi.

[158] A. P. Nirmal, "A Dialogue with Dalit Literature," 68.

The passages from *Manu Dharma Sastra* say that the Shudra was created by the self-existent (*Svayambhu*) to do servile work and that servitude is innate in him. Service is the *Sva-dharma* of the Shudra. Let us remember the fact that in dalits we have peoples who are *avarnas*- those below the Shudras. Their servitude is even more pathetic than that of the Shudras. Against this background the amazing claim of a Christian dalit theology will be that the God of the dalits, the self-existent, the *Svayambhu* does not create others to do servile work, but does servile work Himself. Servitude is innate in the God of the Dalits. Servitude is the *sva-dharma* of the God; and since we the Indian dalits are this God's people, service has been our lot and our privilege.[159]

Peniel Rajkumar comments on this statements, "Nirmal makes hermeneutical purchase of this servant image to affirm the dalitness of the dalits through this commonality of pathos and servanthood."[160]

An integral part of dalit power is *dalit consciousness*, which consists in becoming aware that dalit humanity is constituted by their *dalitness*. A. P. Nirmal's statement about 'dalit' and 'Christian' is also necessary to note here:

> ...the primacy of the term "dalit" will have to be conceded as against the primacy of the term "Christian" in the dominant theological tradition. This means that the non-dalit world will ask us, "What is Christian about dalit theology?" And our reply will have to be "It is the *dalitness* which is 'Christian' about dalit theology." That is what I mean by the primacy of the term "dalit." The "Christian" for this theology is *exclusively* the "dalit." What this exclusivism implies is the affirmation that the Triune God- the Father, the Son and the Holy Spirit- is the God of the dalits and not of the non-dalits. It is the common dalit experience along with other dalits that will shape a dalit Christian theology.[161]

In the words of Peniel Rajkumar, "it is in this pain-pathos that the sufferer knows God, and this experience of pain or pathos should become the epistemological starting point for the dalits' knowledge of God."[162] Thus, the articulation of dalit theology is inextricably interlinked with the issue of *dalitness*.[163]

---

[159] A. P. Nirmal, "Towards a Christian Dalit Theology," in *Indigenous People: Dalits. Dalit Issues in Today's Theological Debate*. Contextual Theological Education Series: 5, edited by James Massey (Delhi: ISPCK, 2006), 224.

[160] Peniel Rajkumar, *Dalit Theology and Dalit Liberation: Problems, Paradigms and Possibilities*, Ashgate New Critical Thinking in Religion, Theology and Biblical Studies Series (Farnham, England: Ashgate, 2010), 52.

[161] Arvind P. Nirmal, "A Dialogue with Dalit Literature," 76.

[162] Peniel Rajkumar, *Dalit Theology and Dalit Liberation*, 49.

[163] M. E. Prabhakar, "Christology in Dalit Perspective," in *Frontiers of Dalit Theology*, edited by V. Devasahayam (New Delhi: ISPCK, 1997), 405.

Justification of the 'dalitness' as the criteria for a dalit Christian could be acceptable. But there is a danger, when theological confession turns to become more exclusivist. For example, "Triune God – the Father, the Son and the Holy Spirit – is the God of the dalits" is an acceptable affirmation where as such passively connotes that Triune God is God *not* of the non-dalits. This anti-caste theology is directly influenced by the casteised interpretation of dalit, that is *dalitvad*. It limits the experience of 'dalitness' as an exclusive experience of a particular people group. The universality of 'condition of dalitness' is neglected in this instance. The attempt of *wholeness* is also discredited here.

Dalitism has been cherishing a historical and cultural heritage that finds an integral place within the broader 'Indic' spiritual resources.[164] Brahmanism, though it is the dominant stream in Indian civilization, never fully succeeded in shaping or limiting Indian culture to become a monolithic or exclusive socio-religious force. Dalitism has to build up dalit identity, which serves not only the purpose of self-definition and theologizing but also involvement of the dalits for social change.[165] The attainment of authentic humanhood or liberation of the last and the least is a precondition for the liberation of all, for there can be no *sarvodaya* (liberation of all) without *antyodaya* (liberation of the least).[166] This should be the motto of dalit theology than carried away with anti-caste agendas. Theology cannot be limited to a particular (either higher or lower) castes. Because, whoever understands the faith as the early faith community of first four centuries does, in universal terms, can no more limit redemption to his/her own caste.[167] Then, dalit theology must be an articulation of the dialogical critical reflection of the dalits arising from their transformative pathos and praxis and its exercise in dalit way.[168] This proposal for re-vision of dalit theology is derived from the meaning of the term 'dalit' - strive for wholeness from the condition of brokenness.

---

[164] See 1.2.1. Ancient Movements.

[165] M. E. Prabhakar, "The Search for a Dalit Theology."

[166] Gandhi drew from the writings of the English liberal social thinker John Ruskin the concept of *Sarvodaya*, which can be translated "the welfare of all." It stands as the designation of a social programme intended to raise the life of every member of society. *Sarvodaya* now designates a loosely-organized movement for social uplift. A. F. Thompson, "Theological Responsibility for our Society: The Christian contribution in terms of a Theology of Society," in *Indian Voices in Today's Theological Debate*, edited by Horst Bürkle and Wolfgang M.W. Roth (Luknow: Luknow Publishing House in collaboration with Delhi/Madras: ISPCK, CLS, 1972), 146. Cf. V. Devasahayam, "Doing Dalit Theology: Basic Assumptions," in *Frontiers of Dalit Theology* (Delhi/Madras: ISPCK, Gurukul, 1997), 274.

[167] Horst Bürkle, "Introduction to German Edition," in *Indian Voices in Today's Theological Debate*, edited by Horst Bürkle and Wolfgang M.W. Roth (Luknow: Luknow Publishing House in collaboration with Delhi/Madras: ISPCK, CLS, 1972), ix.

[168] Anthoniraj Thumma, *Dalit Liberation Theology*, ix.

1.3.2 *Dalitvad* in Dalit Theology

Based on dalitness, dalit theology built up *dalitvad* to lay out its praxis. As dalit militant movements have been actively advocates that, "the pathos should give birth to protest which is so loud as to break down the walls of Brahmanism," can be termed as *dalitvad*.[169] The aggressive nature of dalitism (i.e., *dalitvad*) came to exist, when the dalitism/dalits were threatened by dominant brahmanic philosophical structures like *Hindutvad*.[170] Brahmanical philosophy excluded and isolated dalitism.[171]

In addition, dalit-bahujan of the nation was outraged when the *Hindutvad* or Brahmanism claimed to be the sole Indian philosophy. As an outburst, dalit militant movement emerged to compete with it. This policy can be identified as a tit for tat or retaliation method. In this context, *Dalitvad* built an antagonist image on other dominant traditions of India. Than asserting dalit identity, it went beyond to the annihilation of other identities. It seems to be a fascist/falsified nationalism.[172] Further, the influence of communism which seeks "revolution" as a means of protest and dignity fostered extreme expression of *dalitvad*. Dalit theology has emerged and nourished in this framework of extreme *dalitvad*.

Hindutva and communism, as the two dominant influences that create contemporary *dalitvad*, which presupposes that, for fuller liberation of dalits, annihilating or over throwing brahmanical tradition, is just and must. Indirectly, it also implies a dalit *desiyatha*, a craving for dalit nation. Dalit theologian V. Devasahayam's words also in line with this thought. He writes,

We conceive ourselves as constituting a nationality, *dalit desiyata*, a nationality in bondage, though we do not have an identifiable territory or a common language. We share a common past of glory followed by enslavement and a common hope of redeeming a single self- identity and dignity: "we are once the rulers once, and we shall be rulers again."[173]

---

[169] Cf. A. P. Nirmal, "Towards a Christian Dalit Theology," 222.

[170] S. Alangaram, *Religions for Societal Transformation: Inter-Religious Dialogue from Subaltern Perspectives* (Bangalore: Asian Trading Corporation, 2006), 68-69.

[171] "A particular *Hindutva* definition of nation with the exclusion of certain segments of society, or their relegation to second class citizenship…because they are placed outside of a narrowly formulated concept of nation." Felix Wilfred, *The Sling Utopia: Struggles for a Different Society* (Delhi: ISPCK, 2005), 215.

[172] Felix writes, "Opposing *Hindutva* forces in the name of another religious identity is a dangerous trap. It will only go to strengthen the agenda of *Hindutva*. Participation, dialogue and collaboration in the ambit civil society are the best course the Christian community can follow." Felix Wilfred, *The Sling Utopia*, 221. Also see Simon Samuel, "Decolonising the Biblical Studies," *Theological Research in the Global South: Prospects and Challenges*, edited by P. G. George (West Bengal: South Asia Theological Research Institute, 2015).

[173] V. Devasahayam, "Identity in Theology," in *Frontiers of Dalit Theology* (Delhi/Madras: ISPCK, Gurukul, 1997), 17.

This statement exemplifies that dalit theology is operated by the impetus derived from dalit nation and nationalism. That means, militancy, polemic, isolationist, sectarian and one-sidedness are the characteristics of *dalitvad* in which dalit theology is trapped into.[174]

In dalit theology, unnoticingly or unintentionally, this structure is built around exodus liberation motifs and deuteronomic creed with the non-filtered influence from Latin American Liberation theology and Afro-American Black Theology.[175] The exodus liberation is symbolized by 'a mighty hand', 'an outstretched arm' and by terror, says Nirmal.[176] For him, this implies that a measure of 'terror' is necessary to achieve dalit liberation as it happened with exodus event. In this way, Nirmal employs the Deuteronomic Creed as a paradigm which will affirm the identity of the Dalits and, in the process also, usher in dalit liberation. In this structure, God is seen as Liberator and Redeemer only for dalits and annihilator of dominant brahmanical hegemony. It is parochial and individualistic dalit theologizing. The common narrow definition of dalit theology *by* dalit as authentic theology will also serve the proponents of *dalitvad* that ultimately leads to divisive nationalism.[177] In this juncture, *dalitism* in oppose to *dalitvad* provides an alternative balanced understanding of what and who 'dalit' is.

1.3.3 *Dalitism* in Dalit Theology

The newly emerging spirit of militancy and assertion of their human dignity at any cost, can become the seed bed into which narrow communalism can be

[174] Anthoniraj Thumma emphases on the nature of the dalit movement lead by Ambedkar during pre and post Independent India generally characterized with "polemic, isolationistic, sectarian and one-sided approach," followed by dalit theologians. Dalit theologians much depend on these dalit movements' ideologies in order to have a praxis-oriented theology. Anthoniraj Thumma, *Dalit Liberation Theology*, 156.

[175] Gustavo Gutierrez and James Cone use the Exodus event as a paradigm to the liberation of the people from oppression or alienation. See James H Cone, *A Black Theology of Liberation* (Philadelphia and New York: JB Lippincott Company, 1970). Also Gustavo Gutierrez, *A Theology of Liberation*, Twelfth Print 1988 (London: SCM Press, 2000), 89.

[176] Arvind P. Nirmal, *Heuristic Explorations*, 146-148. Also "Towards a Christian Dalit Theology," in *A Reader in Dalit Theology*, 60.

[177] Christian theological reflection with reference to dalits was of three kinds. Firstly, theology *about* Dalits, or theological reflection among Christians concerning their responsibility to Dalits. Secondly, theology *for* dalits, or the theology of the Christian gospel (that is, good news) they addressed to Dalits, and which dalits responded and thirdly, theology *by* dalits, or the Christian theology which dalit have developed themselves or which has been implicit in their expressions of Christian faith. A radical approach has implied in recent time arguing that dalit theology can be and should be done *by* dalits alone. This exclusive nature of dalit theology built up in the structure of *dalitvad*. John C. B. Webster, *The Dalit Christians: A History* 1992, 4th edition. ISPCK Contextual Theological Education Series No. 4 (Delhi: ISPCK, 2009), 248-249.

fostered.[178] *Dalitvad* is a kind of enslavement of themselves into, in the words of S. Anandan, "the feelings of bitterness, anger and hostility on the basis of caste, race, colour and creed; instead of uniting and empowering them it tends to divide and weaken them."[179] In this regard Joseph Pandiappallil opines that "...I do not agree to the premise that we have to reject the existing philosophies in order to do justice to the dalits."[180] The dominant traditional characteristics of *dalitism*, contrary to *dalitvad*, are hospitality, friendliness, solidarity, communion with earth and nature, non-exploitative and non-dominating attitudes and earning one's livelihood by honest and hard labour which would not allow to parochialise in theologizing.[181] The pro-dalit symbols constructed were brought a 'terror' nature to dalit theological discourse. Dalitism, as its basic tenant, practices non-violence and respect for 'others'. Anthoniraja also agrees with it when he stated that dalit theological articulation must depend on dalitism, because "it [dalitism] determines its [dalit theology's] value system, principles and methodology."[182] Therefore, keeping these recent trends of *dalitvad* and dalitness in dalit theologizing as extreme views, this study focuses on *dalitism* as the launch pad for re-considering and re-structuring dalit theology, its method/ology and dalit historical consciousness. This dalit theology would celebrate the polyphony of theology *of / by / from* dalits. It would also redefine exclusive communitarian nature to inclusive humanitarian nature of dalit theology. Dalit theology's purpose is to become an alternate form of theological endeavor towards nurturing an egalitarian and humane value-system, which would support and sustain the aspirations of the weaker sections of the people relegated to the bottom of the social pyramid.[183]

Further, dalitism invites others to celebrate *with* their rich diversified historical consciousness, not only the pathos, but also all the strivings for future wholeness. This would also be recognition of 'others.' Dalit theology needs to

[178] S. Faustine, "From Exile to Exodus: Christian Dalit Women and the Role of Religion," in *Frontiers of Dalit Theology*, edited by V. Devasahayam (Delhi/Madras: ISPCK, Gurukul, 1997), 92-99.

[179] S. Anandan, in "Dalit Non-violence as a Means of Community Healing," presents reasons for dalits to be *dalitvad* such as of caste, untouchability, illiteracy, poverty, social status, lack of political power and proposes viable and tactic non-violent method of response, in *Building Theologies of Solidarity: Interfacing Feminist Theology with Dalit Theology and Tribal/Adivasi Theologies*, edited by Hrangthan Chhungi, Raj Bharath Patta and P. Mohan Larbeer (Bangalore: BTESSC/NCCI/ SCMI, 2012), 50-59. Also Gnana Robinson, "Theological Education in India To-day: Problems and Challenges," *NCC Review* CXV/4 (April, 1995): 291.

[180] Joseph Pandiappallil, "Need for an Inclusive and Integral Philosophy in the Indian Subcontinent," 152.

[181] S. Faustine, "From Exile to Exodus: Christian Dalit Women and the Role of Religion," 92-99.

[182] Anthoniraj Thumma, *Dalit Liberation Theology*, ix.

[183] M. E. Prabhakar, "Introduction," to *Towards a Dalit Theology* (Delhi: ISPCK, 1988), 4-5.

recognize such legitimate yearnings of broken people. Dalitism is also a liberative spirituality/philosophy. In the midst of hegemonic caste oppression, dalitism maintained to come along with it, as a different stream by correcting, interacting and protesting against dominant traditions. Such long survivality makes dalit a tradition of liberation, sustainability and authentic Indian spirituality.

1.4 A Re-definition to 'Dalit' Theology

When the term 'dalit' is used as an adjective to the 'theology,' it is a pointer to the role of this theological expression in dalit situation.[184] Dalit theology has predominantly used the expression dalit in a narrow sense that refers to the Scheduled Castes with the *primary* focus on them and *secondly* or *simultaneously* on their broken condition.[185] However, K. Wilson, a prominent dalit Christian thinker, regards the social structure and the ideology of caste as a *dalit enemy* without distinguishing between the two gives undue importance to the former. It increases the caste consciousness of the dalits than defeating their fight against castiesm.[186] Hence, Wilson has used the term 'dalit' to refer primarily to the broken human condition of the ex-untouchable communities which is to be healed, and *secondarily* or *simultaneously* to their caste.[187] Further, S. Chatterji uses the term dalit in a wider sense including, "various sections of the oppressed people" under the umbrella of dalit theological thinking.[188] Recently, Clarke Santhinathan has attempted to give the term dalit a broader meaning that embraces a subaltern dalit consciousness, which is more capable of forging bonds of solidarity to accomplish liberative goals.[189] Therefore, in this research, the term dalit, as etymological study proposed, is used *inclusively* in which all people who experience pathos of undefined condition are included and their collective struggle for wholeness must be the hallmark of dalit theology.

In the earlier phase of dalit theology, dalit identity was often seen within the framework of pain and pathos in which caste played a major role. It was similar to one of the etymological meanings of the term dalit as 'pressed down,' 'oppressed' and so on. But now the dalit identity can be *sudalit* or *dala*. In addition to the

---

[184] James Massey, *Down Trodden*, 63.

[185] J. Webster, *The Dalit History*, 192. Also M. E. Prabhakar, "The Search for a Dalit Theology," 201. Also Dionysius Rasquinha, *The Dalit Quest*, 83. Also James Massey, "Ingredients for a Dalit Theology," in *Towards a Dalit Theology*, edited by M. E. Prabhakar (Delhi: ISPCK, 1989), 59.

[186] K. Wilson, *The Twice-Alienated: Culture of Dalit Christians* (Hyderabad: Booklinks Corporation, 1982), 65-66, 88.

[187] K. Wilson, *The Twice-Alienated*, 65-66. Also "An Approach to Christian Dalit Theology," in *Towards a Dalit Theology*, edited by M. E. Prabhakar (Delhi: ISPCK, 1989), 59.

[188] Saral Chatterji, "Why Dalit Theology?"

[189] Santhinathan Clarke, "Subaltern, Identity Politics, and Christian Theology in India," in *Christian Theology in Asia,* Sebastian C. H. Kim, ed., (Cambridge: CUP, 2008), 271-290. Also Santhinathan Clark, Manchela Deenabandhu and Vinod Philip Peacock, eds., "Introduction," to *Dalit Theology in the Twenty First Century*, 7.

condition of brokenness, that is *dalitness,* one need to put the 'condition of wholeness' as the premise for dalit theology.[190] As elsewhere said, there can be two meanings for the term dalit such as brokenness and wholeness.[191] This could be named as dalitness and *sudalit,* which is the complete meaning of the term 'dalit.' Brahmabandhav Upadhaya, a Brahmin convert's poem *The Incarnate Logos,* mentions about Jesus as *sudalitkālakarāla,* which means crusher of fierce death.[192] And this balanced view is rendered by dalitism too. George Gispert-Sauch finds the usage of the term in the writings of a Brahmin convert who addressed Christ as "*sudalita*" literally "totally crushed." The adjective acquire here an active meaning. Christ is not here the one that has been crushed but rather the one through whose life and death the "terrible death" (*kāla-karāla*) has been crushed, or the one who has crushed death through his resurrection.[193] This usage of '*sudalit*' also proposes the positive connotation of something unfolding itself so as to pass from brokenness to wholeness.[194] It is from *dalitness* to '*dala'ness,* from brokenness to 'flowering' or wholeness, in and through the blossoming of the humanizing power and creative spirit of Jesus Christ, as L. Prasad comments.[195] Here, no longer we do construe 'dalit' as a closely guarded marker of either an ontological or biological identity, but rather, 'dalit' is projected as an open and dynamic affirmation of brokenness that invites solidarity from others who commit themselves to breaking down all forms of dehumanization.[196] Thus, dalit theology would articulate not only the brokenness, but also strivings for wholeness for a fuller liberation, having an inclusive framework.

---

[190] Cf. Dionysius Rasquinha, *The Dalit Quest.*

[191] See 1.1.1. Etymology of the term 'Dalit'.

[192] B. Upadhyay, "The Incarnate Logos," in *The Writings of Brahmabandhab Upadhyay,* Vol. 1, Library of Indian Christian Theology – 6, edited and annotated by Julius Lipner and George Gispert-Sauch (Bangalore: The United Theological College, 1991), 191.

[193] George Gispert-Sauch, "Jesus the "Good Dalit"," in *VJTR* 65/7 (July, 2001), 520. Refer also Timothy Tennent, *Building Christianity on Indian Foundations* (Delhi: ISPCK, 2000), 382-3. Also L. Prasad, "Dalit," in *Gems from India,* edited by George Gispert-Sauch (New Delhi: ISPCK/VIEWS, 2006), 174.

[194] George Gispert-Sauch, "Jesus the "Good Dalit"," 520.

[195] L. Prasad, "Dalit," 174.

[196] Nadars in the south India is an example for this *sudalit* experience. Nadars, traditionally a toddy-tapping caste group previously labeled as Shanars of low caste, denied the positioning them as polluted caste by Madras Census Commissioner in 1891. Their agitation against such caste division brought a emancipation and liberation from caste hegemony. They are a model for dalit liberation, who themselves eradicated low dalitness and build up a dignified identity and consciousness opposing to brahmanic categorization. See Nicholas B. Dirks, *Castes of Mind: Colonialism and the Making of Modern India* (Delhi: Permanent Black, 2001), 239.

1.4.1 A Re-consideration of Historical Dalit Consciousness

Dalit theology is built on the historical consciousness of Dalits and seeks to sensitize and further intensify this consciousness.[197] It seeks for a dalit cultural idiom for theological articulation.[198] A. P. Nirmal had deducted and exposed on the dalit philosophical stream in much early stage, but later dalit theologians showed less attention to vast dalit resources. Dalit theologians were concerned more with emphasizing dalitness and advocating *dalitvad*. While asserting the pathos and blaming caste for the same, they had forgotten the vital dalit ways to do theology. In this regard historical dalit consciousness, which cherished not only the pathos, but also distinct philosophical stream (dalitism), can be utilized meaningfully.

History and consciousness are interrelated, since consciousness of being a Dalit and the consequent questions such as why I am a Dalit and how I became a Dalit are unavoidably rooted in the history of dalits.[199] Dalit history is the only means which one can recover dalit past, which has deliberately been destroyed by the other dominant traditions. The historical dalit consciousness becomes established through a process of uncovering the roots, which is bound up with their existence in historic communities which have been suppressed and degraded through the ages and in which there is an awakening for regaining their lost identity. In the words of M. E. Prabhakar, "The dalit search is for community-consciousness, community-identity, community-autonomy and community-progress."[200] The nature of this 'community' so far was an exclusive one with casteist hegemony and anti-caste activities under *dalitvad* with exclusive methodologies. On the contrary, re-evaluating the historical 'dalit consciousness' would bring the 'dalitism' as the consciousness in which 'inclusivism' is emphasized. The dalit consciousness should realize that the ultimate goal of its liberation movement is the realization of full humanness or conversely, full divinity, the ideal of *imago dei*, the image of God in us.[201] In that sense, a renewed historical Dalit consciousness can be the primary datum of a Dalit theology.[202]

A. P. Nirmal uses as *historical dalit* consciousness instead of *dalit historical* consciousness. Here, consciousness is qualified by 'dalit,' as an adjective referring

---

[197] V. Devasahayam, "Formative Factors of Dalit Theology," 12.

[198] V. Devasahayam, "Formative Factors of Dalit Theology," 12.

[199] Charles Singaram, "Can Dalit Theology be Systematized? A Tentative Proposal," in *Moving Forms of Theology: Faith Talk's Changing Contexts*, edited by Israel Selvanayagam (Delhi: ISPCK, 2002), 127.

[200] M. E. Prabahakar, "Beginning and Growth of Dalit Studies in the CISRS and its Joint Programmes," *Religion and Society* XL/1&2 (March-June, 1993): 121.

[201] A. P. Nirmal, *Heuristic Explorations*, 148.

[202] Charles Singaram, "Can Dalit Theology be Systematized? A Tentative Proposal," 127.

to the condition of the consciousness.[203] In 'adjectival noun,' the phrase dalit consciousness could mean a consciousness that is weak, marginalized, step aside and neglected. Then, historical dalit consciousness refers to the *wounded psyche of a person or a community historically carried through.* Further, the meaning of the term 'dalit' is striving for wholeness that gives the historical consciousness as a progression/continuum of *dalitism* in which the aspiration for fuller liberation is attached with. Therefore, historical consciousness of dalit is both of pathos and of progression of dalitism, a distinct way of life in a society.

It means, then, that the dalits are not ashamed of being called dalit, since their history and culture from ancient times of the *bahuajan's* and distinct from elite discourses. Getting rid of their 'inferiority-complex' and 'slave mentality' is an integral part of the dalit consciousness- "Dalit is dignified."[204] It makes the dalits realize that their position in life is not simply to suffer their 'lot' but to take responsibility for themselves. The focus on dalitsm affirms their Dalit power not only for self-definition but also for their involvement on social change. Dalit power is "a clear critique of and a force for fundamental change of systems and patterns in society which oppress or give rise to oppression of dalit people."[205] It can also help to revive dalit symbols and also can create new ones. Dalit solidarity will help us in shaping dalit present economic, social and political existence as well.[206]

In nutshell, the question of dalit consciousness is really the question of dalit identity.[207] The question of identity is the question of the concerned people's roots and their historical consciousness. It considers the sidelined traditions of India that has survived for the wellbeing of weaker sections of society. The historical identity of dalit is not a caste identity, but the identity of the identification with pathos and struggles for wholeness. Therefore, dalit theology must also informed by a social vision which is a caste but inclusive in character.

---

[203] Johnson Puthenpurackal also shares similar concerns when he interprets dalit *perspective* as adjective and noun. "Philosophising from Dalit Perspective," in *Subaltern Perspectives: Philosophising in Context*, edited by George Thadathil (Bangalore: ATC, 2005), 25.

[204] Influenced by the ideas of K. Wilson, the Christian Dalit Liberation Movement (CDLM) which emerged in Madras on the 8th Dec. 1984 articulated the slogan 'dalit is dignified' and the term Christian dalit in 1985 and in 1986-87 the CISRS-CDLM circles chose the term *dalit theology* to name that they were articulating. This qualification of the noun consciousness with dalit can mean anything that is the meaning of dalit, including its etymological meaning.

[205] Cf. Statement in *Social Action Groups and the Churches in India* (ISRS, 1984) cited in M. E. Prabhakar, "The Search for a Dalit Theology," 45.

[206] James Massey, "History and Dalit Theology," *Frontiers of Dalit Theology* (Delhi/Madras: ISPCK, Gurukul, 1997), 181. Also *Down Trodden*, 23-40.

[207] Arvind P. Nirmal, "Towards a Christian Dalit Theology," 59.

1.4.2 Restructuring Dalit Theological Methodology

Theological methodology is a 'three level' endeavor, as Huang Po Ho observes.[208] It includes ways of establishment and organization of a theological structure and framework; methods of analysis and classification for social and historical situations and contexts; and the approaches of interpretation and hermeneutic toward theological resources.

In this way dalit theology would, firstly, have to find out ways and means for dalit theological structure and framework. Class and caste are not the means to frame dalit theology as elsewhere have discussed. Now, theologizing is done in dalit way. For this purpose, dalit symbols interacting with dominant traditions, if necessary, re-dalitizes all the resources. It can help us in framing a concrete dalit theological structure which is inclusive (opposite to exclusive of traditional dalit theology) in nature.

Secondly, method of socio-historical analysis is neither based on Marxist tool nor on castiestic tool, but with the criteria of dalit. Dalit in which *undefined condition of oppression* perceives the brokenness of the people and finds the *sprouts for wholeness* from the so-called weaker sections of the people themselves.

Thirdly, the approach towards the theological resources must be potential enough to re-create dalit myths, re-historicise dalit history and re-dalitise the faith confession. It is done not oppose to any dominant structures, since the method of dalit is not 'anti', but dialogue or *samvad* with dominant traditions.

Summary of Findings

The whole discussion on dalit movements and dalit Christian theological reflections in India can be summarized as follows:

Primarily, the term 'dalit' refers to the condition and status; the condition of undefined oppression and status of overcoming. Thus, dalits are the people who undergo the experience of brokenness and strive for wholeness, which disregards any exclusive connotation of the term based on caste.

Secondly, Dalit Movements have established root in the Indian dalit-bahujan civilization representing *Lokayata* philosophy carried out from pre-Aryan community till contemporary movements. These movements aggressively opposed the dominant brahmanic ideology, considering it as the cause for 'dalitness.'

Thirdly, contemporary dalit epistemology is the result of the historical movements ideology can be termed as *Dalitvad*- an extreme expression of dalitism. It advances a nationalism (dalit *desiyata*) that demands separate territories for Dalits (*dalitsthan*).

---

[208] Huang Po Ho, *No Longer a Stranger: Towards the Reconstruction of Contextual Theologies* (Thiruvalla: CSS, 2007), 51.

Fourthly, this *dalitvad* affected the dalit theological formulations in India negatively. Dalit theology emerged in opposition to the brahmanical theology by critiquing it served as patronizing theology for brahmanic dominance.

Finally, the dalit theology, once unintentionally used casteistic/class interpretation of 'dalit' which served *dalitvad*, must be re-considered on the basis of afresh identity of 'dalit,' which is a-caste based and a-class based. Thus, the renewed methodology of the dalit theology would be solidarity with 'all' those who experience the condition of brokenness (dalitness) and strive for wholeness in a dalit way.

Evaluation

Etymological study and historical usages give afresh meaning to the term 'dalit,' in which the condition of brokenness and strive for wholeness are emphatically emphasized than focusing to the casteic or class interpretation of the term. Thus, the concept of Dalit is not limited to any particular caste groups. Dalit is an inclusive ideology able to identify with anyone who experience the condition of brokenness. However, contemporary dalit movements grabbed it as their title impatiently in order to overcome the condition of 'dalitness.' This extreme spirit led these movements to be 'exclusive' in nature. It caused for *dalitvad* which argued for a separate dalit nation and wanted to always compete with *Hindutva(d)* and other brahmanical ideologies. This militant approach leads to national disintegration.

Dalit theological reflection in India also are limited in many ways. It serves the 'vested interests' of non-brahmanic communities in India than real 'dalits.' By establishing a separate identity in Indian context, the attempts of Phule, Ambedkar and Periyar was a formation of separate domain for dalits.

Possible re-definition of dalit is necessary to contour dalit theology in India. Primarily, caste defines Dalits as outcastes of Indian society. Secondly, Indian class interpretation defines dalits as deprived class. Finding for an alternative definition of dalits is not any total negation of the contemporary two-fold definition, but an integrated and holistic approach towards it. It builds upon them whereas caste and class are not necessarily sole center of this definition. The focal point of definition is 'dalit' itself, not necessarily as people, but as 'condition' and 'status' – condition of brokenness and status of overcoming. Dalitness defines who dalit is. It represents the *undefined exploited sections* of a society. They are not castes neither are they out-caste. They visualize the term dalit as an affirmation of brokenness that openly and dynamically invites solidarity from others who commit themselves to eradicating all forms of dehumanization.

Dalit movements provided Indian theological reflections in line with the dalits and their condition of brokenness. Dalit movements are reaching out to embrace dalit theology as a valid vehicle for the articulation of dalit experience and liberation.[209] In such context, dalit theology should provide right direction towards current dalit trends. Christian theologizing should not be a reason for "hegemonic act on caste people." Because it is not the 'caste people' who do evil, but the satanic structure that is built around them. Thus, this chapter critically looks at the fortress that dalit theologians have been building opposed to 'the others' in the Indian society, which is a war between *dalitvad* vs *Hindutva(d)*. This pragmatic and subaltern shift in theological discourse visibly has affected on the dalit view of Jesus Christ – the core and content of Christian faith. Therefore, there is a need to call back the parochialism of dalit Christology and will find an alternative place for Jesus to be situated in the Indian dalit context.

Evaluating dalit theology from above said perspective, it feels that, to a certain extent dalit theology also tended to the supporters of dalit national separatist movement, who annihilate whatever is non-dalit. Even Dalit theological methodology also served as an exclusive outlook for a defensive purpose, but really served as an offense to the so-called non-dalits who experience dalitness. This trend of dalit theology must be re-considered.

When dalitism becomes the foundation and structure of dalit theology, instead of extreme *dalitvad*, then the claim - "by the emergence of the dalit theology, an authentic Indian theology has emerged-" will be validated.[210] Otherwise, dalit theology would remain merely as a castiest theology that serves the elite people of the society not necessarily weaker ones. Because dalit theology is not a caste/class-based theology, but it is purely 'dalit' theology.

Conclusion

The contemporary use of the term 'dalit' is explicitly overriding of its semantic meaning. With this chapter, a proposal is placed to evaluate and understand the validity of new definition of 'dalit' as a condition of *undefined brokenness* and *status of wholeness*. It is secular in nature, not confined to any caste or religious community.

Dalit discourses (*dalitism*) is understood as the thought pattern of the subaltern, marginalized over the period of time from the mainstream of the Indian society, but now revived in its extreme position of *dalitvad* in opposition to *Hindutva(d)*. On the contrary to the contemporary trend of *dalitvad*, dalitism is a balanced voice of the weaker sections of society. It addresses the condition of brokenness and aspiration for the wholeness in a distinct dalit way. The dalit way, i.e., dalitism, is considered to be a prominent but forgotten tradition of India which has been existing parallel with other Indian traditions.

However, modern India has revived the dalitism from Phule, strongly built by Ambedkar and it still influences Indian society in an emphatic way. The emphasis

[209] Clarke, Manchela and Vinod, "Introduction," in *Dalit Theology in the Twenty First Century*, 11.

[210] Arvind P. Nirmal, "Introduction," in *A Reader in Dalit Theology*, edited by Arvind P. Nirmal (Madras: Gurukul Lutheran Theological College and Research Institute, nd), i.

on *dalitism* helps the dalits belonging to different language groups, ideologies, religions to come together forgetting their differences. This alternative trend is missing in the nationalist philosophical and cultural discourse of contemporary dalit movements and in dalit theological articulations. To sum up, *dalitism* is a dalit-bahujan thought and action process. Dalit *Desiyata* is an opposing nationalism of *hindutva* nationalism. Dalitstan gives the territorial and political landscape identity. Finally, dalitness is the reason for both the above mentioned factuals. In other words, historical development of *dalitivad* is the result of the people's experience of continuous dalitness.

The framework of dalit methodology that is proposed and argued for, in this study, is 'inclusive' in character. This inclusive approach would provide more vistas to dalit theologians in reflecting in the context of *dalitvad* and *hindutva(d)*-divisive nationalistic spirits. For dalit theology to become authentically Indian, the contemporary dalit theology needs a thorough revision and right direction. This dalit framework is used to see the condition of the early faith community (first century Christian church) and their faith confession.

2

The Early Community of Faith and Its Faith Confession: A Dalit Re-Mapping

Introduction

The Christian faith is centered on the historical event of Jesus Christ and different communities' faith on Him. Early Christian community and their faith on Jesus Christ is a raw material for any Christologizing. Studies on the early faith community and their faith confession, in recent time, have been widely discussed in the theological scholarship. Beginning with the eighteenth century C. E., a quest for original/early faith community and their confession has been emerging, which is for example evident in the writings of Herman Samuel Reimarus, G. E. Lessings and others.[1] This quest continues to affect the view on Jesus Christ and poses difficulty in relation between history of Jesus and faith in Christ. The trend of this scholarship has been moving back and forth while supporting either historical Jesus or Christ of faith.[2] It propelled the contemporary Christological

---

[1] Until the eighteenth century faith in Jesus Christ was known only through the religious experience in the church, codified creeds and doctrines about Jesus Christ and did not assess with reason. But with the historicism of the nineteenth century C. E., the quest for 'real' Jesus was posed. It reflected in the writings of Herman Samuel Reimarus. See *Fragments from Reimarus. Consisting of Brief Critical Remarks on the Object of Jesus and His Disciples as Seen in the New Testament*, translated by G. E. Lessing, edited by Charles Voysey (London and Edinburgh: William and Norgate, 1879). Also James M. Robinson, *Jesus According to the Earliest Witness* (Minneapolis: Fortress Press, 2007), 65.

[2] Research upon the 'Life of Jesus' scholarship generally summarize into three phases of development. The first phase is an 'anti-dogmatic,' started with Herman Samuel Reimarus climaxed in the writings of Albert Schweitzer. A second 'new' quest grounded in historical and traditional criticism as well as in Greco-Roman background. Even though the 'new' quest is connected to Ernst Käseman, it is James M. Robinson coined the term 'new' quest. And a 'third' quest rooted in the study of Jesus in his Jewish milieu. However, exact demarcation of this research into three phases

discourses, especially liberation theologies, with more emphasis given on the reconstruction of historical Jesus of Nazareth. Historical Jesus over against Christ of faith is the hero for liberation theologians. Christ of faith played a secondary or minimal role in the liberation theological articulation.[3] Therefore, present study persistently questions the logistics of 'exploring historical Jesus by avoiding Christ of faith' in contextual Christological articulations, and thrives for integration of both. How historical quest for Jesus impacted liberation theologies, especially dalit theology, will deal in the next chapter. Before such an attempt, one has to analyze how the *faith confession* of the early faith community developed in the midst of their existential issue of identity against dominant forces of that time. Did the early faith community demarcate historical Jesus and Christ of faith? How they maintained humanity (historical) of Jesus and divinity (Christ of faith) of Christ in their abysmal *dalit* experiences? Did *Christ of faith* help them to combat their dalit experience, which most liberation theologians disregard? Therefore, this part is not intended to reconstruct Jesus' life from the milieu of first century C. E. and be trapped into the contemporary quest for historical Jesus. Rather, this section regards the *faith confession* of the early church as a decisive factor in their sustenance and growth in midst of their *dalitness*.[4] It is a dalit reading of the early

---

seems ambiguous. See *Fragments from Reimarus*. Also Albert Schweitzer, *The Quest of the Historical Jesus: A Critical Study of Its Progress from Reimarus to Wrede*, translated by W. Montgomery from *Von Reimarus zed Wrede*, 1906 (Np: Suzeteo Enterprises, 2011). Also James M. Robinson, *A New Quest of the Historical Jesus*, Studies in Biblical Theology 1959 (London: SCM Press Ltd., 1970). Also Ernst Käseman, *Essays in New Testament Themes*, translated by Montague (London: SCM Press Ltd., 1964), 15-47. The summary of current trends in this scholarship is explored in M. J. Borg, *Jesus in Contemporary Scholarship* (Valley Forge, P.A.: Trinity Press International, 1994). Also Ben Witherington III, *The Jesus Quest: The Third Search for the Jew of Nazareth*, 2nd Ed. (Illinois: InterVarsity Press, 1997). Also John Dominic Crossan, *The Birth of Christianity: Discovering What Happened in the Years Immediately After the Execution of Jesus* (New York: Harper Collins, 1998), 43-44.

[3] Liberation theologies tend to emphasis historical Jesus and draw liberation motifs. That means, historical Jesus is the primary source of liberation, not necessarily the Christ of faith. For this, liberation theologians consider the necessity of reconstructing of Jesus of Nazareth from the gospel traditions. Arvind P. Nirmal, a pioneer dalit theologian, also maintains such presupposition that reconstruction of historical Jesus is necessary to formulate dalit Christology. Such trend downplays the presence of 'Christ of faith' in the *kerygma* of the early church. See Arvind P. Nirmal, *Heuristic Explorations* (Madras: The Christian Literature Service for the Gurukul Lutheran Theological College and Research Institute, 1990), 151-155. Also Gustavo Gutierrez, *A Theology of Liberation*, translated by Carida Inda and John Eagleson (Maryknoll: Orbis Books, 1988), 130-131. Also James H. Cone, *A Black Theology of Liberation*, (Philadelphia: J.B Lippincott Company, 1970), 197-227. Also Ronaldo Munoz, *The God of Christians*. Liberation and Theology Series 11, translated by Paul Burns (USA/Maryknoll: Burns & Oates and Orbis Books, 1991), 132.

[4] For Rudolf Bultmann, *Kerygma* is the proclamation of the decisive act of God in Christ. This *kerygma* occupies the center of faith confession. Faith confession explains, interprets and affirms the *kerygma* in the form of hymns, creeds, writings, teachings, preaching, in reaction to false teachings, struggle with demonic powers and in the witness of martyrs, exercised in the communal gatherings

faith community and its faith confession. The focus on the early faith community than Jesus, as a historical personality, would differentiate this study from other 'quests'. Hence, the task ahead is to define the early faith community and its situation that would elucidate the framework of early confessions, its contexts, content and significance in the early faith community's dalit experiences.

2.1 Mapping Contours of the Early Faith Community

The early faith community refers to the adherents of Jesus of Nazareth, who confessed Him as the Christ and the Lord, in different geographical area of the world from the first century to the fifth century C. E. This definition of the early faith community will discuss here in detail. Before detailed discussion on the 'early faith community,' a preliminary comment on its usage is necessary for clarity of thought. The phrase 'early' instead of 'earliest' gives an ample scope to enlarge the period till the fifth century C. E.[5] The term 'community' is used as a collective noun. In spite of the existence of geographically different communities, it is the 'faith' (confession) that characterizes and unites them as one "community."[6] These basic assumptions are helpful to draw a possible contour of the early faith community's location, timing, membership and their profession of common faith.

---

such as of Lord's Supper, baptism and others. Thus, comparing to *kerygma* in relation to the in-depth content and characteristics, faith confession is inclusive. Therefore, scope of this research widens from the *kerygma* to the confession of the early faith community. Rudolf Bultmann, et al., *Kerygma and Myth: A Theological Debate*, edited by Hans Werner Bartsch (New York: Harper & Row Publishers, nd.). Also Hans Conzelmann, *An Outline of the Theology of the New Testament* (New York: Harper & Row, 1969), 62. Also Günther Bornkamm, *Jesus of Nazareth*, translated from German edition 1959 by Irene and Fraser McLuskey with James M. Robinson (Minneapolis: Fortress Press, 1995), 189.

[5] There are usually two usages, according to D. H Williams, of the term 'early Christian' in relation to its periodization. First, as a reference to Christian communities of the first and early second century C.E., often called the New Testament church. Secondly, it is used as a way of talking generally about patristic Christianity, that is, the period of the church fathers that immediately followed the apostles and continued for five or six hundred years. This research emphasizes the later usage in which 'early' referring to the era of the formulation of the completed Christian faith and its interpretation in more systematic and advanced way. See for details *Evangelicals and Tradition: The Formative Influence of the Early Church* (Grand Rapids, Michigan: Baker Academics, 2005), 24-25.

[6] A community is a group of people established with shared values. People can belong to a number of different communities like cultural community, religious community simultaneously. In this research, the word 'community' is used to give meaning of the people group of the early church who professed 'common faith.' This common faith united early faith communities together as 'community.' John Behr writes, even though "there were Christian communit*ies*, scattered throughout the Empire, from Edessa in the East to Lyon in the West, displaying a remarkable diversity but also a concern to hold a common faith and pattern of life." [Emphasis added] See "Social and Historical Setting," in *The Cambridge History of Early Christian Literature*, edited by Frances Young, Lewis Ayres, and Andrew Louth (Cambridge: CUP, 2004), 55. Also Roger Haight, *Dynamics of Theology*, (Bangalore: Claretian Publications, 2002), 21. Also J. N. D. Kelly, *Early Christian Creeds*, 1960, 3 Ed. (London, New York: Continuum, 1972), 94. Also Daniel Bell, *Communitarianism and its Critics* (Oxford: Clarendon Press, 1993), 14.

2.1.1 Location

It is difficult to draw a strict geographical line in the sense of identifying a particular locality for the early faith community. Nevertheless, Greco–Roman world[7] provided a premise for the early faith community to view themselves as a part of a wide geographical territory.[8] Geographically, the early faith community as a *continuum* spread throughout Asia, Europe and Africa having prominent centers like Jerusalem, Antioch, Alexandria and so on within a short span of time.[9] This geographical expansion was a reason for the differences in the articulation of faith confessions in the early faith community.[10] Therefore, the geographical location of every community is important in the course of the development of the faith affirmation.[11] In a sense, different locations of the early faith community gave birth to diverse confessions en route for the faith in Jesus, the Christ. However, one has to acknowledge that the early church councils, to some extent, helped the church of different geographical situations to be united in their faith confession.

2.1.2 Timing

The period of the early faith community can be extended from the time of post-resurrection scenario (generally New Testament/Apostolic time) to the council of Chalcedon (451 C. E.). Further, this large phase can be divided into two

[7] Greco-Roman world is characterised by the entrance of Roman Empire mainly into its eastern regions, including Asia Minor, Syria, Palestine, and Egypt where Greek culture was prevailed because of the influence of Alexander the Great and his successors. George D. Dragas, "Greece, Greek," in *Encyclopaedia of Early Christianity*, edited by Everett Ferguson (New York and London: Garland Publishing, 1990), 392.

[8] Even though there was a multiplicity of differences in Greco-Roman world, in the word of Gerald Downing, it was "a common universe of discourse, a common intertexture." Tacitus writes about the first century situation under Roman Empire as "…countries and nations (*gentes*) should form one body under the name of Romans." *Annals*, 11:24 quoted in Terrence, "Gentile," 457. Also Gerald Downing, *Doing Things with Words in the First Christian Century* (New York, London: T&T Clark, 2004), 21. Also Halvor Moxnes, "Landscape and Spatiality: Placing Jesus," in *Understanding the Social World of the New Testament*, edited by Dietmar Neufeld and Richard E. DeMaris (London and New York: Routledge, 2010), 90-106.

[9] John E. Stambaugh and David L. Balch dedicate last part of the chapter of their book *The New Testament in its Social Environment* to talk about the major centers of Christian community. Antioch in Syria, Ephesus and other cities in Asia Minor, Philippi and Thessalonica of Macedonia, Corinth of Achaia, Rome and Alexandria of Egypt. (Philadelphia: Westminster Press, 1986), 145-187.

[10] Geography plays vital role in the formulation of thought pattern and expression of a particular community. In the words of Paul McKechnie, Christianity grew and succeeded, and its vigour lay in diversity as well as in uniformity. The diversity was mainly geography but unity in the faith confession. *The First Christian Centuries: Perspective on the Early Church* (Secunderabad: OM Books, 2001), 14. Also see John Knox, *The Early Church and the Coming Great Church* (London: The Epworth Press, 1957), 63-129. Also Halvor Moxnes, "Landscape and Spatiality: Placing Jesus," 93.

[11] For instance, the Christianity at Antioch emphasized on the humanity of Jesus whereas the Alexandria emphasized on the divinity during the second and third century C. E. See detailed discussion in 2.4.3. Christological-Thematic Analysis of the Faith Confession.

according to the time in which the faith confession is formed. They are, 'the making of Christology' and 'the developed (orthodoxy) Christology,' that is to say, *formative period* of the faith confession and *formed period* of faith confession in the form of creeds and dogmas.[12] Formative period refers to the period from first followers of Jesus to the time when Christianity became the official religion of Rome. Formed period refers to the time between the Council of Nicaea to the Council of Chalcedon.[13] In the formative and the formed periods, faith confession of the early community and the New Testament literature had been in the process of canonization.[14] It means that Christology has been developing both 'outside' of the New Testament and even 'after' the first century C.E. Thus, the zenith of the development of the Christological faith, both structurally and affirmatively, presented in the ecumenical creed of the Church at the Council of Chalcedon must be taken as the scope of this research.

---

[12] Until the fourth century C. E., Christology was in the process of making and in the fourth century C. E, especially of the Chalcedonian Council, Christology formed as established orthodoxy. James D. G. Dunn, *Unity and Diversity in New Testament: An Inquiry into the Character of Earliest Christianity* 1977, 2 ed. (London: SCM Press, 1981), 11-32.

[13] Generally the period of early Christianity is limited from about 30 C. E. to the rise of the state church under Roman emperor Constantine in 313 C.E. However, one can extend the period even beyond that, from the point of view of the developments of the early faith confessions. Delbert Burkett, *An Introduction to the New Testament and the Origins of Christianity* (Cambridge: Cambridge University Press, 2002), 90.

[14] There is a tendency to treat the early Christians as the people of 'the text,' that is, the texts are the central focus of the community for the faith and practice. Though, the early faith community valued the Hebrew Scripture and Christian writings, it received as authoritative text in the sense of exposing their faith affirmation only. Therefore, it could appropriate to argue that 'texts' were used as a means to express their faith affirmations. Further, the texts were not the sole criteria for the development of the faith confessions in the formative period. Primary authority during formative period was the living testimony or living voice. However, the writings of the apostles regarded as important because they bear witness first hand Jesus' experience. In addition, it is to be noted that, even though the New Testament writings and other fragments were written before early 90's, the formation and affirmation of it happened in the third and fourth century with the process of canonization. Therefore, it would be proper to assume about the centrality of the faith and its confession in the early faith community than the centrality of the scripture. Thus, the assumption of early community of 'the text' turns to be the community of 'the faith'. See J. F. Bethune-Baker, *An Introduction to the Early History of Christian Doctrine to the Time of the Council of Chalcedon* 1903, 6th Ed. (London: Methuen & Co. Ltd, 1938). Also Edward Lohse, *The Formation of the New Testament*, translated by M. Eugene Boring (Nashville: Abingdon Press, 1981). Also James Barr, *Holy Scripture: Canon, Authority and Criticism* (Philadelphia: Westminster Press, 1983) 1-22. Also N. T Wright, *The Last Word: Beyond the Bible Wars to a New Understanding of the Authority of Scripture* (New York: HarperSanFrancisco, 2005), 54-58. Also R. Timothy Mclay, "Biblical Texts and the Scriptures for the New Testament Church," in *Hearing the Old Testament in the New Testament*, edited by Stanley E. Porter (Michigan: William B. Eerdmans, 2006), 43. Also Adolf Harnack, *What is Christianity* (New York: G. P. Putnam's Sons, 1901 reproduced by San Diego: The Book Tree, 2006), 10.

2.1.3 Membership

In the earliest period of the early faith community, members were comprised of, predominantly, people of Jewish ethnicity.[15] In the later stage, the influx of gentiles had given a gentile predominance within the 'faith community.'[16] However, the community maintained its inclusive nature by accommodating both Jews and Greek, slave and free, male and female (cf. Gal. 3:28a). That means, the membership of the community was opened to all those who were willing to accept and proclaim the faith confession.[17] This inclusive nature formed the inner consciousness of the community. It is also noted that such inclusive consciousness was the reason for their faith confession – "for *all* of you are *one* in Christ Jesus" (Gal. 3: 28b) – in the community. This inclusive consciousness was one of the characteristics of the early faith community.

2.1.4 Faith Confession

The early faith community had been revolving around the faith in Jesus, as they confessed Him 'the Christ.'[18] The Christian faith confession, according to Rudolf Bultmann, "is the saving faith which recognizes and appropriates God's saving work in Jesus Christ."[19] In other words, the faith confession was communities' authentic expression of belief and understanding.[20] It concentrated into a radical change to those who professed it and therefore it had no systematized intellectual articulation.[21] Consequently, this proclamation of faith is known as the apostolic teaching (Acts 2:42), the Word of Life (Phil. 2:16), the Words of Faith and Good Doctrine (I Tim. 4:6). Later on, the early faith community began to argue the certainty of their faith as they had historically held, called it as 'rule of faith' or 'canon of truth.'[22] Albeit 'rule of faith' was not systematically arranged, it

---

[15] Howard C. Kee, *Christian Origins in Sociological Perspective* (London: SCM Press, 1980), 98. Cf. Donald A. Hgner, "An Analysis of Recent 'Historical Jesus' Studies," in *Religious Diversity in the Greco-Roman World: A Survey of Recent Scholarship*, edited by Dan Cohn-Sherbok and John M. Court (Sheffield: Sheffield Academic Press, 2001), 106.

[16] Recent scholarship rejects the strict division of Jewish and gentile Christianity, because there can be less evidence for such demarcation. See Troels Engberg–Pederson, ed., *Paul Beyond the Judaism/Hellenism Divide* (Louisville: Westminster John Knox Press, 2000).

[17] Hans Conzelman, *History of Primitive Christianity*, 49.

[18] Cf. Philip Schaff, ed., *The Creeds of Christendom with a History and Critical Notes*, Vol. 1: The History of Creeds, Reprint 1931 (Michigan: Baker Book House, 1990), 4.

[19] Rudolf Bultmann, "πιστεύω κτλ," in *Theological Dictionary of the New Testament,* Vol. VI. edited by Gerhard Kittel and Gerhard Frierich (Michigan: Wm. B. Eerdmans Publishing Company, 1968): 208-209.

[20] Kelly R. Iverson, "A Centurion's "'Confession": A Performance-Critical Analysis of Mark 15: 39," *Journal of Biblical Literature*, 130/2 (Summer, 2011): 336.

[21] Paul M. Bassett, "Faith," in *Encyclopaedia of Early Christianity*, edited by Everett Ferguson (New York and London: Garland Publishing, 1990), 338.

[22] Ralph P. Martin, *Worship in the Early Church* (New York: Guideposts, 1975), 55.

bespoke of the universally accepted content – Jesus Christ.[23] The crux of the early faith confession was a pre-Pauline and post-resurrection reality.[24] Articulation and affirmation of the faith confession became more technical, philosophically complex, and ideologically weighted, acknowledged as creeds, when the early faith community had sought for a secure place in a wider plural society with dissent voices like heresies.[25] This historical adaptability of the 'faith' into 'creeds' in a complacent philosophical framework shows preservation of the *kerygma* that combated divisive teachings like of heresies and preserved the community as catholic and apostolic community.

In short, the early faith community was diverse in numerous areas but united in strict sense of the faith confession. With such assumptions, we need to place the early faith community in its wider context. It would help us to understand the external milieu of the early faith community.

2.2 The Positioning of the Early Faith Community in its Strange Context

The wider context of the early faith community is vivid with three dominant forces of that time such as Greece, Rome and Judaism.[26] Formative period for the early Christianity was a period of struggle with these dominations;[27] struggle with cultural domination of Greek,[28] political imperialism of

---

[23] Paul M. Bassett, "Faith," 338.

[24] The *kerygma* was consisted of the faith in historical Jesus, his mission and post-resurrection presence as Christ of faith. Martin Hengel, *Between Jesus and Paul: Studies in the Earliest History of Christianity*, 1983 (Eugene, Oregon: Wipf and Stock Publishers, 2003). Cf. James D. G. Dunn, "Remembering Jesus: How the Quest of the Historical Jesus Lost its Way," in *Handbook for the Study of the Historical Jesus*, Vol. 1: How to Study the Historical Jesus, edited by Holmén and Stanley E. Porter (Boston, Leiden: Brill, 2011), 187.

[25] Paul M. Bassett, "Faith," 340.

[26] It is an unanimous agreement of Biblical scholars that there are three major world powers of the first century Palestinian context that influenced in the growth and development of Christianity. The three nations have their own specialty. For example, while the Rome is known for its military power, Greek in its philosophical hegemony, whereas Judaism for its religiosity with a zeal to conquer the world. This leads to the highly idealized concept of *oikoumenē* of that time. Terence L. Donaldson, "Gentile Christianity" as a category in the study of Christian Origins," *Harvard Theological Review*, 106/4 (Oct, 2013): 454-455. Also J. Dwight Pentecost presents clubbed materials on the background during first century Palestine. *Words and Works of Jesus Christ* (Michigan: Zondervan Publishing House, 1981), 515-571. See also F. Hrangkhuma, *Introduction to Church History* (Bangalore: TBT, 1996).

[27] John Behr writes, "It was a period of struggle for survival and the crucible in which the basic elements of Christian identity and church organization were forged." "Social and Historical Setting," 55.

[28] Hellenisation is a technical term firstly used by J. G. Droysen, referring to the cultural movement after Alexander (333 – 323 B. C. E) resulting that the then world was dominated by

Rome[29] and religious fundamentalism of Judaism.[30] The struggle with these dominant forces did not mean that the early faith community was a by-product of these dominant contexts. Rather, the early faith community held an explicit self-consciousness as a community of distinct faith expression as they interacted with dominant forces of that time.[31] The context of struggle and constant confrontations led to the definition of the early church's identity and their faith affirmation. Some of the characteristics of the early faith community in its formative period in relation to its wider context are worth mentioning.[32] Therefore, here, it is an attempt to find the location of the early faith community in the wider context of first four centuries without downplaying dominant context of that time.

Greek language and civilizations. H. Jagersma, *A History of Israel from Alexander the Great to Bar Kochba* (London: SCM Press Ltd., 1998), 10.

[29] The early faith community witnessed Roman empire's flourishing under Trajan (98 – 117 C. E.) and later its declination due to internal problems and external pressure. They retained the memory of Roman Empire mainly because of two reasons. Firstly, the persecution of Rome towards the earliest faith community such as under the emperor Nero in 70 C. E. and Decius in the middle of the third century C. E. Secondly, royal protection to the early faith community after the conversion of Constantine towards the fourth century C. E. in later stage of the community. Thus, the early faith community's perseverance helped to them to survive in the period of unfriendly political situation of Rome that resulted into the acceptance of Christian faith as royal religion. See Andrew Stephenson, *The History of Christianity: From the Origin of Christianity to the Time of Gregory the Great*, Vol. 1. (Boston: Richard G. Badger, 1919), 254-255. Also F. Hrangkhuma, *An Introduction to Church History*, 33-34. Also Peter Lampe, "Early Christians in the City of Rome. Topographical and Social Historical Aspects of the First Three Centuries," *Christians as a Religious Minority in a Multicultural City: Modes of Interaction and Identity Formation in Early Imperial Rome. Studies on the Basis of a Seminar at the Second Conference of the European Association for Biblical Studies (EABS) From July 8-12, 2001, in Rome*, edited by Jürgen Zangenberg and Michael Labahn (New York, London: T&T Clark International, 2004), 20-32.

[30] One of the struggles of the early faith community with the Jewish context was the exclusivism of Judaism and universalism of the gospel. See Herman Bavinck, "The Catholicity of Christianity and the Church," *Calvin Theological Journal* 27/2 (1992): 225.

[31] For instances, Jesus' movement had constant struggle with other religious sects of Judaism. Apostolic movement was a struggle to find a place in the wider Greco-Roman world. Roman Garrison's statement, "early Christianity firmly rejected Greco–Roman religious and event to the god of the Jews" makes clear picture that the struggle early Christianity with three major world views. *The Greco-Roman Context of Early Christian Literature* (Sheffield: Sheffield Academic Press, 1997), 9. Cf. Ben Meyer, *The Early Christians: Their World Mission and Self-Discovery* (Delaware, Wilmington: Michael Glazier Inc., 1986), 36. Also John Behr, "Social and Historical Setting," 55.

[32] During formative period, the main struggle was with outside communities such as various sects of Judaism, philosophy of Greeks and military power or authority of Rome. Such analysis is important to note that how does the early community uphold faith in Jesus amidst of these constant struggles. Nevertheless, internal struggles also were another factor that Christian community had to respond affirmatively. Here, former struggle is emphasized. James D. G. Dunn, *Unity and Diversity in the New Testament*, 341 ff.

2.2.1 The Early Faith Community's *Glocalisation* and Cultural Hegemony of Greece

The early faith community can be placed in the cultural context of Greece. The features of language, philosophies and other cultural categories of Greek were prominent and were used by Roman Empire to maintain domain over eastern people, though the Greek context of Hellenism had to undergo attempts of annihilation by Romanism.[33] Hellenistic world for some Romans was a place of learning, initiations and travels and tours and for others a place to remain after renouncing Rome.[34] That is to say, Greek culture was in the process of deterioration, yet engaged in an intense dialogue of 'cultural mapping' of mutual self-definition and aggressive maintenance of boundaries with Rome.[35] An affinity with things of Hellenic culture and a desire for integration of Roman were the two predominant tendencies during this time.[36] It was a fusion of cultures which characterized Greco-Roman world.[37] The early faith community was sandwiched in between the synthesis of Greece's culture and Roman's politics.[38] The language as a carrier of culture and philosophy (worldview), Greek offered universal umbrella for the early faith community to amalgamate their faith with Greek philosophical stream. It became quite evident later when the apologists and spokespersons of Christian faith had to combat with the Grecian philosophical imposition over the faith community. For instance, Gnosticism, a Greek worldview, assimilated the early

---

[33] Elisabeth Schüssler Fiorenza, "Critical Feminist Historical Research," in *Handbook for the Study of the Historical Jesus*, Vol. 1: How to Study the Historical Jesus, edited by Holmén and Stanley E. Porter (Boston, Leiden: Brill, 2011), 541.

[34] See C. R. Whittaker, "Imperialism and Culture: The Roman Initiative," in *Dialogues in Roman Imperialism: Power, Discourse, and Discrepant Experience in the Roman Empire*, (JRA Supp. Series, No. 23), edited by D. J. Mattingly (Portsmouth: JRA, 1997), 143-163. Also Simon Samuel, "A Postcolonial Reading of Mark's Story of Jesus," 97.

[35] Simon Samuel, *A Postcolonial Reading of Mark's Story of Jesus* (New York: T&T Clark International, 2007), 55. Cf. S. E. Alcock, "Greece: A Landscape of Resistance?," in *Dialogues in Roman Imperialism: Power, Discourse, and Discrepant Experience in the Roman Empire*, (JRA Supp. Series, No. 23), edited by D. J. Mattingly (Portsmouth: JRA, 1997), 109. See also Stanley E. Porter, "The Context of Jesus: Jewish and/or Hellenistic?," in *Handbook for the Study of the Historical Jesus*, Vol. 2: Study of Jesus, edited by Holmén and Stanley E. Porter (Boston, Leiden: Brill, 2011), 1441-1463.

[36] Simon Samuel, *A Postcolonial Reading of Mark's Story of Jesus*, 59.

[37] Simon Samuel writes, "...Greek generally responded to the Roman advances, invasions and colonization in an ambivalent manner accepting and rejecting Rome and also appreciating and disrupting their native Greek/Hellenistic culture almost simultaneously." in *A Postcolonial Reading of Mark's Story of Jesus*, 65.

[38] A Horsley, "Jesus-in-Context: A Relational Approach," in *Handbook for the Study of the Historical Jesus*, Vol. 1: How to Study the Historical Jesus, edited by Holmén and Stanley E. Porter (Boston, Leiden: Brill, 2011), 214.

faith community's confession with mythical orientation.[39] It shook the skeleton of the early faith community, which disregarded humanity of Jesus and held mythical understanding of Jesus with Greek mythical thoughts of *Aeons*.[40] In addition to this ideological blow, the oppression faced by the early faith community was more of psychological in nature. Greek philosophical hegemony negatively affected the total consciousness of the early faith community since it challenged their core faith itself. Philosophical oppressors wanted to synchronize with their agenda of relating Jesus either to human alone or to divine alone. However, the early faith community utilized the energy of Greek in the attempt of globalizing their philosophy to produce universal affirmation. The result of it was the production of 'creeds' as the universal Christian declaration. These reactions helped the early faith community to maintain and cherish the *complete consciousness* of Jesus, his historical human existence and his current existence as the Christ of faith. This made the community of faith to be harbingers of unified faith confession.[41] In a way, the Greek cultural-philosophical domination was compelling the early faith community to merge with the mainline prevailing worldview, but the community refused such globalizing attempt of the cultural imperialists by maintaining a local, yet universal faith confession of Jesus of Nazareth as the Christ of their faith. Thus, this period witnessed emergence of an alternative hybrid philosophical structure from the early faith community to combat any intrusion of oppressive philosophical thoughts.

2.2.2 The Early Faith Community's Initiative for Integration and Roman Imperial Regime

Rome was the world's first territorial empire which tightly integrated military, economic, political and ideological strands of social power better than any earlier empires.[42] Rome placed its legions on the periphery of every territory that they own for an unified operation. This nature of empire helped Rome to interfere much more intensely in local affairs, lives, customs, and traditions of that time.[43] Although, in the early phase of the early faith community got special considerations

[39] Gnosticism can be seen as a world view of Hellenistic culture. Cf. Joseph B. Tyson, *The New Testament and Early Christianity* (New York and London: Macmillan Publishing Company, 1984), 376-377.

[40] Joseph B. Tyson, *The New Testament and Early Christianity*, 379.

[41] Richard A. Norris, Jr., "Articulating Identity," *The Cambridge History of Early Christian Literature*, edited by Frances Young, Lewis Ayres and Andrew Louth (Cambridge: CUP, 2004), 71.

[42] The view about emperor helped Roman Empire to execute its imperial ideology tightly embracing the whole world. Augustus, for instance, was Divine, Son of God, God, and God of God. He was Lord, Redeemer, Liberator and Savior of the world. Roman concept of emperor motivated to conquer the whole world. John Dominic Crossan, "Context and Text in Historical Jesus Methodology," in *Handbook for the Study of the Historical Jesus*, Vol. 1: How to Study the Historical Jesus, edited by Holmén and Stanley E. Porter (Boston, Leiden: Brill, 2011), 165.

[43] John Dominic Crossan, "Context and Text in Historical Jesus Methodology," 165.

from the Roman Empire because of their affinity with Jewish sects of that time, in the later period, Rome censored the early faith community as *illicit religio* (illegal religion).[44] The early faith community's firm rejection of Greco-Roman traditions, and their gods and goddesses, resulted into severe persecution. Jewish community also betrayed them before Roman Empire, which intensified the persecution and isolation.[45] In this context of struggle, the early faith community maintained its faith claims emphatically and more meaningfully.

Roman empire started to consider the early faith community as a threat to popular convictions.[46] Persecutors branded Christians as a communal sect, who practices unconventional rituals.[47] Notwithstanding persecution, the early faith community emerged to be more resistive and intrepid to the imperial dominance of Rome in order to explain the purpose of their existence, than politically overthrow the Roman imperialism. The early faith community's presentation of Jesus as the Lord and Son of God was stemmed from the images of Roman political context of that time, which was a positive affirmation and constructive response to the existing Roman reign.[48] Drawing oppressive images from the Roman political oppressors show the *adaptability*, not uncritical-admiration, of the early faith community. It also was an invitation to the Roman imperialism to see how an oppressed community look at oppressive imageries and utilizing creatively to preserve their faith confession.[49] For instance, Jesus was addressed as Lord, who supposed to be ruler, but the early faith community utilized particular imagery of 'Lord' to share the 'serving' or 'ministering' attitude of Jesus (Mark 10:45). This attempt denotes the early faith community's deliberate response

---

[44] The official religion of Roman Empire was emperor worship. Nevertheless, Rome had paid a special consideration to Jews to continue their religious practices irrespective of its contradictory nature towards Roman Emperor worship. The early faith community enjoyed same freedom in the beginning stage till the Synagogue community betrayed them. Everett Ferguson, *Background of Early Christianity,* 2 Ed. (Grand Rapids, Michigan: William B. Eerdmans Publishing Company, 1993), 556-571.

[45] Refer Scott Cunningham, *Through Many Tribulations: The Theology of Persecution in Luke-Acts* (England: Sheffield Academic Press, 1997).

[46] Roman Garrison, *The Greco-Roman Context of Early Christian Literature*, 9.

[47] R. E Brown, Carolyn Osick and Phem Perkins, "Early Church," *New Jerome Biblical Commentary*, edited by Raymond E. Brown (Bangalore: TPI, 1991), 1342.

[48] Adam Winn, "Tyrant or Servant? Roman Political Ideology and Mark 10.42-45," *Journal of the Study of the New Testament* 36/4 (June, 2014): 330-331.

[49] Cf. Gary Gilbert, "Roman Propaganda and Christian identity in the Worldview of Luke-Acts," in *Contextualising Acts: Lukan Narrative and Greco-Roman Discourse*, edited by Todd Penner and Caroline Vender Stichele, Society of Biblical Literature: Symposium Series No. 20, edited by Christopher R. Matthews (Atlanta: Society of Biblical Literature, 2003), 233-256 especially 237. Also Milton Moreland, "Jerusalem Community in Acts: Mythmaking and the Sociorhetorical Functions of a Lukan Setting," in *Contextualising Acts: Lukan Narrative and Greco-Roman Discourse*, edited by Todd Penner and Caroline Vender Stichele, Society of Biblical Literature: Symposium Series No. 20, edited by Christopher R. Matthews (Atlanta: Society of Biblical Literature, 2003), 303.

to the oppressing or persecuting nature of Roman imperial power. The images that derived from their oppressors creatively converted in the form of faith confessions.[50] The political, social and economic oppression did not destroy the faith confession or the community, rather produced occasions to interact and dialogue with dominant structures of the period, which promoted harmonious and healthy co-existence of different people groups. Thus, political isolation and persecution, a *dalit* condition of the early faith community imposed by Roman imperialism, overcame with the imageries of oppressors themselves. That means, the early faith community was a corrective force to regulate the political, military, economic and ideological currents of that time.[51]

2.2.3 The Early Faith Community's Inclusive Identity and Divisive Spirituality of Judaism

The time of the early faith community overlaps two distinct periods of Jewish religion/history such as second temple Judaism and Rabbinic Judaism.[52] Judaism during the time of the early faith community was more of a Hellenistic nature.[53] While all Jews believed in one God and followed the Torah, great diversity existed with respect to other beliefs and practices. Such differences led to the formation of different religious groups, parties, or sects such as of the Pharisees, the Sadducees, and the Essenes. Therefore, the early faith community was (mis)understood as one among other Jewish sects in its early phase.[54] As a result,

---

[50] Adam Winn, "Tyrant or Servant? Roman Political Ideology and Mark 10.42-45," 349.

[51] Cf. Peter Oakes, ed., *Rome in the Bible and the Early Church* (Grand Rapids: Baker, 2002). Also Howard Kee, *Christian Origins in Sociological Perspective*, 120.

[52] In the former period, religion revolved around the Temple, and the leading religious figures were priests. This period extended from the completion of Jerusalem's second temple in 516 B.C.E to its destruction in 70 C.E. After the destruction of the Temple, religion focused on study of Jewish Law (the Torah), and the leading religious figures were rabbis (scholars of the Law). These two periods are generally designated Second Temple Judaism and Rabbinic Judaism, respectively. Delbert Burkett, *An Introduction to the New Testament and the Origins of Christianity*, 32.

[53] James H. Charlesworth says that "Philo mixed Jewish traditions in the caldron of Greek ideals and myths. Josephus explained Jewish theology as if it was like Greek philosophy. These examples refer that Judaism in the later period was amalgamation of Greek and Judaism of that time." "The Historical Jesus: How to Ask Questions and Remain Inquisitive," in *Handbook for the Study of the Historical Jesus*, Vol. 1: How to Study the Historical Jesus, edited by Holmén and Stanley E. Porter (Boston, Leiden: Brill, 2011), 119. Also Stanley E. Porter, "The Role of Greek Language in Historical Jesus Research," in *Handbook for the Study of the Historical Jesus*, Vol. 1: How to Study the Historical Jesus, edited by Holmén and Stanley E. Porter (Boston, Leiden: Brill, 2011), 362-404 especially 375. Also Teresa Okure, "Historical Jesus Research in Global Cultural Context," in *Handbook for the Study of the Historical Jesus*, Vol. 2: Study of Jesus, edited by Holmén and Stanley E. Porter (Boston, Leiden: Brill, 2011), 962.

[54] Pharisees, Sadducees, Essenes, Scribes and others were similar sects within the larger Jewish religious tradition with an exclusive perspective. The context of isolation and sectarianism prevailed even in this wider Jewish religious tradition; some sects agreed with mainline Judaism, for example

the early faith community became a minority sect comparing to other Jewish sects of that time.[55] While Jewish community, at large, embraced synagogue community of Judaism, they had excluded/ex-communicated the early faith community. The sectarianism, parochial attitude, and extreme vituperation of Jewish religious tradition could not accommodate Christianity, a Jewish offspring, in later stage with its faith confession.[56] In the words of Williston Walker "By the last decade of the first century, the rabbis who reorganized and reinvigorated Judaism after the destruction of the temple had inserted in the synagogue prayers an anathema which made it impossible for a "Nazarene" to participate officially in the liturgy."[57] It was a deliberate attempt to seclude and isolate the early faith community from the mainline religious tradition of nation Israel and betraying to Roman political authorities. However, this condition of exclusion and isolation from the popular religious tradition of that time, can also be termed as a *dalit* condition, the early faith community had maintained the conscious as the messianic community (*ekklesia*), where all were included irrespective of ethnicity, nationality and religiosity.[58] The distinctive feature of the early faith community was its ecumenical orientation over against the parochial nature of Judaism. The faith claims that emerged in this condition of *dalitness* shows inclusive and ecumenical characteristics, for instance, "...there is no distinction between Greek and Jew, circumcised and uncircumcised, barbarian, Scythian, slave and freeman, but Christ is all, and in all" (Col. 3:11). This statement represented the inclusive and ecumenical nature of early faith community and their faith confession.

In short, Greek's ideology to assimilate the early faith community with its philosophical universalism was responded with the particularity of the faith confession and its universalistic implication. The Roman context also demanded

---

Rabbinic, some deliberately separated from mainline Judaism such as Qumran, Essene communities. Usage of Jewish scripture, use of synagogues, monotheistic belief and other matters contributed to the view that Christian faith is similar to that of a Jewish sect. The early faith community was in the middle of these two extremities. Neverrheless, Christianity moved beyond its original sectarian Jewish environment. Howard Kee, *Christian Origins in Sociological Perspective*, 108. Also Emil Schürer, *The History of the Jewish People in the Age of Jesus Christ (175 B.C.-A.D. 135)*, Vol. II, revised 1979 and edited by Geza Vermes, Fergus Millar and Matthew Black (Edinburgh: T&T Clark Ltd., 1986), 550-590.

[55] Jewish Christians were considered among the *mînîm*, gradually they were excluded from synagogue worship sometime between 85–130 C.E. The Rabbinic distaste for sectarians (*mînîm*) was enshrined by a curse against them introduced into synagogue prayer (the expanded 12th of the Eighteen Benedictions) later.

[56] James H. Charlesworth, "Exploring Opportunities for Rethinking Relation among Jews and Christians," in *Jews and Christians: Exploring the Past, Present and Future*, edited by James Charlesworth (New York: Cross Road, 1990), 37.

[57] W. Walker, *History of the Christian Church*, 4th Edition (New York, 1985), 33.

[58] Christians were taught to think of themselves in collective terms and as a distinctive from other cultic religious group. Cf. Larry W. Hurtado, *At the Origins of Christian Worship: The Context and Character of Christian Devotion* (New York: Guideposts, 1999), 54-55.

the early faith community to be uncritical obedient and assimilate with Roman political regime. But the early faith community maintained critical approach in the process of integrating with the mainline society and kept a unique identity within the society. That is to say, the early church had an integrative approach. While Roman ideology interfered at peripheries of the society to force margins to join with them by demanding uncritical obedience, Jewish got a special consideration. However, the special considered Jewish community excluded 'others.' Conversely, the early faith community responded with accommodativeness to include both Jews and non-Jews alike. Thus, the early community of faith was a *dalit* community isolated from the mainstream of society, yet they strived for an integration to present their confession vividly.

2.3 The Early Faith Community and their Immediate Settings of Faith Confession

Study on the early faith community's interaction with its strange contexts brings forth important distinctiveness of the community – a struggling (dalit) community within dominant structures, which maintains a separate but united identity within themselves. The struggle of the early faith community with the dominant forces produced "newer forms of ideas."[59] These ideas were confessed and developed in the precise backgrounds of the early faith community. Hence, before analyzing the content of the confession, it is necessary to expound the immediate locale of the early faith community's confession. Describing these immediate contexts would also help us to recognize the distinctive characteristics of the early faith community and context in which the early faith confession is made.[60]

2.3.1 Context of 'Household' Gathering

The cultic setting of the early church, mainly, was in the house setting that provided direct engagement and participation of all the community members.[61] The breadth of participation transcended the lines of differentiation and marginalization which was in operation outside of the worship setting.[62] This domestic setting, the size of the house-church group, and shared meal in the worship practice contributed to the social intimacy and strong solidarity among the members of the early church. It furthered with the persistence of the early confession in the form of prayer, teachings, hymns and so on.[63] By participating in

---

[59] Jonathan Knight, *Christian Origins* (New York: T&T Clark, 2008), 322.

[60] See for more detail on the implication of the faith confession in the setting of early faith community in 2.4.2. Functional Analysis.

[61] Larry W. Hurtado, *At the Origins of Christian Worship*, 41.

[62] Larry W. Hurtado, *At the Origins of Christian Worship*, 46.

[63] W. O. E. Oesterlay, *The Jewish Background of the Christian Liturgy*, 1925 (London: Oxford University Press, 1965), 149. Also Bruce D. Chiton and Jacob Neuser, *Classical Christianity and*

worship, a person, along with the community actively involved in the confessing activity.[64] In the words of Larry Hurtado, the little house-groups saw themselves as bearing of salvation in the history and as God's *ekklesia* being called together in response to the divine summons issued in the gospel message. Their worship assembly was itself an event of eschatological meaning, a foretaste of the blessings of the coming age, and participation of the heavenly realities, which included the presence of holy angels and the presence and power of Christ experienced through the phenomena that they saw a manifestations of divine power.[65] Thus, the faith confession became more relevant to the household setting but transcended its scope beyond the household gathering.

2.3.2 Context of Fellowship Meal

Fellowship meals were another context of the early faith community that expressed group solidarity regardless of their individual social status, economic standing and gender (Gal. 2:28 cf. Col. 3:11), feel of equality, acceptance and recognition in the community.[66] Christians referred to one another as brothers and sisters, children of the same heavenly Father, or members of one body (I Cori. 12:27). Fellowship meal, thus, provided inclusive forum of participation regardless of the people from various social levels. It included women, slaves and others who were regarded as socially inferior.[67] The portrayal in Acts 2:45-47 reveals the nature of the early faith community as the community of sharing and of equality. Members were allowed to openly participate in public liturgical life and leadership of the community. The fellowship meals were, often, centered on faith confession of the community.

2.3.3 Context of Cultic Practices

Since "the Christology took birth in the context of worship," as Ralph Martin states, the early faith community's worship life also needs some discussion here.[68]

Rabbinic Judaism: Comparing Theologies (Grand Rapids, Michigan: Baker Academic, 2004), 29. Also Harry Emerson Fosdick, *The Man from Nazareth: As His Contemporaries Saw Him* (New York: Harper and Brothers, 1949), 35. Also Wayne A. Meeks, *The First Urban Christians: The Social World of Paul*, 1983, 2 Ed. (New Haven and London: Yale University Press, 2003), 157-162.

[64] Wayne A. Meeks, *The First Urban Christians*, 150-157. See also 2.2. The Positioning of the Early Faith Community in Its Strange Context.

[65] Larry W. Hurtado, *At the Origins of Christian Worship*, 62.

[66] Larry W. Hurtado, *At the Origins of Christian Worship*, 44.

[67] In this regard, the status of women in the early faith community needs some comments. They enjoyed considerable acceptance and respect inside the community. The gospel narratives that daringly mention the first apostle of Jesus was a woman (John 20:17). A similarly open participation by those of lower social and economic status, even slaves, including visible participation in corporate worship, seems to have been widespread among the early Christian groups. Cf. I Cori. 11: 17-22. Larry W. Hurtado, *At the Origins of Christian Worship*, 45.

[68] Ralph P. Martin, *Worship in the Early Church*, 33.

The early faith community experienced mystical dimension in the congregations. Miracles were etiquette of the earliest community. Teaching and preaching was the method of communication. Even the letters were also preached (read) in the churches. Further, the language of the earliest Christian discourse used in collective worship was the expression of intimacy. Seemingly, outlook of the early community was scholastic in nature, the early faith community lacked complicated components as of the colourful Roman religiosity like, sacrifices and offerings to idols.[69] The symbolic act of baptism or Lord Supper remained a simple act, but gave importance to the meaning of such symbolic acts. Later, Greek philosophical affinity provided useful intellectual framework for the faith community's religious practices in the worship.[70] Therefore, cultic practices were fertile place for emergence of confessions in a more systematic way as liturgy(ies).

2.3.4 Context of Persecution

In the early period of the faith community, persecution was a local affair. In 64 C. E., Nero persecuted Christians with false allegations can be noted as first official persecution over the early faith community.[71] However, persecution continued sporadically throughout the second and third centuries because of hostility from pagan and support from local Jewish authorities.[72] Persecution provided the early faith community "a greater sense of cohesion and belonging as they realize they are all in it together."[73] In addition, it is interesting to note that, even in the midst of this *dalitness*, feeling of ostracized by society at large, people were willing to join the community and to suffer with one another.[74] In a way, the context of persecution functioned to strengthen the early faith confession and community together. For instance, the writings of Apologetic Fathers' confessions in the midst of persecution would throb with logical and emotional movements. However, the Edict of Milan, which was issued by Constantine, a Roman emperor, ended official persecution in 313 C. E. granted complete freedom of worship.[75] With

---

[69] E. A. Judge, "The Early Christians as a Scholastic Community," *Journal of Religious History* 1 (1960/61): 4-15.

[70] Thomas P. Rausch, *Who is Jesus? An Introduction to Christology* (Minnesota: Liturgical Press, 2003), 149.

[71] Later, Roman emperors began to issue edicts against the Christians, forbidding them to make converts, ordering them to sacrifice to the gods, and forbidding Christian worship. Such edicts resulted in new waves of martyrdom. The persecution climaxed under the emperor Diocletian and his successors, during the years 303-313 C.E. Bart D. Ehrman, *The New Testament: Historical Introduction to the Early Christian Writings* (Oxford: OUP, 2000), 396.

[72] Delbert Burkett, *An Introduction to the New Testament and the Origins of Christianity*, 102-3.

[73] Bart D. Ehrman, *The New Testament: Historical Introduction to the Early Christian Writings*, 399.

[74] Bart D. Ehrman, *The New Testament: Historical Introduction to the Early Christian Writings*, 399.

[75] Delbert Burkett, *An Introduction to the New Testament and the Origins of Christianity*, 103.

Constantine's support, Christianity became the favored religion of the state of Rome.[76]

These concrete contexts would help to unravel the structure of the faith confession and provide way out to analyze the content of the faith confession and its function and significance in the early faith community.

2.4 The Early Faith Confession: Structural – Functional and Thematic Analysis

'Confession' usually signifies a statement of belief that expresses certain basic convictions about God and Jesus. Statement of belief can be in various forms depending on particular circumstances in which it is used. For instance, theological statements or confessions during the time of worship, prayer, preaching, liturgy, teaching, catechism, and apology are different.[77] This section tries to analyse the content of the early faith confession. For that, previous analysis of the wider and immediate contexts of the early faith community would serve here as the concrete background to examine the faith confession structurally, functionally and thematically.

2.4.1 Structural Analysis

In order to understand what the early faith community meant (i.e., significance of confession) when they confess Jesus (i.e., content) in their particular contexts, it is appropriate to study structure of the confession of the early faith community. The structure is the carrier (husk) of the content, i.e., view about Jesus Christ, who gave meaning to the existence of the life and worship of the early faith community. This would help us to identify the early Christology of the community that carried along with their struggle of subsistence and made them an authentic community.

Scholars have often used such terms as creed, formula of faith, *kerygma*, *paradosis* (that is, tradition), hymn, prayer, confession, liturgical formulations, ecclesial tradition, narrative portion, story or saying when trying to establish a nomenclature for faith confessions. Richard N. Longenecker argues for the existence of 'confessions' prior to any other developments such as *kerygma* (proclamation), *parenesis* (ethical exhortation), *didache* (teaching), and different forms of the faith confession, in the early faith community.[78] Nevertheless, Ethelbert Stauffer observes that "many confessions were hymn-like and many hymns were creed-like."[79] Technically this classification of confession comes

---

[76] Delbert Burkett, *An Introduction to the New Testament and the Origins of Christianity*, 103.

[77] It is already discussed in 2.3 Immediate Settings of Faith Confession in the Early Faith Community.

[78] See *New Wine Into Fresh Wineskins: Contextualizing the Early Christian Confessions* (Peabody: Hendrickson Publishers, Inc., 1999).

[79] Ethelbert Stauffer, *New Testament Theology*, translated by J. Marsh (London: SCM Press, 1955), 237.

under the titles – formulaic prose portions (often called as *homologiai*, a Greek word for confessions) and poetic portions (hymn), as Longenecker suggests. This genre classification seems to overlap since the early faith confessions were transferred, mainly, in the oral form and preserved in written form. In addition, single-statement affirmations and early creeds can also add to this list of structural analysis as a unanimous and popular confession of the early faith community.[80] Single statement as the shortest form of the early faith confession and early creeds as the longest or precise explicit statement of the early community provide to include in the earliest and last in the list of structural analysis of early faith confession respectively. Thus, we find four prominent confessional models in the early faith community such as titular (single statement affirmations), *homologai*, hymns and creeds.

2.4.1.1 Single-Statement Affirmations (Titular)

Most often single-statement affirmations ascribed to the titles of Jesus Christ appear in the poetic and prose confessional portions. Single-statement confessional affirmations spoke about the work or the person of Christ. Chief among the titles were, for example, as "the Christ," "the Son of God," or "the Lord."[81] The early community of faith, therefore, "denied this sort of status to the Roman ruler."[82] Larry Hurtado says that "the characteristic use of the definite article in the New Testament acclamation of Jesus with these titles carries an implicitly exclusive connotation."[83] Frequently, titles of Jesus, as single-statement affirmation, are taken to reconstruct early Christology by contemporary Christian theologies.[84]

---

[80] Richard N. Longenecker, *New Wine Into Fresh Wineskins*, 6-26.

[81] Richard N. Longenecker gives example for important confessional titles of the early community. Primarily for Christ Mark 8:29b- Peter's confession: "You are the Christ"; John 1:15-27, 41; 7:41; 9:22b; 11:27; 20:31; Acts 9:22; 17:3b; I John 2:22a; 5:1a. can be considered as the early confession noted in New Testament. For Son of God title, Mark 15:39; Matt. 16:16; John 1:34, 49; 11:27; 20:31; Acts 9:20; I John 4:15; I John 5:5, and for Lord Rom 10:9; I Cor. 12:3; II Cor. 4:5; Phil 2:11; Col 2:6. are the examples. *New Wine Into Fresh Wineskins*, 21.

[82] Larry W. Hurtado, *At the Origins of Christian Worship*, 117.

[83] Larry W. Hurtado, *At the Origins of Christian Worship*, 117 fn. 27.

[84] It is a general trend among scholars to concentrate only the titles without regarding its usage in the early faith community to develop early Christology. For instances see Oscar Cullmann, *The Christology of New Testament* (Philadelphia: Westminster John Knox Press, 1963). Also F. Hahn, *The Titles of Jesus in Christology* (London: Lutterworth, 1969). Also Reginald H. Fuller, *The Foundations of New Testament Christology* (New York: Charles Scribner's, 1965). This would be seen as an imposition of present historical scholarship on the Christological titles than regarding how the community perceived it. Michael J. McClymond also tells the danger that Jesus' title alone cannot be valid to formulate Christology, since the titles are relative and original intention of them is missing. However, the context of the titles can provide us the nature of Christology that they professed. Michael J. McClymond, *A Familiar Stranger: An Introduction to Jesus of Nazareth* (Grand Rapids, Michigan: William B Eerdman's Publishing Company, 2004).

However, the existence of other forms, such as in prose and poetic forms of early faith confession, allow us to be aware of the danger to limit early Christology to the titles of Jesus alone.[85] Certain linguistic features commonly appear in the introductions to confessional materials, such as the use of (1) the verb confess (ὁμολογέω), (2) other verbs of a kerygmatic, didactic, or confessional nature, (3) a double accusative, or an infinitive (often in combination), i.e., *hoti recitativum*, and (4) a participial construction or relative clause.[86] By recognizing this, we can overcome the jeopardy of particularization of the early faith confession into single statement confession alone.

2.4.1.2 *Homologiai* (Formulaic Prose Portions)

Homologiai means an agreement to the declarations of another.[87] To identify early formulaic confessional materials, many of the form-critical criteria used. Longenecker lists them as follows:

> (1) The presence of *parallellismus membrorum*, even though the material is not poetry; (2) the presence of *hapax legomena*; (3) a preference for participles over finite verbs; and (4) an affirmation regarding the work or person of Jesus Christ. Further, there are some linguistic indicators such as (5) the noun ὁμολογία (confession) to signal the content of such early Christian material, either expressed or implied; (6) the verb ὁμολογέω (confess) with a double accusative or an infinitive to introduce a direct or an indirect quotation; (7) the word ὅτι (the *hoti recitativum*) to introduce a direct or indirect quotation; (8) verbs for preaching (εὐαγγελίω, κηρύσσω, or καταγγέλλω), teaching (διδάσκω), or witnessing (μαρτυρέω or μαρτύρομαι) to introduce confessional material; and (9) a participial construction or a relative clause are used to introduce the material in question.[88]

Longenecker also gives an example from 1 Cor. 15:3b–5. He writes,

> the material is introduced by a fourfold use of the *hoti recitativum*, and the two crucial points of death and resurrection are highlighted by the repetition of the *hapax legomenon* expression "according to the Scriptures":

[85] The titles of Jesus express one or the other characteristics of Jesus, which need further explanations to be away from exclusive Christology. Ben Witherington III writes, "no one title or label adequately explains a figure as complex as Jesus." *Jesus the Seer: The Progress of Prophecy* (Peabody: Hendrickson, 1999), 246.

[86] Adopted mainly from Richard N. Longenecker, *New Wine Into Fresh Wineskins*, 15.

[87] Vernon H. Neufeld, *The Earliest Christian Confessions*, New Testament Tools and Studies, Volume V, edited by Bruce M. Metzger (Netherland: Brill Archive, 1963), 14.

[88] Richard N. Longenecker, *New Wine Into Fresh Wineskins*, 15.

> [That] Christ died for our sins according to the Scriptures;
> [that] he was buried;
> [that] he was raised on the third day, according to the Scriptures;
> [that] he appeared to Peter and then to the Twelve.[89]

Another example Longenecker gives from Colossians 1:15–20.[90]

2.4.1.3 Hymns (Poetic Portions)

Poetic portion is also one of the confessional structures in the early faith community. Eduard Norden proposed the following criteria for identification of hymn-like confession: (1) the presence of *parallelismus membrorum* (i.e., parallel structures), (2) the use of second- or third-person singular pronouns at the beginning of such portions, (3) the use of participial predications and relative clauses throughout these materials, and (4) an elevated, celebratory style.[91] Longenecker finds some of the common features of poetic portions as follows:

> (1) The presence of parallel structures *(parallelismus membrorum)* that reflect Jewish or Hellenistic poetic conventions; (2) The presence of words and phrases not used elsewhere in an author's writings *(hapax legomena),* or not with the meaning or in the manner found in his other writings— which suggests that the material in question was probably composed by someone else; (3) A preference for participles over finite verbs, suggesting an original oral provenance; (4) The frequent use of the relative pronoun ὅς ("who") to begin passages; (5) Contextual dislocations: poetic material in a prose section or doctrinal material in an ethical section; (6) The continuance of a portion after its content has ceased to be relevant to its immediate context; and (7) the affirmation of a basic Christian conviction, usually concerning the work or person of Jesus Christ.[92]

For hymn form of confessional examples, Longenecker gives from Phil. 2:6–11, I Tim. 3:16b, and I Pet. 2:22–23.[93] Ralph P. Martin also writes about major content of the poetic structure of confession would be:

> They are related to the person and mission of Christ Jesus and tell how He existed in the pre-existent glory of His Father and was the Agent

---

[89] Richard N. Longenecker, *New Wine Into Fresh Wineskins*, 16.

[90] Richard N. Longenecker, *New Wine Into Fresh Wineskins*, 16.

[91] Mentioned in Richard N. Longenecker, *New Wine Into Fresh Wineskins*, 9.

[92] See Richard N. Longenecker, *New Wine Into Fresh Wineskins*, 10-11.

[93] Ralph P. Martin, *Worship in the Early Church*, 48-49. Also James Ian Hamilton McDonald, *Kerygma and Didache: The Articulation and Structure of the Earliest Christian Message*, Society for New Testament Studies Monograph Series, 37 (Cambridge: CUP, 1980), 64-68. Also Hans Conzelmann, *An Outline of the Theology of the New Testament*, 80. Cf. Richard N. Longenecker, *New Wine Into Fresh Wineskins*, 12.

> in creation. He became Man [*sic*] and accomplished redemption for the world through His suffering and death. At length He is exalted and enthroned and receives from God in a solemn acclamation the supreme name.[94]

Thus, traditional hymns as faith confessions were used to keep away from the error and from lapsing into heresy other than cultic purpose.

2.4.1.4 Creeds

The word creed is derived from the Latin term *credo*, means "I Believe."[95] This short definition of creed helps to place the early faith confession, in the form of creeds, much earlier date than any declaratory creeds.[96]

The process of 'creedization' began even in the earliest period of the early church, when they proclaimed – "*I Believe* in Jesus as Lord and Saviour" (Baptismal Creed) – at the time of baptism that can be generally named as interrogatory creed.[97] However, the declaratory creeds emerged later, such as the Apostolic Creed,[98] the Nicene-Constantinopolitan,[99] and the Athanasian Creed, played vital role in the early church to preserve and maintain the content of the early faith confession. However, these creeds did not represent complete statement

---

[94] Ralph P. Martin, *Worship in the Early Church*, 52.

[95] Here, present researcher differs from the definition of J. N. D. Kelly on creed as "a fixed formula summarising the essential articles of their religion and enjoying the sanction of ecclesiastical authority" and goes for etymological meaning of 'I believe'. J. N. D. Kelly, *Early Christian Creeds*, 1.

[96] There is some ambiguity in the way the phrase "declaratory creed" is used in the literature. On the one hand, the phrase is consistently set over against "interrogatory" confessions such as in early baptismal confessions. Kelly defines declaratory creeds as "short statements, couched in the first person, asserting belief in a select group of facts and doctrines regarded vitally important." However, this does not distinguish between expressions of the rule of faith, which were typically single-authored, ad hoc, and local, and conciliar creeds, which were multi-authored (or at least presented as multi-authored), more formal in presentation, and to which conformity was expected. Kelly, *Early Christian Creeds,* 3:31. Also Craig A. Blaising, "Creedal Formation As Hermeneutical Development: A Reexamination of Nicaea," *Pro Ecclesia* XIX/ 4 (from ATLA accessed on 21-08-13): 374.

[97] The baptismal creed, in early period, was in the form of question answer form. Graham Keith, "The Formulation of Creeds in the Early Church," *Themelios* 24/1(October, 1998): 14-17.

[98] The Apostolic Creed seems to have had three uses, first as a confession of faith for those about to be baptised, secondly as a catechism (an instruction for new Christians in the essentials of the faith), and thirdly, as a 'rule of faith' to give continuity to orthodox Christian doctrine. It has existed essentially since the second century C. E. and was first referred to in the fourth century C. E. See W. Sanday, "Recent Research on the Origin of the Creed," in *The Journal of Theological Studies* 3-20. Accessed from http://www.biblicalstudies.org.uk/pdf/jts/001_003.pdf on 21-11-14.

[99] The Nicene Creed is an example for fixed declaratory creed, which became the model for all later declaratory creeds beginning with Constantinople in 381 C. E. W. Sanday, "Recent Research on the Origin of the Creed," 5.

of the Christian faith as a whole.[100] This limitation of incompleteness in creeds' content can be seen as a functional one. That means, creeds were used in its *Sitz-im-Leben*[101] and functioned as a tool for instruction, apologetic and worship as well as philosophical discourses. In that way, creedal formulas were limited in its linguistic style to explain fully the content of the faith.[102] Since, the struggle of the early faith community was not only over proper theological terminology and its use, but also for the effort to bring the mystery of Jesus, the Christ into a philosophically conditioned language. That means, creeds cannot be taken as normative value, even though they were expressed in the language of certainty.[103] It can run the risk of each affirmation being also a denial of some other aspect of the mystery.[104] Therefore, in short, existence of variety of creeds and other confessional formulas to express one faith confession gives the ambiguity and plurality of the content of the faith confession.

2.4.2 Functional Analysis

The function of the faith confession also gives meaning to the content of it. This section, therefore, would analysis the usage of the faith confession in the early faith community's life and worship. This would help us to reflect on how the faith confessions were meaningful in relation to its function in a particular occasion such as in the contexts of worship, wrong teachings, and also in the contexts of persecution and public witness.

---

[100] Geoffrey Grogen, *The Christ of the Bible and the Church's Faith* (Np: Mentor, 1998), 229. Also Ernest Best, "The Use of Creedal and Liturgical Materials in Ephesians," in *Worship, Theology and Ministry in the Early Church: Essays in Honor of Ralph P. Martin*, edited by Michael J. Wilkin and Terence Paige (Sheffield: Journal for the Study of the New Testament Press, 1992), 53.

[101] *Sitz im Leben* is a German term referring to 'setting of life'. Donald K. McKim, *Westminster Dictionary of Theological Terms* (London: Westminister John Knox Press, 1996), 262.

[102] One example of such limitation mentioned by James M. Robinson, "It [Apostolic Creed] begins with what was done *for* Jesus, "conceived by the Holy Spirit, born of the virgin Mary," and then skips to what was done *against* Jesus, "suffered under Pontius Pilate, was crucified, died and buried." But what is skipped in the middle is what was done *by* Jesus- as if that were not important enough to include what we believe about Jesus!" Also Geoffrey Grogen writes, we must treat the ancient creeds in their historical settings (not in the setting of sophisticated modern psychological or philosophical discussion). They had their own technical terminology available.... James M. Robinson, *Jesus According to the Earliest Witness*, viii. Also Geoffrey Grogen, *The Christ of the Bible and the Church's Faith*, 226. See also Delbert Burkett, *An Introduction to the New Testament and the Origins of Christianity*, 128.

[103] Edward Schillebeeckx, *Jesus: An Experiment in Christology*, translated by Hubert Hoskins (New York: The Seabry Press, 1979), 55.

[104] Thomas P. Rausch, *Who is Jesus?*, 154.

2.4.2.1 Liturgical Function

As already argued somewhere, the liturgical context of the early faith community was the fertile place for the emergence of Christology and its confession.[105] The faith confessions were so strategic and meaningful exercise in the community's activities. In the community, during the time of sacraments, such as of baptism and Lord's Supper, pronounced their confession. At the time of baptism, a participant and baptizer would confess the Lordship of Jesus and affirm it by pronouncing 'in the name of Jesus Christ.'[106] The emergence of Baptismal Creed must also read along with the function of the confession in the liturgical context.[107]

In addition, particular acts such as of baptism represent death and resurrection of Jesus as historical event. It is also same with Lord's Table, which trace back to the historicity of institution in relation to Jesus and proclaims 'Jesus' death until he comes' (Cf. I Cor. 11:26). Further, the early faith community's *prayer*, *kerygma* (preaching), *parenesis* (ethical exhortation), and *didache* (teaching) embodies strong Christological conviction.[108]

2.4.2.2 Apologetic Function

The reason behind the persecution was, in a sense, the confession of the early faith community.[109] When they were put on trials, it was demanded to recant their faith in Jesus and perform certain cultic gestures, such as invoking their gods, offering incense to the image of emperor and ritually cursing Jesus.[110] It was in this context of religious ritualism that the early faith community was asked to present their faith (Acts 7:1-53). Such contexts, they would publically confess their faith more with polemic nature (cf. Acts 5:29-32). For instance, the confession of Stephen about Jesus as "the Son of Man standing at the right hand of God" would indicate the nature of confession in the context of persecution (Acts 7:56). V. H. Neufeld connects the confession – Jesus is the Lord – an act to the situation of trial, conflict and persecution.[111] Those who suffered death for their faith came

---

[105] See. 2.3.3 Context of Cultic Practices. Also Ralph P. Martin, *Worship in the Early Church*, 33.

[106] Geevarghese Mar Osthathios, "Cosmic, Communitarian and Kenotic Dimensions of the New Man in Christ," 177-185. Available from http://www.biblicalstudies.org.uk/pdf/ijt/27-3-4_177.pdf accessed on 12-02-15. Also see Vincent Taylor, *The Person of Christ in New Testament Teachings* (London: Macmillan & Co., 1958), 203.

[107] For more details, see 2.3.3. Context of Cultic Practices and also 2.4.1.4. Creeds.

[108] Mike Highton, "Christology," *The Cambridge Dictionary of Christology*, edited by Ian A. McFarland and et.al. (Cambridge: Cambridge University Press, 2011), 100.

[109] It is usually argue that Christians put to death not because of their odd practices, but because of what they believed. Gerald Bray, *Creeds, Councils and Christ: Did the Early Christians Misrepresent Jesus?*, 1984 (Scotland: Mentor, 1997 reprinted in 2009), 75.

[110] Pliny, *Epistles* 10.96 Martyrdom of Polycarp 8-9 cited in Larry W. Hurtado, *At the Origins of Christian Worship*, 3.

[111] V. H. Neufeld, *The Earliest Christian Confessions*, 60-67.

to be known as 'martyrs' ("witnesses"). Tertullian, an apologist and church father of second century C. E., understood persecution and death for the sake of the Name (of Christ) primarily as a *confession*.[112] Faced with this situation, Christian intellectuals began to write defenses of the Christian faith known as *Apologies*.[113] These Apologists sought to show that the popular antagonism toward Christianity was unfounded.[114] The language of the expression of the faith confession would be more definite, rendering the linguistic help from surrounding contexts.

2.4.2.3 Anti-Heretical Function

While persecution was an external setting where the confession was made, internally, wrong teachings also molded and sharpened the faith confessions about Jesus Christ in the early faith community. The recent discovery of *The Didache of the Twelve Apostles* points out to the context of false teachers and fraudulent Christian leaders of the early second century C. E.[115] Heresies were a kind of philosophical oppression, as elsewhere stated, tries to assimilate and reduce the meaning and content of the confession.[116] The early faith community rejected any perversion and extremity in the early faith confession. For example, Gnostic Christianity and Montanist represented two extremities of perversion of the faith confession, where former attempted to syncretise with Gnostic philosophy and later with an extreme which demanded ascetic life.[117] While the extreme of both positions was renounced to preserve apostolic witness (the early faith confession), and the episcopate, the canon, and the creed were developed accordingly.[118] It is to say that church councils were very particular in the formation of creeds, which is developed out of early faith confessions to compete heresies of that time. The council's assertion in creedal forms represents the general confession of the early

---

[112] Geoffrey D. Dunn, *Tertullian: Early Church Fathers* (London: New York: Routledge, 2004), 27-31. Cf. Gerald Bray, *Creeds, Councils and Christ*, 75.

[113] The apologists are a group of early writers who wrote apologies or a justification of the faith to those outside of the church. Some of the notable example of Apologies are (1) Epistle to Diognetus. (2) The Apology of Aristides. (3) The Works of Justin Martyr. (4) The Apology of Athenagoras. (5) The Muritorian Fragment. (6) The Works of Tatian. See James L. Papandrea, *Reading the Early Church Fathers* (New Jersey: Paulist Press, 2012).

[114] Delbert Burkett, *An Introduction to the New Testament and the Origins of Christianity*, 103.

[115] Bart D. Ehrman, *The New Testament: Historical Introduction to the Early Christian Writings*, 412-415.

[116] James M. Robinson says, "heresy is so tenacious and unbending not because of the hardening of its heart, but because of its *relatively valid claim* to be rooted in an original Christian point" (Italics is mine). James M. Robinson, *Jesus According to the Earliest Witness*, 29. Also Cyril C. Richardson, "Introduction to Early Christian Literature and Its Setting," in *Early Christian Fathers*, translated and edited by Cyril C. Richardson (New York: Touchstone, 1996), 24. See also 2.2.1. The Early Faith Community's *Glocalization* and Cultural Hegemony of Greece

[117] Cyril C. Richardson, "Introduction to Early Christian Literature and Its Setting," 24-26.

[118] Cyril C. Richardson, "Introduction to Early Christian Literature and Its Setting," 26.

faith community concerning the person and work of Jesus Christ as reliable and historical document.

2.4.2.4 *Kerygmatic*/Evangelistic Function

Early public proclamations were fruitful moment for the confessing community's faith confession.[119] It is done either in public preaching and discourses (cf. Acts 17:16-33; 19:8-10) or in personal house-to-house level (Acts 5:42).[120] The whole development of Christological perception progressed parallel to the evangelistic work of the early faith community in their hostile surroundings.[121] It was a context for affirming the faith and relating it to the socio-political, religious and philosophical context of the people. In the process of decipher the early faith confession to another context was a hard task. The early faith community had to choose right language in order to express their faith clearly. At the same time, however, they had to avoid compromising their essential beliefs to any particular context.[122] The interaction with the outside world provided more logical and polished pattern of the faith confession that was reflected in its language, form, and structure of the confessions of the early faith community.

To sum up, the early faith confession was objective or universal and at the same time subjective or contextual. It was objective, because of its content and subjective, because of its appropriation/function to particular contexts of usage such as the contexts of worship, teachings, persecution and evangelization.

2.4.3 Christological-Thematic Analysis

The structural analysis concluded with an assumption that the complete content of the early faith confession cannot be fully expressed in particular forms. The functional analysis shed light to the oscillation of the objective faith confession with its subjective appropriation to particular contexts. In a way, the early faith community recollected known (revealed) facts about the mystery and was trying to relate (interpret) it to the *dalit* experiences of the early faith community. Principally, theme wise, then, there would be three parts in the early faith confession. Primarily, the mystery of the person Jesus Christ such as his pre-existence, incarnation, resurrection, divinity, etc. Secondly, the known facts about the historical person Jesus of Nazareth such as his baptism, ministry, teachings

[119] G. N. Stanton says that, "if there had been no initial preaching there would have been no worshipping community" (177). That means, the early faith community is the result/product of the evangelistic preaching or proclamation. A detailed study on the missionary preaching of the early faith community that carried Jesus/Gospel tradition, see G. N. Stanton, *Jesus of Nazareth in New Testament Preaching*, Society for New Testament Studies Monographs Series. 27 (Cambridge: CUP, 1974).

[120] Vincent Taylor, *The Person of Christ in New Testament Teachings*, 194-197.

[121] Oscar Cullmann, *The Christology of New Testament*, 321. See also 2.2. The Positioning of the Early Faith Community in its Strange Context.

[122] Gerald Bray, *Creeds, Councils and Christ*, 71.

and death transferred through reliable traditions. Finally, the confession included implications of *mysterium Christi* and Jesus of Nazareth (one at the same time) to the immediate and larger context of *dalitness* of the early faith community. For instance, affirming Jesus as 'the logos, which was in the beginning, now made flesh dwelt among us,' (mystery) or 'Jesus died on the cross for the salvation of humankind' (known fact) and so on that relates Jesus (of history) Christ (of faith) into the *dalitness* of the early faith community at large is a classical formulation of the early faith confession. In short, mystery of Jesus Christ and revelation of him as historical person; significance of both mystery and revelation in the context of *dalitness* of the early faith community is the content of the faith confession.

2.4.3.1 *Absconditus* Christ: *Mysterium Christi*

The plurality of the early faith confession on Jesus Christ provides the impracticability to understand fully who Jesus is – He is a mystery.[123] The common to the *Mysterium Christi* or *Absconditus* Christ is a firm recognition of Jesus' transcendence and his central position in the salvation history.[124] With the faith confession, the early faith community was trying to unravel and clarify *Mysterium Christi*. It had important consequences for the early Christology and context in which was confessing. *Mysterium Christi* proved to be both a powerful driving force to theological progress and a favorite starting point for heresies. Aloys Grillmeier writes,

> Certainly the massiveness of the *Mysterium Christi* continued to remain the source of impulses leading to new formulas and efforts to give new expression to the inexpressible. Men [*sic*] were conscious that the *Mysterium* was something beyond words.... [T]he Church grasped the totality of the picture of Christ more in a kind of spiritual intuition than in words and formulas which apparently contradicted each other. The Church measured newly-emerging doctrines as much by her intuition as by her formula made from them new fixed forms for her proclamation.[125]

---

[123] Aloys Grillmeier writes that New Testament itself shows the diversity of content in the faith confession. He mentions the understanding of Origen about Christ is a 'plurality.' *Christ in Christian Tradition: From the Apostolic Age to Chalcedon (451)*, translated by J. S. Bowden (London: A. R. Mowbray & Co Limited, 1965), 36, 82. Also John Young, *The Christ of History: An Argument Grounded in the Facts of His Life on Earth* (New York: Robert Carter & Brothers, 1857), 193. And also Andreas J. Köstenberger and Michael J. Kruger, *The Heresy of Orthodoxy: How Contemporary Culture's Fascination with Diversity has Reshaped our Understanding of Early Christianity* (Illinois: Crossway, 2010).

[124] *Absconditus* is used to refer the 'hiddenness' of Jesus, the Christ. Aloys Grillmeier, *Christ in Christian Tradition*, 36.

[125] Aloys Grillmeier, *Christ in Christian Tradition*, 40.

The *conception and birth of Jesus* from Mary were the first Mysteries in the life of Jesus.[126] The early faith community's literature developed a mythical understanding of the incarnation gained a footing in the same way as the legends which adorned and expanded the Gospel narratives about Jesus of Nazareth.[127] Theologically, this mystery of incarnation lucidly explained in the statement – "*Logos* become flesh and dwelt among us" (John 1:14).[128] In the fourth Gospel, though the language is Greek (*Logos*), the concept is profoundly Hebraic (*Dabar*);[129] like Wisdom, the Word was present with God in the beginning, active in creation, and took on flesh in Jesus, that means, beginning of beginning was God himself. Thus, Hebrew Word had a *soteriological* principle, as argued by Thomas Rausch.[130] In the Greek philosophical tradition, it was referred to a cosmological principle.[131]

Further, the mystery was continued with the statements such as "Jesus is the Savior." It was closely related to the primary abstract way in which refers to the effect of the Christ-event, namely "salvation."[132] Although, *sōtēr* was used in the contemporary Greco-Roman world to refer god, philosopher, statesman, or king, it also had a Jewish background. In Jewish tradition, savior was used of individuals whom God had raised up for the deliverance of Israel (Judg. 3:9, 15) and also of God himself (I Samuel 10:19; Isaiah 45:15, 21), where he was called in Hebrew *môšîă* and in Greek *Sōtēr*. Hence, in this instance the background of this

---

[126] Here the mystery is related to the birth of Jesus Christ, and not on Mary in which Catholic and Orthodox Liberation theologians argue for. Cf. Ivone Gebara and Maria Clara Bingemer, *Mary: Mother of God, Mother of the Poor*, Liberation and Theology Series. 7, translated by Philip Berryman (USA/Maryknoll: Burns & Oates/ Orbis Books, 1989), 93-100. Also Aloys Grillmeier, *Christ in Christian Tradition*, 77. Tissa Balasuriya, *Mary and Human Liberation: The Story and the Text*, edited by Helen Staton (Harrisburg: Trinity Press, 1997), 77-78.

[127] Aloys Grillmeier, *Christ in Christian Tradition*, 77.

[128] Though the term *Logos* was common to the church, given in its Jewish heritage, and to Greek philosophy, it had different connotations in each. In relation to Logos concept, there emerged another Christological strand known as 'Wisdom Christology' in earliest Christian theological reflection that tend to project feminist characteristic of Christology, later discarded for its Gnostic connection. James D. G. Dunn, *Did the First Christians Worship Jesus?*, 117-120. See also James M. Robinson, *Jesus According to the Earliest Witness*, 81. And Aloys Grillmeier, *Christ in Christian Tradition*, 31.

[129] "In the Hebrew tradition, which valued the word of a person, "word" (in Heb. *Dabar*) was understood as a dynamic extension of the person's personality and power. Similarly, the divine Word was an embodiment of God's power, going forth to accomplish the divine will, in creation (Gen. 1 -2:4a; Isa. 55:11)." Thomas P. Rausch, *Who is Jesus?*, 150.

[130] Thomas P. Rausch, *Who is Jesus?*, 150.

[131] Thomas P. Rausch, *Who is Jesus?*, 150.

[132] The title savior (*sōtēr*) is more or less exclusive to Lucan writings. Although, John uses it once (4:22), it is found in the Synoptics only in Luke (2:11). It occurs again in Acts 5:31; 13:23, 24. Joseph A. Fitzmyer, *To Advance the Gospel: New Testament Studies* 1981, 2nd edition (Grand Rapids and Michigan: William B. Eerdmans Publishing Company, 1998), 258.

Christological title can be disputed, whether it was Jewish or Hellenistic in origin. As applied to Jesus, it designated as the deliverer, the one who rescues human beings from evil, be it physical, psychic, political, cataclysmic, or moral evil (sin).[133] Then, the title Jesus as the savior referred for soteriological understanding of *Mysterium Christi*. However, the early Christian theology united these two concepts; it is active in both creation and salvation.

Consequently, the dynamic presentation of the mission of Christ in the economy of salvation was impregnated more with a static-ontological awareness of the reality of Christ as God and human.[134] It was a transition of Christology from functional base (economic) to ontological Christology. This mystery of relation between *Logos* and Jesus resulted in the emergence of controversies like Docetism.[135] Apart from the early Christian affirmation of Jesus is the Son of God in a polemic usage against the Docetic tendencies of Gnosticism,[136] Apostolic Father Ignatius, Bishop of Antioch responded with the incarnation as a central tenet of the Christian faith and asserts the coming of Jesus in the flesh. He explained that "no doctrine of the heavenly Christ could be formulated if not based on the historical Jesus and therefore any Gnostic system that denied that Jesus Christ truly was flesh and blood is defective and heretical."[137] Ignatius of Antioch repeatedly emphasized that humanity of Jesus is "truly, and not in appearance," while Iraneaus supported that the references to the Logos, the beginning (*arche*), and the only begotten (*monogenes*) were added to the prologue of the Gospel of John in direct reaction to the Gnosticism.[138] In this way, the early

---

[133] Joseph A. Fitzmyer, *To Advance the Gospel*, 258-259.

[134] Aloys Grillmeier, *Christ in Christian Tradition*, 40.

[135] Docetism was a Christological expression of Gnosticism. While the Docetist easily saw Christ as a mediator, what they could not accept was that the divine Word had become flesh, with all its earthly connotations. Thus, they taught that Jesus only "seemed" or "appeared" (Greek *dokeo*, "to seem") to have a human body. James W. Garrett, *The New Testament Church and Heresy* (Tulsa, Oklahoma: Doulos Press, 2004), 30.

[136] The confession of Jesus Christ as the Son of God demanded a twofold demonstration: first that it was compatible with Jewish monotheism, and secondly that it was different from pagan polytheism. The solution of this problem depended on the possibility of combining in God a true unity with a true distinction (between Father, Son, and Spirit). This sonship of Jesus is understood in legal, and not in physical terms. The formula does not distinguish two 'natures', but two stages in the existence of Jesus. J. N. D. Kelly, *Early Christian Creeds*, 14. Also Thomas P. Rausch, *Who is Jesus?*, 152. Cf. Grillmeir, 106. And Hans Conzelmann, *An Outline of the Theology of the New Testament*, 77.

[137] Issa A. Saliba, "The Bishop of Antioch and the Heretics: A Study of a Primitive Christology," *The Evangelical Quarterly* (ATLA Series assessed 21-08-2013): 65-76.

[138] Quoted in Harold O. J. Brown, *Heresies: Heresy and Orthodoxy in the History of the Church* (Peabody: Hendrickson Publishers, 1988), 52. Also Daniel Hoffman, "The Authority of Scripture and Apostolic Doctrine in Ignatius of Antioch," *Journal of the Evangelical Theological* Society 28/1 (March. 1985): 71-75.

faith community was formulating the mystery of Christ's humanity and filial union with his Father more systematic and affirmative.

Two schools are to be noted for this codification of the *Mysterium Christi* formula of relation between humanity and divinity of Jesus Christ- Alexandrian and Antiochian schools. Alexandrian theology[139] with its reverence for the transcendence and unity of God, placed great emphasis on the Logos which somehow "enters into" or becomes "attached" to human flesh. The focus is always on the Logos. Thus, Clement speaks of Christ as having "clothed Himself with a man," being "God in the form of a man," unsullied. And Origen, who believed that human souls preexisted in a world of spiritual beings, taught that the Logos became fused with the soul of Jesus.[140] However, the theologians at Antioch tended to stress the reality of the humanhood of Christ. Antiochan community developed a framework of *Logos-anthropos* Christology which emphasized the full humanity of Jesus that is focused on Jesus of Nazareth in opposite to the *Logos-sarx* Christology of Alexandria.[141] This constant struggle between these two communities helped in articulating a balanced *Mysterium Christi* creedal statements in the early councils of the church regarded as the common faith of the early faith community. The common content of the early faith confession read like this,

> We believe in one Lord, Jesus Christ, the only son of God, eternally begotten of the Father, God from God, Light from Light, true God from true God, begotten, not made, of one being with the Father. Through him all things were made. For us and for our salvation he came down from heaven: by the power of the Holy Spirit he became incarnate from the Virgin Mary, and was made man. For our sake he was crucified under Pontius Pilate; he suffered death and was buried. On the third day he rose again in accordance with the Scriptures; he ascended into heaven and is seated at the right hand of the Father. He will come again in glory to judge the living and the dead, and his kingdom will have no end. (Nicene Creed)[142]

The content of *Mysterium Christi* becomes the total person of Jesus condemning other teachings stand against this notion, especially Arianism.[143] The

[139] The catechetical school at Alexandria was founded in 195 C. E. by Clement of Alexandria (d.215 C. E.), but its great name was Origen (Ca.185-254 C. E.).

[140] See J. N. D. Kelly, *Early Christian Doctrines*, 1958, 4th Ed. (London: Adam & Charles Black, 1968), 153-155.

[141] Thomas P. Rausch, *Who is Jesus?*, 153.

[142] Quoted in Philip Schaff, ed., *The Creeds of Christendom with a History and Critical Notes*. 1931. Vol. 1 The History of Creeds, 6th edition (Michigan: Baker Books, 1998), 27.

[143] The Council of Nicaea condemned several Arian propositions such as 'There once was when he was not,' and 'before he was begotten he was not,' and 'that he came to be from things were

Council of Nicaea (325 C.E.) affirmed in certain terms the divinity of Jesus – "God from God, Light from Light, true God from true God, begotten, not made, of one being/consubstantial (*homoousion*) with the Father."[144] It is to affirm with unambiguous clarity that Jesus is to be identified as God incarnate – God has not merely come *in* a human being but *as human*.[145] Second half part of the creed talks about the humanity of Jesus, his birth, ministry, death and ending with hope of futuristic kingdom.

Another characteristic of *Mysterium Christi* is its mythical nature. *Mysterium Christi* is also a mythical expression of the early faith community.[146] Aloys Grillmeier also agrees that the transcendent nature of Christ-event in the history can only be expressed in mythical ground.[147] However, Bultmann's attempt of demythologization, in this particular context, will not be a useful tool, in the words of Aloys Grillmeier, since the process of de-mythologization may erode the content of the faith confession itself.[148] Because the whole of the Christ-event as understood by the early faith community is 'myth' and valid in the existential community's self-understanding before God in Christ.[149] However, the mythical expression of *Mysterium Christi* struggled to find proper theological language to express the content fully.

Then, *Mysterium Christi* as the content of the faith confession, is a totality of Christology, carried throughout centuries in traditions, creeds and texts (literatures). In another away, the *Mysterium Christi* was regulated by authentic testimonies of the past (apostolic tradition) in both oral faith affirmations and written texts can be called as gospel traditions.

2.4.3.2 *Revelatus* Jesus: Jesus the Disclosed

Jesus, as the content of the early faith confession, is not only a mysterious phenomenon, but also a disclosed and disclosing personality. He is disclosed in the sense of the act of revealing (revelation) of himself to/in the early faith

---

not, or from another hypostasis or substance,' 'affirming that the Son of God is subject to change or alteration.' *Decree of the Ecumenical Councils*, Vol. 1: Nicaea I to Lateran, edited by Norman P. Tanner (Washington: Georgetown University Press, 1900), 5. Mentioned in Thomas P. Rausch, *Who is Jesus?*, 153.

[144] Alan Torrance, "Jesus in Christian Doctrine," *The Cambridge Companion to Jesus*, edited by Markus Bockmuel (Cambridge: CUP, 2001), 207.

[145] Alan Torrance, "Jesus in Christian Doctrine," 200.

[146] Alan Torrance also tells that the impossible task of codification of *Mysterium Christi* is a "a form of activity better described as 'mythology' than 'theology'." Here the myth is not the world view of the first century C. E. as Bultmann has explained, but the inseparable content of the confession itself is a 'myth'. Alan Torrance, "Jesus in Christian Doctrine," 207. See also Henry F. Lazenby, "The Mythical Use of the Bible by Evangelicals," *JETS* 34/4 (Dec., 1991): 485-494.

[147] Aloys Grillmeier, *Christ in Christian Tradition*, 75. Cf. Bultmann, *Kerygma and Myth*.

[148] Aloys Grillmeier, *Christ in Christian Tradition*, 75. Cf. Bultmann, *Kerygma and Myth*.

[149] Aloys Grillmeier, *Christ in Christian Tradition*, 75.

community's confessions. He is disclosing personality is in the sense of his act of revealing Father to the early faith community. Therefore, at the heart to the content of confession lies not so much a set of abstract ideas or beliefs but revealed person Jesus of Nazareth.[150]

The gospel traditions carried the words and deeds of Jesus.[151] That is to say, the initial disclosure of Christ of faith as experienced by the early Christians presented freshly in the New Testament via reliable traditions. In another words, the early faith community's faith confession was a recollection of the earthly Jesus, of what he said and did as experienced by His disciples.[152] Jesus' sayings cannot be separated from Jesus himself, because, in Jesus, the message and the messenger are one and the same.[153] Thus, the person of Jesus and his work of salvation by suffering and death become an important and revealed part in the early faith confession.

Oscar Cullmann says, the person of Jesus is "recognized only in the light of the new events of his death on the cross and the experience immediately following his resurrection."[154] Thus, the gospel tradition confessed by the early faith community was, mainly, in relation to Jesus' suffering and death or work of Jesus. After an exegesis on the Christological formula in I Cori. 15:13 ff, Conzelman comments that the content of faith is "Jesus was really dead and he was raised from the dead. It is explicit and revealed content."[155] When the name Jesus is used as the object of their confession, the consciousness of the early faith community would trace back to the historical event that some of them witnessed, heard and believed. The first generation of Christians believed that this Jesus (that is a historical reality) is the Christ (that is a 'disclosure') expressed in a Jewish term evocative for the Jews.[156]

The other titles for Jesus of Nazareth, implicitly and explicitly, qualify this proper noun establishing the revealed identity of Jesus of Nazareth. The title Christ (Χριστός) is used as a second name for Jesus as having lost its

---

[150] Jesus (Ἰησους) is used in the early community of faith as the name of historical person, referring to Jesus of Nazareth. The early community's portrayal of earthly life of their object of confession used the proper noun Jesus. This name along with the place designation 'of Nazareth' affirms the historical existence of the person. Alister E. McGrath, *Studies in Doctrine* (Michigan: Zondervan Publishing House, 1997), 14.

[151] Delbert Burkett, *An Introduction to the New Testament and the Origins of Christianity*, 126.

[152] Edward Schillebeeckx, *Jesus*, 47.

[153] Walter A. Elwell and Robert W. Yarbrough, *Encountering the New Testament: A Historical and Theological Survey*, 2nd ed. 1998 (Grand Rapids: Baker Academic, 2005), 203. Also Alister E. McGrath, *Studies in Doctrine*, 15. See also Alan Torrance, "Jesus in Christian Doctrine," 207.

[154] Oscar Cullmann, *The Christology of New Testament*, 318-319.

[155] Hans Conzelmann, *An Outline of the Theology of the New Testament*, 66-67. Also Alan Torrance, "Jesus in Christian Doctrine," 207.

[156] Edward Schillebeeckx, *Jesus*, 58.

titular sense.[157] The meaning of the title Messiah or *Christos* when applied to Jesus, however, was determined primarily by *Christian* conceptions of Jesus rather than by conventional *Jewish* messianic notions.[158] That means that the Christian conception of the *heavenly* coronation of Jesus as Messiah represents a spiritualization of the traditional Jewish understanding of an *earthly* coronation of the ideal king of the future. It was the death of Jesus, however, which the early faith community regarded as the primary obstacle preventing the general Jewish recognition of Jesus as the Messiah of Jewish expectation. The early faith community therefore tried to revise the Jewish conception of the Messiah by arguing from OT proof texts that both suffering and death were integral aspects of the divinely ordained role of the Messiah (Luke 24:46; Acts 3:18, 17:3, 26:22-23; I Cor. 15:3). For this reason early creeds or confessions placed the motif of the *death* of Jesus in close association with *Christos,* which already tended to be used as a proper name for Jesus in pre-Pauline Hellenistic-Jewish Christianity (Cf. I Cor. 15:3) as revealed and implicit identity of historical Jesus.[159] This is similar with the title Son of Man, which refers to round about Hebraic saying "a human being" (Psalm 8:4; 80:17).[160] Some of the Son of Man sayings related to the suffering of Jesus Christ, even though a mention for heavenly human being is implied because of the developments in inter-testamental period (Daniel 7:13-14).[161]

---

[157] The term *Christos* is found 80 times in the Gospels and Acts – 16 times as a proper name for Jesus (e.g. Mk 1:1; John 1:17; 17:3) and 64 times as a title either as a general designation for eschatological Davidic king or less frequently but more importantly as a title predicted of Jesus (e.g. Mark 8:29 = Matt. 15:16 = Luke 9:20). D. E. Aune, "Christian Prophecy and the Messianic Status of Jesus," in *The Messiah: Developments in Earliest Judaism and Christianity*, The First Princeton Symposium on Judaism and Christian Origins, edited by James H. Charlesworth (Minneapolis: Fortress Press, 1992), 405-406. Also Joseph A. Fitzmyer, *To Advance the Gospel*, 259.

[158] The term Christ is a translation from the Hebrew word *messiah*. During Jesus' time the concept kingdom of God differed widely. The Pharisees imagined it to be the complete fulfilment of the Torah; the Zealots thought of a political theocracy which they thought they would install by force of arms; and the apocalyptic looked forward to the coming of the new eon, the new heaven and the new earth. Walter Kasper writes, "Jesus cannot be easily attached to any of these groups. His way of talking about the kingdom of God is remarkably open." *Jesus the Christ* (New York: T&T Clark International, 2011, first edition 1976), 60.

[159] The problem of identifying Jesus as the Messiah, however, did not simply center on the fact of the Messiah's death, as though the fact that he died before accomplishing the tasks traditionally associated with the ideal future Davidic king. However, early Palestinian Christianity did not *deny* the traditionally messianic role to Jesus, but simply *postponed* that role into the imminent (though indefinite) eschatological future (Acts 1:6; 3:20-21; Rev 11:15; 12:10; 20:4, 6).

[160] John Howard Yoder, *Preface to Theology: Christology and Theological Method* (Michigan: Brazos Press, 2002), 63.

[161] Wilhelm Bousset, *Kyrios Christos: A History of the Belief in Christ from the Beginnings of Christianity to Irenaeus*, translated by John E. Steely (Nashville: Abingdon Press, 1970), 31-35. Also Delbert Burkett, *The Son of Man Debate: A History and Evaluation* (Cambridge: CUP, 2004).

In addition, the full-fledged meaning of the confession Jesus as the 'Lord' (κύριος), in the context of the early community, could be the remembrance of historical death and resurrection of Jesus Christ and its implication of his present status of Lordship over all the creation.[162] Further, the titles Second Adam, High Priest ["in all points tempted like as we are..."], (Heb.4:15), and other titles used for Jesus by the early faith community's faith confession refers to the work of Jesus more related to the suffering, death and resurrection. These events of suffering, death and resurrection caused the recognition of the importance of Jesus' personhood.[163] In a way, Jesus' message was given weight and status because of who the early faith community recognized Jesus to be. Jesus is God's revealed human identity.[164] The early stage of the faith community itself they made the startling assertion that, in Jesus, God himself had taken human form (i.e., disclosed).[165] This language of faith meant the actual Jesus of Nazareth, a concrete and historical reality that disclosed to the early faith community.[166]

It is interesting to note that controversies over the humanity of Jesus Christ is emerged *not over the historicity* of the person called Jesus [because it is already an established fact], but the *human nature* that present in historical person Jesus. For example, Roman Williams finds, "the language of early Alexandrian theology...emphasizes the role of Jesus as the visible manifestation of the invisible God...."[167] Nicene debate also, as elsewhere mentioned,[168] unintentionally left with one-sided Christological interpretation emphasized with the divinity of Jesus to avoid any Arian controversy but detriment all-important stress on humanity of Jesus.[169] Additionally, fear of confusing Jesus' divinity with a humanity conceived as "transitory, changeable, corruptible, mortal and capable of suffering" generated a tension.[170] To affirm the *humoousion* involved the insistence that Jesus was 'of one being with the Father.' At the same time, the incarnation could not mean the collapse of the divine into the human. In this regard, one cannot over simplify the

---

[162] Vincent Taylor, *The Person of Christ in New Testament Teachings*, 6. Also Oscar Cullmann, *The Christology of New Testament*, 320.

[163] Alister E. McGrath, *Studies in Doctrine*, 15.

[164] Richard Bauckham, "The Future of Jesus Christ," in *The Cambridge Companion to Jesus*, edited by Markus Bockmuel (Cambridge. CUP, 2001), 275.

[165] Walter A Elwell and Robert W. Yarbrough, *Encountering the New Testament*, 203.

[166] Edward Schillebeeckx, *Jesus*, 44.

[167] Roman Williams, "A History of Faith in Jesus," in *The Cambridge Companion to Jesus*, edited by Markus Bockmuel (Cambridge: CUP, 2001), 221.

[168] See 2.4.3.1. *Absconditus* Christ: *Mysterium Christi*

[169] Henry Bettenson, ed., *Documents of the Christian Church* (NY, London: Oxford University Press, 1967), 44. Also Alan Torrance, "Jesus in Christian Doctrine," 207.

[170] Alan Torrance, "Jesus in Christian Doctrine," 210.

contribution of Cappadocian Fathers.[171] Most useful was their formula in reference to the Godhead, one divine nature (*ousia*) and three hypostases (*hypostasis*). The strategy adopted by the Council of Chalcedon (451 C.E.) is also important to mention in this juncture. It safeguarded the divinity and the humanity of Jesus by repudiating any confusion of the two, on the one hand, and any separation of the two on the other. The Council stated:

> We, then, following the holy Fathers, all with one consent, teach men to confess one and the same Son, our Lord Jesus Christ, the same perfect in Godhead and also perfect in manhood; truly God and truly man, of a reasonable soul and body; consubstantial with the Father according to the Godhead, and consubstantial with us according to the Manhood; in all things like unto us, without sin; begotten before all ages of the Father according to the Godhead, and in these latter days, for us and for our salvation, born of the Virgin Mary, the Mother of God, according to the Manhood; one and same Christ, Son, Lord, Only-begotten, to be acknowledged in two natures, inconfusedly, unchangeably, indivisibly, inseparably; the distinction of natures being by no means taken away by the union, but rather the property of each nature being preserved, and concurring in one Person and one Subsistence, not parted or divided into two persons, but one and the same Son, and only begotten, God the Word, the Lord Jesus Christ, as the prophets from the beginning [have declared] concerning him, and the Lord Jesus Christ himself has taught us, and the Creed of the holy Fathers has handed down to us.[172]

The Council of Chalcedon (451 C.E.) represented a synthesis of the best insights of two competing theological schools. Alexandrians who continued to emphasize the union of the divine and the non-divine, making clear the presence of God in Jesus and thus in the Word, the Antiocheans, with their emphasis on the humanity of Jesus, resisted any tendency to see Jesus as less than a full, integral human being.[173] In the words of V. C. Samuel,

> Council of Chalcedon's made clear that, Christ was declared as to his divinity "consubstantial with the Father," and as to his humanity "consubstantial with us in manhood." On unity of natures, the divinity and the humanity of Christ exist "without confusion, without

---

[171] Basil the Great of Caesarea (ca. 330-379 C. E.), Gregory of Nyssa (335-394 C. E.), and Gregory of Nazianzas (330-389 C. E.) played a major role in securing the proper relationship between the Father and Son; they taught that the Son was fully and equally God, not a subordinate reality (as in Arius), but eternally begotten while the Father is unbegotten. Thomas P. Rausch, *Who is Jesus?*, 158.

[172] Quoted in Philip Schaff, ed., *The Creeds of Christendom,* Vol. 2: 62-65.

[173] Philip Schaff, ed., *The Creeds of Christendom*, 29. Cf. Thomas P. Rausch, *Who is Jesus?*, 163.

change, without division, without separation." Thus, the two natures coalesced in one person (*prosopon*) and one substance (*hypostasis*).[174]

The content of most of the early faith confessions witness the historical particularity of Jesus of Nazareth at the same time universality of Christ's existence as the object of faith. Historical particularity is important at the same level of Christ of faith. The early faith community as the witness to the historical particularity of Jesus, then concentrated on the Christ of faith as their object of devotion. Thus, the early faith confession mediates between two extremes, on the one hand the reduction of Christology to history and on the other abandoning history as irrelevant to faith.[175] It is worthwhile to read along with the observation of Aloys Grillmeier,

> So to-day...a synthesis is being sought between the extremes (pure Jesus of history-pure Christ of faith); the Jesus of history is taken as a presupposition of the Christ of faith. There is recognition that the primitive community itself already achieved this conjunction. It identified the humiliated Jesus of Nazareth with the exalted *Kyrios*. With this twofold recognition it was in a position to withstand the error of Docetism on the one hand and the denial of the transcendence of the *Kyrios* on the other.... The understanding of primitive church 'the history of Jesus was decisive for faith, because the earthly and the exalted Lord are the same.'[176]

In nutshell, Jesus is both God's *truly human* identity and *truly God's* human identity.[177] These polyphonic confessions show the integrity and unavoidability of the two movements as Torrance tried to explain:

> Whereas the Father had emphasized that in Christ we have God coming to humanity *as God* (the *anhypostastic* or God-humanward movement), their integral and attendant emphasis that the incarnation simultaneously denotes the incarnate Son's presentation of humanity to the Father *as fellow-human* (the *enhypostatic*, human-Godward movement) was weakened in the Nicene debate. Without this twofold movement, the essential grammar of the early faith confession, namely, that Jesus represents both God's coming to humanity *as God*, and God's reconciliation and representation of humanity to himself as

[174] V. C. Samuel, *The Council of Chalcedon Re-Examined: A Historical and Theological Survey* (Delhi: ISPCK, 2001).

[175] Joseph Ratzinger, *Introduction to Christianity* (New York: Herder and Herder, 1971), 144-47 cited in Thomas P. Rausch, *Who is Jesus*, 4.

[176] Aloys Grillmeier, S.J. *Christ in Christian Tradition*, 5-6.

[177] Richard Bauckham, "The Future of Jesus Christ," 275.

> the true human (*eschatos Adam*, the 'Last' or 'Second' Adam) the early faith confession is lopsided.[178]

That means, neglecting either one aspect of the person of Jesus would bring the faith confession 'lopsided.'

2.4.3.3 Jesus Christ, the Distinct and Relevant

Deepened by constant reflection on meaning of the Christ-event as a mystery and revelation for the community of disciples, the process also reflects different moments in the life and faith of the early church.[179] It is, in another term, a 'contextual confession' of the early faith community in their particular *dalit* situations.[180] The *Mysterium Christi* and Disclosed Jesus also can be considered as the 'contextual' theology of that time. However, the early faith community considered most of their faith affirmation as 'givenness' than contextual one. It is given once for all. The attempt here is to draw out gist of the contextual relevance of given Christology. That means it is an attempt to understand the significance of the content of the confession in the life and consciousness of the early faith community. Consciousness of the early faith community means the remembrance and maintenance of the confession, that is, Jesus Christ himself in their *Sitz im Leben*.

The formation of historical consciousness of the early faith community had begun with the event of Jesus Christ, developed by the apostolic witness about it, and later, interpretation of it by the adherents of this tradition. It was the Christological consciousness of the early faith community that determined their historical consciousness other than their dalit surroundings.

The center of community consciousness the early faith community treasured Jesus of Nazareth and Christ of faith inseparably. It was evident, as already stated, in the faith confessions of the early faith community. Early faith confessions helped the early faith community to side with 'continuing' relationship between historical Jesus and Christ of faith. The life and worship of the early faith community was regulated by both passing tradition of historical Jesus and the continuing presence of Christ of faith. In short, the early faith community's consciousness about Jesus Christ was indivisible. Embryo form of such in-divisive Christology can trigger from the early faith confessions that widely used even before New Testament writings and continued throughout the early periods of the community.

Further, the life context of the early faith community and their view about Jesus constituted their historical consciousness. The early faith community's

---

[178] T. F. Torrance, *Theology in Reconstruction* (London: SCM Press, 1965), 131-132. Cf. Alan Torrance, "Jesus in Christian Doctrine," 207.

[179] Thomas P. Rausch, *Who is Jesus?*, 28.

[180] "Situation" refers to "the scientific and artistic, the economic, political, and ethical forms in which they (*individual and groups*) express their interpretation of existence." Paul Tillich, *Systematic Theology*, Vol. 1 (Chicago: The University of Chicago, 1951), 3-4.

loftiest expectations and utopias which they see realized concretely in Jesus.[181] For instance, the title messiah in the early community of faith is the fulfillment of the Jewish expectation of messiah who would restore and save the righteous people, overthrow evil powers and establish reign of God. However, the Jewish expectation had more of a political overtone. Nevertheless, the community remembered universal implication of 'Christ' as happened in past – a historical event and having contemporary and future implication.[182] Another example is the usage of the title 'Lord' (κύριος) in the early faith community is to affirm the 'present lordship of Jesus of Nazareth.'[183] The Aramaic reference of *maranatha* also needs to read in this direction.[184] It consists of an apocalyptic and eschatological experience of the early faith community in present tense. In addition, this confession can be placed *in contra* to the usage of emperor worship and the Hebraic allusion of Lord in Psalms 110:1.[185] The affirmative nature of this faith confession was tactical assertion in the Roman and Judaistic context of 'lordship.' It identified the consciousness of the early community's faith about Jesus' past [in contra to Judaism], of the present [in contra to Roman emperor worship] and of the futuristic [usage of the *maranatha*] in the struggled context with dominance and established their space of discourse.

To speak of Jesus in the language of faith is to express what the historical Jesus had come to signify for his disciples and how this is anchored in Jesus himself.[186] The important thing is that, in the words of Schillebeeckx, "on the basis of their communal experiences these believers are obliged to grasp for the loftiest titles provided by their religious and cultural milieu, so as to be able in some degree to express in words their past and present experience with Jesus and arising from him."[187] The titles, hymns, and other Christological formulas/confessions "were developed polemically as persuasive strategies to encourage believers to remain faithful to Jesus, especially in the time of trail and persecution."[188] They celebrated

[181] Edward Schillebeeckx, *Jesus*, 58.

[182] Hans Conzelmann, *An Outline of the Theology of the New Testament*, 73.

[183] During earthly ministry of Jesus, this title signified as a salutation as 'sir', but the proper and full expression emerged in the context of early faith community, says James D. G. Dunn, *Did the First Christians Worship Jesus? The New Testament Evidence* (London: SPCK, 2010), 103. Also Hans Conzelmann, *An Outline of the Theology of the New Testament*, 84. Also S. E. Johnson, "Lord (Christ)," *The Interpreters' Dictionary of the Bible: An Illustrated Encyclopaedia*, Vol. 3 (New York: Abingdon Press, 1962), 151.

[184] A. Wikgren, "Maranatha," *The Interpreters' Dictionary of the Bible: An Illustrated Encyclopaedia*, Vol. 3 (New York: Abingdon Press, 1962), 262. Also Oscar Cullmann, *The Christology of New Testament*, 320.

[185] James D. G. Dunn, *Did the First Christians Worship Jesus?*, 103.

[186] Edward Schillebeeckx, *Jesus*, 44.

[187] Edward Schillebeeckx, *Jesus*, 46.

[188] Teresa Okure, "The Global Jesus," in *The Cambridge Companion to Jesus*, edited by Markus Bockmuel (Cambridge: CUP, 2001), 242.

suffering, death, and resurrection of Jesus, the Christ in their confessions, hymns, preaching, and teaching in midst of their *dalit* situations. The four Gospels also is the end products of these confessing activities, says Thomas Rausch.[189]

It also constitutes the community's present experience of historical Jesus. In the words of Richard Baukham, "[t]hus in his life, death and resurrection, the exalted Christ has established his identity as one of open identification with others, open in principle and potential to all who will identify with him in faith."[190] It is confessed that, "[u]ntil the parousia his identification to all remains open to all."[191] "For those who have sought their own identity in his identification with them, his parousia will be the revelation at once of who he finally is and of who they themselves finally are: 'your life is hidden is Christ with God. When Christ who is your life is revealed, then you also will be revealed with him in glory' (Col. 3:3b-4; cf. I John 3:2)."[192]

Thus, Jesus' identity at the end is inclusive of others, but not in a way that dissolves his properly human individuality. As the one who has identified in love with all other human in their stories, his story finally includes also theirs. Since his loving identification with them is prevenient but not preemptive, that is, it is open to all but actualized only in the living of their own lives, his own identity as the one human whose identity is found in story of his relatedness to all others remains to that extent open until his parousia.[193]

Thus, the early faith confession becomes a means and end, as elsewhere mentioned, to the early faith community to be inclusive and open to all.

Then, in the wider context of isolation and seclusion (dalit), even though they were having an oppressed consciousness (wounded psyche), they cherished the consciousness of Jesus, who is both mystery and disclosure. It was mysterious consciousness in which the outsiders like Jewish-Greco-Roman world could not understand - either the confession of the community or the reason for their existence.

Origin of Christian mystic tradition in the early faith community can also draw out from such consciousness. It was also a consciousness of disclosure, where the early faith community openly pursued the oppressors with their faith affirmations.[194] Thus, the early faith community maintained the mysterious and disclosure consciousness that the faith confession itself projected. In short, Schillebeeckx meaningfully put the relationship between the early faith

[189] Thomas P. Rausch, *Who is Jesus?*, 28.

[190] Richard Bauckham, "The Future of Jesus Christ," 277.

[191] Richard Bauckham, "The Future of Jesus Christ," 277.

[192] Richard Bauckham, "The Future of Jesus Christ," 277.

[193] Richard Bauckham, "The Future of Jesus Christ," 277.

[194] In the context of persecution, one has to either affirm the *kerygma* and be martyred or reject the *kerygma* and save life. Therefore, the faith community lived in the context of life and death because of the faith affirmation about Jesus Christ.

community and the interaction with the content of their faith confession like this – "Neither Jesus nor the earliest 'church community' constitutes the fount and origin of Christianity, but both together as offer and response."[195] That is to say, the meaning and content of the early faith confession came alive when the early faith community's dalit situation encountered with Jesus of Nazareth revealed to them Lord over their dalit situation.

Summary of Findings

To sum up the finding of this chapter,

The condition of 'dalitness' and *the faith confession* are the two common factors that united and characterized the early faith communities of different regions and period into one community.

The condition of 'dalitness' was experienced in all sphere of their life, such as physical oppression by persecution, psychological subjugation by dominant philosophies and isolation from the mainstream of the society.

The early faith confession was proclaimed in such a *dalit* context in order that they may transfer the situation of brokenness to the condition of wholeness in the mainstream of the society.

Different structures of the early faith confession were limited in relation to its full expression on the content of the faith, and acted as only a carrier of the faith confession.

The confession functioned in and outside of the early faith community to maintain a healthy consciousness about themselves and about others.

The complete content of the faith confession comprises of three elements – mystery, revelation and relevance of Jesus Christ. That is to say, historical Jesus and Christ of faith are in in-divisive relationship, and any separation of them would be lopsided Christology.

Evaluation

It is an attempt to layout the early faith community and their confession.

The early faith community was a minority and was under constant pressure to assimilate with the dominant socio-political, cultural and religious systems of that time. It was likely such context, confessional proclamation played an important role in maintaining some level of solidarity and inclusive nature in the early community of faith. This nature helped the early faith community in the period of transition of minority to state religion to be more inclusive and solidarity with others. This reflected in the early faith confessions. However, this argument can be proved wrong in the context of the exclusion of wrong teachers from the early faith community and exclusive faith confessions. Why such exclusions in an inclusive community and why exclusive faith claims? Reasons have to be stated clearly. In this study, the researcher argued that the faith confession - Jesus in his

[195] Edward Schillebeeckx, *Jesus*, 58.

full humanity and divinity – of the early church is a holistic faith confession. The other teachers (heretics) were not willing to accept this holistic faith confession. They follow a lopsided Christology. Such lopsided approach was not only limited Jesus into a particular deity of the group such as of Gnostics or Arians, but also created the community of exclusive and conclusive claims. In this regard, the early catholic faith community was totally different. They were ready to accept any one who is ready to profess the full Christian faith – that is Jesus of Nazareth as the Christ of their confession. Thus, holistic or complete faith confession signified the early community of faith.

The language and structure of the early faith confession was distinct but compatible with the mainstream discourses of that time which helped the early community of faith to relate and dialogue with dominant structures. Symbols of the early faith community functioned as carrier of the community's identity and consciousness. By the usage of the dominant symbols of that time, the early faith community was trying to affirm themselves in the mainstream of the society. The 'confession' which they profess must be proclaimed and heard by others so that others can also understand and join with them in process of wholeness in their *dalit* situations.

Contemporary scholarship on historical Jesus starts with the consciousness of Jesus, and interprets the movement of Jesus as the apocalyptic movement and Jesus as eschatological prophet and so on.[196] This framework is alien to the early faith community.[197] The study on early Christology is not considered as how Jesus thought of himself rather "what do the people say that who He is?" The central challenge for the present thesis was the identity and relevance of Jesus Christ for the early faith community. Jesus of Nazareth was the Christ of faith that professed by the early faith community in which the Christ of faith is mysterious, that is

[196] See Bart Ehrman, *Apocalyptic Prophet of the New Millennium* (New York: Oxford University Press, 1999). Also Dale C. Allison, *Jesus of Nazareth: Millenarian Prophet* (Minneapolis: Fortress Press, 1998). Also Burton L. Mack, *A Myth of Innocence: Mark and Christian Origins* (Philadelphia: Fortress Press, 1988). Also Paula Fredriksen, *Jesus of Nazareth, King of Jews: A Jewish Life and the Emergence of Christianity* (New York: Vintage Books, 1999). Also John A. T. Robinson, "The Last Tabu? The Self Consciousness of Jesus," in *The Historical Jesus in Recent Research,* Sources for Biblical and Theological Study Vol.10, edited by James D. G. Dunn and Scot Mcknight (Winona Lake, Indiana: Eisenbrauns, 2005), 553-566.

[197] Donald A. Hgner criticizes the current trend in Jesus research that, "it is working with a set of presupposition totally alien to the first century." Donald A. Hgner, "An Analysis of Recent 'Historical Jesus' Studies," in *Religious Diversity in the Greco-Roman World: A Survey of Recent Scholarship*, edited by Dan Cohn-Sherbok and John M. Court (Sheffield: Sheffield Academic Press, 2001), 106. Also Michael J. McClymond concludes his study by pointing out the limitation or danger of presenting Christological reflection is that "the interpreter's most common and most characteristic error regarding Jesus is to narrow down the figure in the Gospels until he fits into some box chosen by the interpreter." As he argues that, the first century context could not confirm Jesus into any limited category such as of healer or guru etc. Jesus was and is uncategorizable. Michael J. McClymond, *Familiar Stranger*, 152.

Jesus the *absconditus* and the Jesus of Nazareth is the *revelatus*. The early faith confession propounded in-divisive nature of these two natures of Christology. This tension between revelation and mystery kept the early faith community's confession as distinct from others. This approach disregards the issue of continuity and discontinuity of historical Jesus and Christ of faith also.

The trend to limit Jesus Christ into specific framework is a lopsided approach. The purpose of this chapter is not to totally disregard the lopsided Christological affirmations, but invitation to have a balanced approach. The Christian community is the site not just of the manufacture of images (about Jesus) but also of controversy about them. Even in the earliest records of the New Testament, we have an interpreted Jesus. The early faith confession is not sided with Pauline faith, but included Petrine, Johannine and other faith affirmations that gives a paradigm of balancing act in doing christologies. This wider inclusion of the faiths characterizes the early faith community as well as its Christology.

Conclusion

The early faith community was unique community in two ways. Primarily, they were experienced the *dalitness* of isolation, exclusion, and oppression of undefined character. The situation that they faced was very hostile dominated by Greco-Roman-Jewish, cultural-political imperialism and religious fundamentalism. Secondly, the community was unique in relation to the faith confession. In their faith affirmation, they declared Jesus as the Lord, the Christ in the midst of persecutions and oppressive situations, that is, 'dalit conditions.' Over against the early faith community's dalit situation, they had kept faith affirmations in structured creeds and other confessional statements. These confessional materials were, in a way, explained and defended the complete faith confession. The complete faith confession was the center of the community's consciousness. The community was watchful to keep the complete faith confession intact, though the language and other structures were limited in nature. However, the major content of the early faith confession comprises of integral ingredients. They are the mysterious nature of Jesus Christ, his disclosure of himself and of the Father to the early 'dalit' faith community. Thus, the core and content of the early faith confession upheld a balanced view of Jesus of history and the Christ of faith by affirming both divinity and humanity of Jesus.

3

A Critique of Contemporary Dalit Interpretations of Jesus Christ in the Light of the Early Faith Confession

Introduction

The early church professed their confession, as argued in the previous chapter, in the explicit context of their 'dalitness' in all spheres of life. Dalitness of the early faith community stands similar with the conceptualization of 'inclusive dalit' as defined in the first section. This convergent factor leads one to critically look at the contemporary dalit faith confession, its content, structure, and function in the existing context of caste conflicts and communalism in India. Major premises of the previous chapters are: firstly, the 'original' meaning of the 'dalit' is one who experience *dalitness* and secondly, the complete content of the early faith confession is an inseparable historical Jesus with the Christ of faith. With these two assumptions, this chapter evaluates whether contemporary dalit discourse on Jesus Christ is complete in its content in relation to early faith confession or lopsided. And also whether it (contemporary dalit faith confession) promotes and foster caste conflicts in India, which is not really 'dalit' way of doing Christology. After analyzing the contemporary dalit faith confession thematically, functionally and methodologically, researcher proposes 'inclusive' dalit methodology at the end as a remedial alternative method for constructing an inclusive dalit Christology.

3.1 Contemporary Dalit Interpretations of Jesus Christ

Broadly, the 'living theology' in the context of dalit speaks of the Dalit Christ and Christ, the Liberator of the Dalits.[1] These two prominent aspects in the dalit

[1] M. E. Prabhakar, "Christology in Dalit Perspective," in *Frontiers of Dalit Theology*, edited by V. Devasahayam (New Delhi: ISPCK, 1997), 411.

Christology are expounded here in order to understand the existing dalit faith confession that would help us to construct a valid criticism of it. Particularly, dalit Christology ventures to understand the dalitness of Jesus and his mission for the subaltern outcastes.[2] It is usual to point out caste or class elements in the dalit interpretation of Jesus Christ.

3.1.1 Jesus: The Dalit *Par – Excellence*

Generally, dalit theologians point out five features in the life and ministry of Jesus to establish dalitness of Jesus Christ.[3] Firstly, like the dalits, Jesus is also counted among ill reputed ancestors.[4] Secondly, Jesus used to refer to himself as the "Son of Man," who like the Dalits, encountered rejection, mockery, contempt, suffering and finally death at the hands of the powerful priest and political rulers. Thirdly, during his ministry Jesus understood that he was sent specifically to the dalits of his times (Luke 4:16-29) and he shared table fellowship with them, to the scandal and anger of those who considered themselves ritually pure. Fourthly, in cleansing the temple, Jesus opened up access to the Temple for the gentiles or outcastes.[5] Finally, in his death on the cross, like the dalits, Jesus was 'broken, the crushed, the split, the torn, the driven asunder man' - the dalit in the fullest possible meaning of the term.[6] These statements on Jesus Christ affirm the *dalitness* of Jesus and identify Him in the contemporary dalit context.

Besides, A. P. Nirmal suggests that Jesus' dalitness is the key to the mystery of the divine human unity.[7] Although, Nirmal has not offered much explanation as how 'dalitness' is the key to understand the mystery of Jesus' humanity and divinity except to say that Jesus' cry on the cross, "My God, My God, why hast

---

[2] Anthoniraj Thumma, *Springs from the Subalterns: Patterns and Perspectives in People's Theology* (Delhi: ISPCK, 1999), 3.

[3] See A. P. Nirmal, *Heuristic Explorations* (Madras: CLS published for The Gurukul Lutheran Theological College and Research Institute, 1990), 151-155. Following Nirmal, dalit theologians expounded on five dalit features in the life and ministry of Jesus Christ. Cf. M. E. Prabhakar, "Christology in Dalit Perspective," 414-417.

[4] Jesus' genealogy comprises of the names of Tamar, Rachel, Solomon which in those days shows an ill repute in the ancestry line (Matt. 1:1-17). In addition, the pejorative reference to Jesus as a carpenter's son is also pointed out to show 'dalit' experience of Jesus at a hereditary inheritance. A. P. Nirmal, "Towards a Christian Dalit Theology," in *A Reader in Dalit Theology*, edited by Arvind P. Nirmal (Madras: Gurukul Lutheran Theological College and Research Institute, nd), 65-69.

[5] Cleansing of temple is another incident, where Nirmal stands with Lightfoot's interpretation that Jesus get angry at the temple court, which is reserved for gentiles (dalits) turned into *bazar*. He interprets it for dalits who struggle for temple entry rights in India or a prefiguration of the vindication of the Indian dalit struggle for their prayer and worship rights. A. P. Nirmal, *Heuristic Explorations*, 151-55. Also "Towards a Christian Dalit Theology," 225.

[6] A. P. Nirmal, *Heuristic Explorations*, 151-55. Also "Towards a Christian Dalit Theology," 225. Also M. E. Prabhakar, "Christology in Dalit Perspective," 414.

[7] A. P. Nirmal, "Towards a Christian Dalit Theology," 225.

thou forsaken me?" – seem to indicate a sense of God-forsakenness.[8] Peter C. Phan says, "Nirmal seems to suggest, obliquely, that the relationship between Jesus' divinity and humanity should be understood in dialectical rather than ontological terms."[9] The feeling of being rejected or 'God forsaken' is the core of dalit experience and consciousness also.[10] Therefore, a thorough study on the dalitness of Jesus Christ in relation to his divinity and humanity is needed. Jesus becomes a dalit in dalit theology by virtue of his dalitness, which is identified in terms of his 'pathos' experience as the suffering servant. This pathos is recognized as the epistemic key to Dalit identity too.[11] It is "an integral link between dalit Christology and dalit anthropology"[12] that is interwoven here.

3.1.2 Jesus: The Pro-Dalit Liberator

In the contemporary dalit Christology, Jesus Christ is confessed not only as Jesus the dalit but also a 'pro-dalit' Christ. In this confession, the person of Jesus cannot be separated from his praxis and his struggle for dalit liberation, since "his praxis was subversive, creative and transformative counter-cultural action."[13] That means, Jesus Christ is understood as to be an inspirer for the ongoing struggle of dalit counter-culture. Jesus becomes an advocate for dalits. In addition, Jesus' dalitness and dalit experiences did not lead him to resignation, fatalism, despair, pessimism, escapism and inferiority in his status, but rather "he was energized and empowered by dalit experience to revolt against the oppressive system."[14] It is a dalit Christology of counter culture. In this dalit counter cultural interpretation, Jesus Christ is placed not only as friends of dalits, but one who sheds blood for dalits on the cross. The praxis of Jesus Christ intended for the liberation of the *daliton* (Luke 4:18). Thus, every act of Jesus need to be interpreted from dalit liberation perspective. Jesus focuses more sharply on the poor, meek, the sorrowful and the persecuted as the agents of God's redemptive activity.[15] They are "the ones

---

[8] A. P. Nirmal, "Towards a Christian Dalit Theology," 229.

[9] Peter C. Phan, "Living for the Reign of God; Liberation, Culture, Religions. A Theology of Liberation for the Asian Churches," in *Movement or Moment: Assessing Liberation Theology Forty Years After Medellin*. Studies in Theology, Society, and Culture Vol. 1, edited Patrick Claffey and Joe Egan (Switzerland: Peterlang, 2009), 84.

[10] A. P. Nirmal, "Towards a Christian Dalit Theology," 229.

[11] Peniel Rajkumar, *Dalit Theology and Dalit Liberation: Problems, Paradigms and Possibilities*, Ashgate New Critical Thinking in Religion, Theology and Biblical Studies Series (Farnham, England: Ashgate, 2010), 64.

[12] Peniel Rajkumar, *Dalit Theology and Dalit Liberation*, 54.

[13] Anthoniraj Thumma, *Springs From the Subalterns*, 3.

[14] Anthoniraj Thumma, *Springs From the Subalterns*, 12.

[15] V. Devasahayam, "Theologising in Context," in *Frontiers of Dalit Theology*, edited by V. Devasahayam (New Delhi: ISPCK, 1997), 24, 25.

made powerless and those who have been domesticated to serve the purpose of their oppressors."[16]

In short, dalitness, counter-culture and pro-dalitist Christ are some of the prominent characteristics of contemporary dalit Christology. One can find two extremities in these arguments of the contemporary dalit faith confession, such as narrow communalism and masochism of extreme dalitness.[17] The common adversary in the contemporary faith confession is brahmanical caste people. With these assumptions, one needs to carefully evaluate the above mentioned two dalit traditional understandings of Jesus Christ to find out its strength and weakness, especially with the help of the early faith confession.

3.2 Thematic Critique of Contemporary Dalit Faith Confession

Thematically or content wise, contemporary dalit interpretation of Jesus Christ as dalit and pro-dalit brings forth the danger of incomplete and misguided early faith confession in the contemporary dalit context. Primarily, it is a relation to the lenience towards the historical Jesus than the Christ of faith. Secondly, there is an attempt to make Jesus as a local dalit deity.

3.2.1 *Casteicization* of Jesus Christ and Incomplete Dalit Faith Confession

One of the Christolgoical-thematic critiques to the contemporary dalit faith confession would be its lopsidedness. When Jesus is termed as dalit *par-excellence* in particular castiest context, it is imposed caste reading on Jesus Christ. When Jesus is interpreted from a caste perspective, the whole idea of dalit is missing from the content of the contemporary dalit faith confession. It would serve as a caste ideological expansion than dalit understanding of Jesus Christ. Casteist interpretation of Jesus Christ is, mainly, Christ of faith or dogmatic Christ. When dalit emphatically interprets Jesus Christ's humanity, it becomes a supplement to the dominant casteist Christology, which mainly focus on the divinity of Jesus Christ. This process of accommodating dalitisation of Jesus Christ by brahmanical tradition can be termed as *casteisation* of Jesus Christ. To become a dalit Christology, it must be liberated from such attempt of *casteization* on Jesus Christ.

However, attempts have been made to overcome this limitation by adopting preventive measures from liberation theology.[18] Liberation theology's

---

[16] Devasahayam, "Theologising in Context," 25.

[17] Sundar Clarke, "Dalit Movement- Need for a Theology," in *Towards a Dalit Theology*, edited by M. E. Prabhakar (Published for CISRS and CDLM by Delhi: ISPCK, 1988), 30-34.

[18] M. Gnanavaram, "Dalit Theology and the Parable of the Good Samaritan," *Journal for the Study of the New Testament* 50 (1993): 66-67. Accessed through ATLA on 09-10-2014. Also Samuel Jayakumar, *Dalit Consciousness and Christian Conversion: Historical Resources for a Contemporary Debate* (Chennai: Mission Educational Books, 2004, first published 1999), 30.

understanding of historical Jesus is the liberator and Christ of faith is less important in the process of liberation.[19] Though the contemporary dalit Christology does not visibly participate in this problem of historical Jesus vs. Christ of faith in its theological discourses, by the influence of liberation theologies, there is a tendency to lean on to historical Jesus alone. Dalit interpretation of Jesus Christ cannot be a separatist one subscribing to the 'historical Quest for Jesus' scholarship. The danger of separating Christ of faith from historical Jesus in dalit context will make a crippled dalit theology, since dalit way of doing theology is not separatist or broken rather to fix it into its wholeness. In order to analyze this situation, one needs to make the early faith confession as criteria.

In the early faith confession, mainly three ingredients were necessitated to interpret Jesus Christ: firstly, the mysterious characteristic of interpreting Jesus, the Christ, secondly revealed aspects and thirdly his relevance to the then 'dalit' situations. Contrarily contemporary Dalit Christology revises the order of the faith confession in which relevance of Jesus in the dalit context is emphasized much, giving revealed aspects of Jesus as focus for dalit Christology and less to the mystery of Jesus Christ. Christology as the product of these (mystery-revelation-relevance) interactions lacks in the contemporary dalit faith confession. Dalit theologians less expound this dalit *mysterium Christi* or Christ of faith. Explicit absence of the Christ of faith and the imposed liberation Christology make the contemporary dalit faith confession incomplete. Therefore, here, the researcher argues for the inevitability of 'Christ of faith' in dalit Christological discourse so

---

[19] Richard Baukam brings three senses of the term historical Jesus such as: (i) It could mean Jesus as he really was in his earthly life, (ii) not all that Jesus was, but Jesus in so far as his historical reality is accessible to us, and (iii) not the Jesus of the Gospels, but the allegedly real Jesus behind the Gospels. Richard Bauckam, *Jesus and the Eyewitness: The Gospel as Eyewitness Testimony* (Grand Rapids, Michigan: William B. Eerdmans Publishing Company, 2006), 2-3. But liberation theologians understood this division as a established fact. Based on this they argue, the 'historical Jesus' will in one sense only be 'the Jesus whom our sources enable us to reconstruct'. And Christ of faith is a new expression to Jesus Christ presented in dogmas and creeds of Christianity. Francis Watson puts in this way, "Christ who has little or no connection with particular historical figure of Jesus of Nazareth." Francis Watson, "The Quest for the Real Jesus," in *The Cambridge Companion to Jesus,* edited by Markus Bockmuehl (New York: Cambridge University Press, 2001), 166. That means Christ of faith does not bind by history, period and any culture. In a way, Christ of Faith is an object of Christian faith and confession and the *kerygma* of Church. Millard J Erickson, *Christian Theology* 2nd ed. (Grand Rapids, Michigan: Baker Books, 2002), 682. Bultmann, champion of such division argues that the early community that formed after Jesus' movement had a little relation to Jesus' consciousness. Rudolf Bultmann, *Theology of the New Testament,* translated by Kendrick Grobel (New York: Charles Scribner's Sons, 1951), 26. Gustavo Gutierrez, *A Theology of Liberation*, 130 ff. Also James H Cone argues that Christ of *kerygma* may distort the whole Christology in its existential situation of a community. Therefore, historical Jesus is the indispensable foundation of Christology. *A Black Theology of Liberation*, 201, 212. Also Juan Luis Segundo, *Jesus of Nazareth Yesterday and Today* Vol. II The Historical Jesus of the Synoptics, translated by John Drury (Maryknoll: Orbis Books, 1985), 23.

that Christology can be a liberative prolegomena for dalits as it was in the early faith community.

> The faith confession of the early Christian community affirms the historical reality of Jesus of Nazareth through the Christ of faith (*kerygmatic* Christ).[20] In this regard, M. M. Thomas, an Indian lay theologian has said as follows:

This argument finds its validity when the Christ of faith becomes a carrier and knower of historical Jesus. The present know–ability of Jesus of Nazareth is the result of the continuance of Christ of faith through texts, traditions, and creeds. The historical fact of Jesus of Nazareth and his significance as God's saving act for men [*sic*] are held together and cannot be separated in the fundamental core of the Christian *kerygma*.[21]

Hence, dalit theologians can draw out liberative resources from these raw-sources than lending from other liberation theologies. This could be an authentic dalit view of Jesus Christ and also a firsthand attempt to unravel the traditional sources of oppression into full liberation. In other words, the Palestine metaphors and imageries need to be interpreted in the philosophical and cultic perspective of dalits.[22] This would be an attempt of any 'dalit' theologian to understand Christ in complete sense. The Christ of faith is less recognized reality or truth in the dalit Christological reflection. This attempt sheds light into this unnoticed area of dalit theology- Christ of faith and dalit theology, and screws up the agenda or propaganda of "historical Jesus" as a lopsided approach. In a way, one has to admit that Dalits' bias towards caste and uncritical belief in liberation theology are the reasons for *casteicization* of Jesus Christ which results in an incomplete dalit faith confession.

3.2.2 Dalitist Jesus and Local Dalit Deity

When Jesus is presented as the dalit *par-excellence* and pro-dalit liberator, this presentation is not only identifying him with dalit situations, but Jesus himself is a true dalit. When this dalit Christological argument read in the context of 'dalit hero worship,'[23] there is a tendency to limit Jesus to be a 'truly local dalit hero.' Dalit theologians, by expounding dalitness of Jesus Christ, foster a 'sacrificial heroism' to Jesus Christ. For instance, to identify Jesus in servant language is to recognize

---

[20] See 2.4.3. Christological-Thematic Analysis.

[21] M. M Thomas, *The Acknowledged Christ of Indian Renaissance* (Madras: CLS, 1970, third edition, 1991), 294. Also Antony Mookenthottam, *Indian Theological Tendencies* (Las Vegas: Peter Lang, 1978), 144.

[22] Herbert Jai Singh, "Toward a Relevant Gospel in India," in *Indian Voices in Today's Theological Debate*, edited by Horst Bürkle and Wolfgang M.W. Roth (Luknow: Luknow Publishing House in collaboration with Delhi/Madras: ISPCK, CLS, 1972), 130.

[23] Satyanathan Clarke, "Subaltern Cultures as Resource for People's Liberation: A Critical Enquiry into Dalit Culture Theory." *Religion and Society* 44/4 (December, 1997): 89.

and identify Jesus as 'a truly dalit deity.'[24] This attempt is done on the basis of 'methodology of exclusivism', where Jesus is only meant for local dalits alone, and not for non-dalits. It is a parochial understanding of Jesus Christ as a local dalit deity, who is exclusively dalitist. It can be termed as dalit captivity of Jesus or dalit imprisonment of Jesus. Parochialising of dalit faith confession diminishes the 'universality' of the early church faith confession and 'inclusiveness' of dalits.

Another limitation of the contemporary dalit faith confession is that it contributes to the reinforcement of the status quo given by caste system rather than challenging it.[25] Peniel Rajkumar also argues when he says, "the contemporary dalit faith confession becomes a passive acceptance of their religiously imposed inferiority and acquiescence to the prevailing status quo."[26] He writes, "There is a possibility of glorifying the condition of dalitness and has potential to reinforce masochistic acceptance of their present suffering."[27] That means, dalitist Christ could be a counter-productive image for practical liberation since there is the risk of idealizing dalitness.[28] Thus, in the contemporary dalit faith confession Jesus is understood as exclusive *dalitist* in which universality of Jesus Christ is denied. Perhaps, this would also serve as a basement for another functional danger of the contemporary dalit Christology which views Jesus as the annihilator of other dominant non-dalit structures and non-dalit people.

3.3 Functional Critique of Contemporary Dalit Faith Confession

Functionally, one must critically look at the contemporary dalit faith confession's function in the context of *dalitvad*. Perhaps, there could two-pronged functional dangers in the contemporary dalit faith confession such as annihilation of whatever is non-dalit and disintegration among the sub-caste groups.

3.3.1 Annihilation of Non-Dalits

When Jesus is presented as 'pro-dalit liberator' in emerging *dalitvad* context, contemporary dalit faith confession would function not only as a defense for dalits, but also implicitly an offence to the non-dalits. It is an offence aimed at 'whatever breaks' or the structural evil that cause for the dalitness. This 'anti' nature, which is one of the characteristics of *dalitvad*, is evident when dalit theologians refer to the exodus event. The dalit Christological paradigm influenced from exodus motif, turned out to be Christ who is full of vigor, and against the non-dalits.[29] The danger of such presentation is that Christ becomes a tool for subjugation for some (dalits) and oppression for others (non-dalits). This way of perception

[24] A. P. Nirmal, "Towards a Christian Dalit Theology," 224.

[25] Peniel Rajkumar, *Dalit Theology and Dalit Liberation*, 67.

[26] Peniel Rajkumar, *Dalit Theology and Dalit Liberation*, 67.

[27] Peniel Rajkumar, *Dalit Theology and Dalit Liberation*, 65.

[28] Peniel Rajkumar, *Dalit Theology and Dalit Liberation*, 65.

[29] Peniel Rajkumar, *Dalit Theology and Dalit Liberation*, 64.

is quite paradoxical to *dalitism* and an uncritical subscription to the brahmanical ideology. The god-images of brahmanical tradition are seen by dalit-bahujan as the propagators of violent wars against them.[30] Thus from 'dalit' point of view Jesus cannot be annihilation of others, but respecter of life or *jeeva*.[31] In the words of Peniel Rajkumar, "from the early faith confession, Jesus is 'saviour for all, and destructor of none.' In Christ, there is no antagonistic and polemic binarism of 'us' and 'them' but all who are suffering and all who are weary."[32] He challenges that "this inclusive nature of faith confession must be therefore forefront in the contemporary dalit faith confession." Peniel Rajkumar suggests an alternative to this situation. He writes, "there is need for a more integrative model where both the 'oppressed' and the 'oppressors' are critically challenged to work in an integrative and dialogical manner for a non-exclusive and non-humanizing society."[33]

3.3.2 Disintegration among Dalits

Class or caste interpretation of 'dalit' and such dalit interpretation of Jesus Christ brings ambiguous situation to the function of Jesus as pro-dalit liberator in the context of *dalitvad*. Contemporary understanding of 'dalit' is a caste or class interpretation, in which dalit becomes low caste or class in the society. Multiplicity of castes and classes in the Indian society make contemporary dalit faith confession more ambiguous. When dalit is identified from caste perspective, there is dilemma in identifying rural sub-castes, which sometimes deny their low position in the caste hierarchy.[34] Then the question of practicality of the dalit faith confession in the caste-dalit nexus context arises.[35] This further divides the people groups and promote rivalry of 'high' and 'low' castes. It is similar with the class interpretation on dalit context and Christian faith in which communal tension can be seen as the aftermath. Thus, as already discussed, dalit interpretation is an unique way of interpretation in which caste-class interpretation is challenged all together for an integrated approach. The liberation that Christ gives is not only for the oppressed castes or classes, it is inclusive in nature which embraces other oppressed groups and resist other forms of oppression. Therefore, the dalit

---

[30] Kancha Ilaiah, *Why I am Not a Hindu: A Sudhra Critique of Hindutva Philosophy, Culture, and Political Economy*, 2nd ed. (Calcutta: Samy, 2005), 100-101.

[31] Kancha Illiah, "Dalitism vs Brahmanism, 114-121.

[32] Peniel Rajkumar, *Dalit Theology and Dalit Liberation*, 64.

[33] Peniel Rajkumar, *Dalit Theology and Dalit Liberation*, 64.

[34] A. M. Abraham Ayrookuzhiel, "Dalit Theology: A Movement of Counter-Culture," in *Towards a Dalit Theology*, edited by M. E. Prabhakar (Delhi: ISPCK, 1988), 94-95.

[35] In Vincent Manoharan John Packianathan "Towards a Practical Dalit Theology: A Study on the Status and Relevance of Dalit Theology among Grass Roots Dalit Christians in their Struggle against Caste Oppression," A thesis submitted to the University of Birmingham for the degree of Doctor of Philosophy (January, 2012) from e-theses repository, 237.

Christology can function in solidarity in relation with any other theologies.[36] Limiting Christ just to particular caste or class will be Christology of class and caste, not necessarily dalit Christology. Dalit Christology on the one side, need to take seriously the economic and social oppression from caste-class nexus, and on the other side embrace and include 'all' broken people, that is, 'dalit' in inclusive terms. Dalit theology should be an initiated theology with inclusiveness so as to strive for a holistic expression of Indian theology.[37]

When dalit interpretation of Jesus can foster communal tensions, it can also work as an isolating dalit imagination from the rest of Indian Christian faith affirmations. Therefore, one needs to recheck *dalitvad* framework and methodologies of traditional dalit Christology that seeks for separatist dalit Jesus. Such faith affirmations need to be integrated with the wider Christological tradition, especially with that of other third world theologies. This would protect theological isolation, and hopefully it may also be able to contribute to a more holistic understanding of the significance and function of Jesus Christ in *dalit* context.

3.4 Methodological and Structural Critique of Contemporary Dalit Faith Confession

Contemporary dalit interpretations of Jesus Christ face a tremendous torrent from *dalitvad* in which method of advocacy and method of exclusivism are used and abused in many ways. These two methodologies, such as method of advocacy and method of exclusivism, can weaken the complete content of the faith confession in the dalit context. One of the possible dangers of contemporary dalit Christology is that it advocates for a particular caste people in its methodology. As elsewhere mentioned, methodology of advocacy is predominant in the dalit interpretation of Jesus Christ, that is, Jesus 'for' particular caste people and unintentionally turns out to be Jesus 'against' particular (another) caste people. This 'exclusive' methodology in dalit Christology is insufficient in many ways. This framework must read along with the methodology of dalit theology proposed by Nirmal. He writes,

> In order to remain counter theology, it is necessary that it [dalit theology] is exclusive in character. This exclusivism is necessary because the tendency of all dominant tradition – cultural or theological- is to accommodate, include, assimilate and finally conquer others. Counter

[36] In the attempt to construct a contextual Christology, it is nonetheless important to maintain the inter-connectedness of various theologies, to preserve the integrity and universal nature of the gospel. Sundar Clarke, "Dalit Movement- Need for a Theology," 32. Also L. H. Lalpekhlua, *Contextual Christology: A Tribal Perspective* (Delhi: ISPCK, 2007), XXIII.

[37] Sundar Clarke, "Dalit Movement- Need for a Theology," 32.

> theologies, therefore, need to be on their guard and need to shut off the influences of the dominant theological tradition.[38]

Charles Singaram and other dalit theologians also support Nirmal's methodological exclusivism as a necessary tool for doing dalit theology.[39] However, when the dalit faith confession – Jesus is "for Dalits and dalit *alone*" – is made in the framework of *dalitvad*, can bring methodology of exclusivism as servant of extreme *dalitvad*. Nirmal's interpretation of Nazareth Manifesto, the gospel of Jesus brought was the gospel for "Dalits and *not* for non-dalits,"[40] also can contribute to foster *dalitvad*. Here, the exclusivist *sola* nature of *dalitvad* is already jolted with dalit Christological articulations. As one concentrates on the Jesus' message and life as a complete antithesis to Brahmanism (countering whatever brahmanism), which will diminish dalit's dignified way of interpreting Jesus Christ.[41] This exclusive framework and counter culture connotation can misrepresent dalit Christology in the Indian context, which is characterized with caste conflicts and communal violence.

Another matter that contemporary dalit faith confession is at crossroad is that the structure of their faith confession. There would be chances for uncritical subscription to the structure of early faith confession like of creed into the dalit context. M. E. Prabhakar has suggested dalit creed, especially the part that deals with Christology as follows:

> ...
> ...came to us in Jesus Christ
> To live with us and save all people from their sins
> We believe in Jesus Christ, born to Virgin Mary
> And anointed by God's Spirit as the Son of God
> To unseat the proud and unjust rulers
> To bring down the rich and mighty
> And to exalt the poor and oppressed
> He will bring justice to all humanity
> Suffering as the Human One and Servant of God
> He took our oppression and pain upon him
> And laid down his life in the cross to redeem us
> He was dead and buried but rose again to live forever
> He created a new humanity and a new future under God
> To realise our full humanity and image of God in us
> Jesus Christ is our Lord, Saviour and Liberator.

---

[38] Arvind P. Nirmal, "Towards a Christian Dalit Theology," in *A Reader in Dalit Theology*, 59.

[39] See Charles Singaram, *The Question of Method in Dalit Theology*, 126-221.

[40] A. P. Nirmal, "Towards a Christian Dalit Theology," 227.

[41] Joseph D'Souza, *Dalit Freedom: Now and Forever: The Epic Struggle for Dalit Emancipation* (Centennial: Dalit Freedom Network, 2004), 90.

...
We believe in the Church, the Body of Christ
And His fellowship to create equality and justice on earth.
We believe that Christ will come again
To judge all nations, according to their deeds to justice
And to establish God's rule of righteousness,
Forever and ever, Amen.[42]

Prabhakar's attempt of dalit creed and its statements seem more traditional and lack of potential for dalit full humanness, since it uncritically adopted the structure from the early church's faith creed. No particular formulation of the Christian faith is adequate for all times and situations as Russel Chandran and others argue for.[43] In the early church councils were busy with denying heresies than in making positive affirmations, since concepts and symbols are not adequate to the mystery of the divine.[44] Therefore, any attempt to canonize structure of the faith confession should be invalid. The argument here is that, structurally, dalit should use dalit structures that derived from their context such as folksong, folklores, etc., and at the same time the content of the early church's faith confession also should not to be reduced. This is a crucial point in which contemporary dalit Christology needs to be safeguarded. That is to say that, the creed for dalits Christology would be more of inclusive in nature, thus it could be named as confessions. It is when an attempt is made to canonize any of these formulations for all times that they become inadequate. The 'inclusive dalit' creed would look like more of inclusive and solidarity in its parts or structure.

As already observed, the contemporary dalit faith confession provides a castiest-*dalitvad* and class-communism. The faith affirmation of dalit theology is structured or formed in the mechanism of caste-class of other dominant traditions. That means, dalit interpretation depends upon the structure of other traditions to express the content of faith such as either of *sanskritization* or rendering class ideology.[45] Such tendency is criticized here by pointing towards the need for original dalit structures like dalitism that could be fruitfully constructed purely on 'dalit' faith confession. Thus, the contemporary dalit faith confession is at crossroads and needs new directions to be an authentic 'dalit' Indian Christology.

3.5 Dalit Christology at Crossroads

Here, an attempt is made to create a rapport for an 'inclusive dalit Christology,' which would be faithful to the early faith confession and to the 'dalit' context. In this preliminary attempt, three things have been done. Primarily, to find out the

---

42 M. E. Prabhakar, "Christology in Dalit Perspective," 419-420.

43 J. Russel Chandran, "The Theological Task of the Church in India," 113.

44 Michael Amaladoss, *The Asian Jesus* (Chennai/Delhi: IDCR/ISPCK, 2005), 6.

45 See Ghanshyam Shah, "Dalit Movements and the Search for Identity."

common sources of the early faith community and of the dalits that can bring forth 'inclusive dalit Christology'. Secondly, from the common resources, suggesting a possible re-visioning dalit faith confession inclusively. Thirdly, proposes a viable inclusive Christological methodology of *samvad* to have dialogue with distinctive dalit resources and the early faith confession. This would include the 'inclusive' approach to the text, tradition and Jesus Christ from the 'dalit' point of view. It would provide scope for suggesting new directions to the contemporary dalit Christology from the early faith community and their confession.

3.5.1 The *Samvad* between the Early Faith Confession and the Contemporary Dalit Christological Discourse

The interpretation of Jesus Christ as dalit and pro-dalit liberator from the dalit tradition in India will be distinct from the contemporary faith confession because of the following reasons.

Primarily, Dalit in contemporary dalit-caste interpretation is against the spirit of dalitism. Arul Raja says, "Dalits respond to only that brand of the divine which seeks to transform their vulnerabilities into empowerment."[46] Dalit Jesus Christ also the same but cannot limit only to particular caste groups, rather solidarities with all who experience, a condition of brokenness. This leads to the 'prime' meaning of the term 'dalit,' that is, any condition of brokenness and striving for wholeness. Because dalits are not people of 'caste' profile, but people who experience brokenness and have potential catalyst to change brokenness into wholeness. Dalit tradition is not at all full of pathos, but with a valid and vivid stream of thought that can have a parallel stand with other dominant traditions in India.

Secondly, the contemporary dalit faith confession challenges the early faith confession that maintained a high Christology in the functional and structural level in midst of their 'dalit' situation within the dominant traditions of that time. The early 'dalit' community of faith proclaimed an inclusive Christ, who was in solidarity with all that is 'dalit'. In other words, contemporary dalit faith confession is stagnant or limited from within and outside. From within, the confession itself is a casteist and particularistic in nature, and from outside, the dalit framework (*dalitvad*) serves annihilation pattern as opposed to all that is non-dalit. To overcome these dangers, the dalit Christology needs to turn its facade mainly towards the early faith community and prime connotation of dalit.

By understanding the distinctiveness of the inclusive dalit faith confession and contemporary dalit faith confession, one needs to seek viable images of dalit Christ, since the place of Jesus Christ is symbolized with the images of the dalits. How dalit imageries do play an important role in theologizing and how far early

[46] A. Maria Arul Raja, "Living Streams Across the Parched Land: Some Tenants of Dalit Spirituality," in *CTC Bulletin*, 3, http://daga.dhs.org/cca/resourse/ctc/ctc01-04/ctc0104d.htm. Also Peniel Rajkumar, *Dalit Theology and Dalit Liberation*, 67.

imageries relevant for dalit context is the matter of discussion. The *samvad*[47]/ interaction of the early faith community's faith confession and the contemporary dalit Christological discourses brings forth fresh sources mainly from the early faith community which is the product of the then 'dalit' condition. The new found resources can be integrated to the dalit resources for christologizing which shares similar motifs and trends.

The early faith community's single statements, poetic, and prose confessions are chosen in the oral context of dalits. Because the 'oral' tradition of the early church is parallel or congruent with the dalit oral culture. Thus, the early faith community's discourses can identify with the present dalit discourses (especially of the pre-literate discourse of the dalits).[48] The early confessional statements, not necessarily the structure itself, become a liberative force for the early faith community. For instance, creed, poem, prose and so on are the structures or formats to carry and communicate the content of the faith confession. And the dalit discourses has to grab and carry the liberative message from these sources.

However, when the sources become central than the content of the confession, the hegemonic activity of dominance come to play meta-narrative over dalit enterprise of theologizing. For instance, Nicaean Creed cannot be a 'structural paradigm' for dalit context, but it can be a 'content paradigm' for the dalit faith confession. Hence, precaution must be taken in such tendency of dominant structures of the faith confession over the contemporary dalit faith confession. In addition, systematization of content is necessary, but the purpose of it must be liberation, and fullness of humanity, not necessarily to exclude and isolate 'others' as the early church councils had done with heresies. Thus, the sources of the early faith confession are important to dalit Christologising as far as the content of the faith confession is concerned. The complete content of the sources signifies the sources itself.

3.5.2 Re-visioning Dalit Faith Confession Inclusively

The proposal here is a *re-vision of dalit Christology* from the vast resources that can interact with Dalitism and the early faith community. The task of theology is essentially revisionist which keeps on examining and revising its models and metaphors. Any theology, which refuses to engage in a critical revision in its concept, becomes idolatrous, says A. P. Nirmal.[49] The task of an authentic dalit Christology would be to reverse and revise meaningfully and utilize the hegemonic

[47] See the methodology of *samvad* explained in 3.5.3.1. Ways of Framing Inclusive Dalit Christology/Faith Confession.

[48] See A. Maria Arul Raja, "Some Reflections on a Dalit Reading of the Bible," in *Frontiers of Dalit Theology*, edited by V. Devasahayam (New Delhi: ISPCK, 1997), 337.

[49] Arvind P. Nirmal, *Heuristic Explorations*, 24.

ideology and mythology of the oppressors.[50] Vinod Peacock writes, "as part of this (dalit revisal) enterprise, inclusion instead of exclusion, unity and community [of plurality] instead of division,"[51] must be characterized in the future dalit faith confessions. Thus, it is clear that dalit Christology is a diaological Christology which always interacts with the dominant traditions and existing unbiased sources[52] for viable and suitable model.

Critical study on the contemporary faith confession and the early faith community also has given convergence vistas between them. The concept of 'dalit' is a common rapport between early faith community and contemporary dalit discourses. 'Dalitness' as experienced by the early faith community and the contemporary dalits are similar in relation to the meaning of the term dalit, that is, oppression of undefined character. Further, the cultural hegemony, imperial regime and divisive spirituality of the dominant structures of then and now bring forth another converging factor of oppression and feeling of oppressed to the forefront. Though the ways and the means of oppression have changed, but the common platform of 'condition of brokenness' still exists as rapport that both communities meet together.

Three areas that can be pointed out to re-vision the dalit faith confession in inclusive terms. Primarily, re-mythologizing is the pre-requisite for dalit Christology. The myths of the dominant traditions happened to see other streams of the society merely existential one. But dalit tradition tried to de-mythologize the myth. By de-mythologizing, dalit potentials as myth maker denied and faith confession become one-sided.[53] The proposal, here, is to 're-mythologize' the faith confession in the dalit way, since dalit tradition has the capacity to create meta-narratives.[54] Dalitism, as unique tradition in India, becomes a realization of "authentic dalit and authentic Indian" consciousness or philosophy. Dalitism is a creative and dynamic myth-maker that has power to interact with dominant traditions. The myth-maker is not a mere spectator but one who shares and interacts with the myth. He is both a helper and a witness in the words of John

---

[50] Vinod Peacock, "Impact of the Context: Dalit Perspective," in *Dalit-Tribal Theological Interface: Current Trends in Subaltern Theologies*, edited by James Massey and Shimreingam Shimray (Jorhat and New Delhi: TSC/WSC and CDS, 2007), 147.

[51] Vinod Peacock, "Impact of the Context: Dalit Perspective," 147.

[52] Sources of dalit Christology are early faith community's sources and dalit contextual materials. These materials are not biased to any particular ideology. Therefore, these resources can be termed as unbiased or neutral sources.

[53] For instance, when contemporary dalit faith confession subscribed liberation theologies of Latin America, brought the divided faith confession of historical Jesus and Christ of faith. The argument is that, dalits have all the potentiality to unravel and profess undivided faith confession in dalit way.

[54] John G. Arapura, "Rediscovering the Meaning of the Symbol," in *Indian Voices in Today's Theological Debate*, edited by Horst Bürkle and Wolfgang M.W. Roth (Luknow: Luknow Publishing House in collaboration with Delhi/Madras: ISPCK, CLS, 1972), 90.

G. Arapura.[55] The distinct dalit tradition which survive from ancient times can offer much to re-mythologize Christian faith in dalit terms. Therefore, inclusive dalit Christology is an attempt to re-construct myths, which are deconstructed, in a dalit way.

Secondly, re-historicizing the dalit origin and development. Re-historicizing from dalit terms is not intended to deconstruct dominant histories, but to see the history from dalit-*bahujan* perspective. In this sense, dalit Christology should be built on both the historical heritage and the living experiences of dalits.[56] Historical affinity between the different sections of the indigenous community is regarded here for inclusive dalit framework.[57] Therefore, there must be a *samvad* in re-historicising dalit histories.

Thirdly, re-dalitising (philosophize) dalit ideology inclusively. This inclusive dalitising can be seen from the nature of the common Indian spirituality of integration or *samvad.* Contemporary dalit ideology is nurtured in *dalitvad* context, in which is against Indic spirituality. Then, the proposal must be to re-dalitise dalit theology from the 'inclusive' meaning of the term dalit. Thus, when the contemporary dalit ideology learns lessons from the dalit localities, re-dalitisation extends the scope towards all localities in search of 'dalitness' to acquire inclusive consciousness.[58] Further, dalit consciousness is not of its oppressors' like brahmanic consciousness. Dalit consciousness is not intended to create a separate or a sectarian philosophy of the oppressed or the aborigines.[59] Dalit consciousness is a distinct philosophy of India developed over many centuries. This survivability of dalitism in India makes inclusive dalit Christology more authentic and Indian. While considering these three revised areas – myth, history and ideology – one can suggest a possible inclusive methodological framework for contemporary dalit Christology.

---

[55] John G. Arapura, "Rediscovering the Meaning of the Symbol," 90.

[56] When James Massey tells the need of dalit history, he had in mind that the criticism of Indian Christian church history written mainly from dominant western tradition and need of Indians to write Indian Christianity from their own point of view (not that of missions and missionaries). See "Ingredients for a Dalit Theology," 340-341.

[57] S. K. Chatterji, "Some Aspects of Dalit Ideology," in *Towards a Common Dalit Ideology* (Madras: Gurukul, 1989/91). Also *Religion and Society* XXXVII/3 (1990).

[58] Sebastian Alackapally, "A Philosophy of Education for Dalit Assertion," in *Indigenous Philosophizing: Indian Horizons*, Dharmaram Philosophy Series: 5 (Bangalore: Dharmaram Publications, 2010), 71.

[59] Joseph Pandiappallil, "Need for An Inclusive and Integral Philosophy in the Indian Subcontinent," in *Indigenous Philosophizing: Indian Horizons*, Dharmaram Philosophy Series: 5 (Bangalore: Dharmaram Publications, 2010), 159.

3.5.3 Inclusive Dalit Christological [Methodology/ical] Framework

There are some expectations required on dalit Christology to be an authentic Christology in the Indian dalit context. In other words, what is implicit in dalit Christology is "the attempt to make the dalits realize their own humanness and dignity through the dalitness of Jesus Christ."[60] According to M. M. Thomas, a living theology is 'situational' or 'contextual' in which the presence of Christ has been recognized and interpreted in the light of Jesus of Nazareth who is Christ incarnate in another situation.[61] In addition, a living theology is formulated with three major ingredients such as Jesus Christ, context and interpretation.[62] That means, in order to develop a living contextual dalit theology the core of the Christian faith (Jesus Christ) need to be interpreted (hermeneutics) in terms of dalit situations (context). Thus, the essential point of dalit theology should be Jesus Christ,[63] then, the dalit contexts of brokenness (*Dalitness*) and striving for wholeness are the ingredients for dalit living theology. These three ingredients were analyzed in previous two chapters separately. This section would use these ingredients to construct an inclusive dalit methodological outline with the tool of *samvad* and solidarity. It would help us in final section to propose an authentic inclusive Dalit Christology.

3.5.3.1 Ways of Framing Inclusive Dalit Christology/Faith Confession

The contemporary dalit faith confession, as already argued elsewhere, has the potential to operate as a palliative inuring the dalitness to their existing suffering through marginalisation and make the Dalits masochistic in their attitude towards suffering. Three precautions can be taken to avoid such danger.

Primarily, inclusive dalit faith confession must interpret Jesus in dalit terms that involve a dalit paradigm of transformation. In the words of Peniel Rajkumar,

> Primarily, inclusive dalit faith confession must be 'dalit' in dalit terms not in caste or class basis. Paradigms which inordinately and exclusively focus on pathos can reinforce the slavish mentality and deeply inculcated sense of inferiority among the dalits. This would be one of the overarching reason impeding dalit initiative in accepting responsibility for self-transformation and the positive realization of their inherent worth and dignity. Thus, if one uses the rhetoric of ethical imperative in relation to the dalits then it should mean an imperative

[60] M. E. Prabhakar, "Christology in Dalit Perspective," 402-432.

[61] M. M. Thomas, *The Acknowledged Christ of the Indian Renaissance*, 293-300.

[62] M. M. Thomas, *The Acknowledged Christ of the Indian Renaissance*, 293-300. Also James Massey, "Ingredients for a Dalit Theology," in *Towards a Dalit Theology*, edited by M. E. Prabhakar (Delhi: ISPCK, 1988), 59.

[63] M. Azariah, "The Church's Healing Ministry to Dalits," *Towards a Dalit Theology* (Delhi: ISPCK, 1988), 120.

that makes them consciously reject their psychological enslavement and gives them impetus to work towards self-emancipation.[64]

Secondly, the dalit theology is no longer a reaction to mainstream theology/ies, but it has attained the stature of setting the trends itself. James Massey says that, "dalit theology should not be seen as a 'counter-theology' to western and traditional Indian Christian Theology, but should be seen as a dialogic theology/Christology. Therefore, we are back in a pre-Chalcedonian situation, where we enjoy the freedom to formulate our confession relevant and meaningful to the context of dalitness."[65] It is no longer obsessed with deconstructing 'upper' caste illusions of the world. It is now in a position to set agenda. It is engaged in multiple other dialogues, (i.e., heterologue/*Samvad*), with not only theologies of the oppressed people but also with other philosophies and ideologies.[66] When this dialogue will take place by the initiative of dalits in the context of caste conflicted India, then Christ will be presented as a dalit who seeks harmony and integration. For this purpose, three qualities are necessary, such as right attitude, correct information and openness to the views of other.[67]

Thirdly, the methodology of solidarity and *samvad* are the two ways that can frame an authentic inclusive nature of dalit theological faith confession since the contemporary dalit Christologies either sideline with dalitness or overpowered by *dalitvad*. It also regulates the extremities in the contemporary dalit faith confession and finds commonplace for interaction and interfacing[68] for fuller humanness with dalit people in their dalitness. In addition, Dalitism is the methodological framework for dalits and provides tools for interpretations.

As one remove dalit'*vad*' from dalit'*ism*', the shift in dalit hermeneutics is from 'advocacy' to 'solidarity'- *vad* to *samvad*.[69] Keeping in mind the positive role

---

[64] Peniel Rajkumar, *Dalit Theology and Dalit Liberation*, 115.

[65] James Massey, *Down Trodden The Struggle of India's Dalits for Identity, Solidarity and Liberation* (Geneva: WCC Publication, 1997), 78. Cf. R. H. S. Boyd, "The Philosophical Context of Indian Christian Theology with Special Reference to P. Chenchiah," in *Indian Voices in Today's Theological Debate*, edited by Horst Bürkle and Wolfgang M.W. Roth (Luknow: Luknow Publishing House in collaboration with Delhi/Madras: ISPCK, CLS, 1972), 69.

[66] Sathianathan Clarke, Deenabandhu Manchala and Philip Vinod Peacock, "Introduction," in *Dalit Theology in the Twenty First Century: Discordant Voices, Discerning Pathways*, edited by Clarke Santhinathan, Manchela Deenabandhu and Vinod Philip Peacock (New Delhi: OUP, 2010), 11.

[67] Herbert Jai Singh, "Toward a Relevant Gospel in India," 138-39. Also Bhagat Oinam, "Philosophy in India: An Agenda for an Alternative Mode of Philosophising," *Journal of Indian Council of Philosophical Research* XXVIII/2 (April-June, 2011): 83.

[68] Hrangthan Chungi, "Interfacing Tribal and Adivasi Theology with Feminist Theology for Building Theologies of Solidarity," in *Building Theologies of Solidarity: Interfacing Feminist Theology with Dalit Theology and Tribal/Adivasi Theologies*, edited by Hrangthan Chhungi, Raj Bharath Patta and P. Mohan Larbeer (Bangalore: BTESSC/NCCI/SCMI, 2012), 6-14.

[69] The term *vad* is used to refer one person's argument or advocacy, whereas *samvad* refers to agreement or a disagreement to the *vad* in a context of debate. *Samvad* is kind of dialogue in which

of advocacy in raising the conscience of the dalits as people groups could not go beyond of solidarity with the people who experience the condition of 'dalitness'.[70] Commitment to dalit (as people groups) cause is the foundation of advocacy reading as followed in Latin American Liberation theologies.[71] James Massey also agrees and says, "advocacy approach has been employed by dalit theologians on behalf of the Dalits from liberation theologies, but mostly it has failed, as it lacked a comprehensive approach to the issue."[72] Advocacy is more of a method either for or against someone. However, the epistemology of dalitism proposes more comprehensive solidarity approach that commitment to the 'right' cause is emphasized.[73] It is also the concept of *communal solidarity* in which Indian constitution stands for; vanishing of majority and minority, elite and low class or caste people. When B. R. Ambedkar talks about the Indian constitution and constituent assembly, he envisioned a 'merging of majority and minority someday into one.'[74] However, Ambedkar's vision must be critically looked at, since the minorities will continue or will vanish must depend on the habit of the majority. The moment the majority loses the habit of discriminating against the minority, the minorities can have no ground to exist.[75] That is why the conversion must take place simultaneously involving both the majority and the minority at the same time, so that they can live harmoniously.

This paradigm of solidarity can be derived from the early faith confession which states that Jesus Christ was in the form of God, emptied himself and dwelt among us (Cf. John 1:14 and Phil. 2:6). This incarnational methodology is the solidarity scheme, which serves as the critical principle for the liberation of dalits.[76]

---

integration of the arguments is prominent than advocating for one's argument. Mutual respect and mutual understanding are the main characteristics of *samvad*. A prominent new emerging trend in philosophizing in India is Daya Krishna's idea of "philosophy as *samvād*." The term "*samvād*" itself is rooted in Sanskrit signifying the idea of "dialogue." Defining philosophy as dialogue (*samvād*) highlights several aspects of the Indian philosophical traditions. Bhagat Oinam, "Philosophy in India: An Agenda for an Alternative Mode of Philosophising," 83.

[70] James Massey, "Paradigm Shift in Theological Education: Advocacy to Solidarity," *From Truth to Truth: A Journey through Faith, A Selection of Representative Essays by Dr. James Massey*, edited by Deepak Seth (Noida/New Delhi: CDS/Academy Press, 2008), 81.

[71] Gustavo Gutteriz, *Theology of Liberation*, iv.

[72] James Massey, "Paradigm Shift in Theological Education," 82.

[73] Philip Vinod Peacock, "Impact of the Context: Dalit Perspective," 144.

[74] B. R. Ambedkar, "Communal Deadlock and a Way to Solve It: Address delivered at the Session of the All India Scheduled Castes Federation held in Bombay on May 6, 1945," in *Selected Works of DR. B. R. Ambedkar*, 647.

[75] Arvind Sharma, "Dr. B. R. Ambedkar on the Aryan Invasion and the Emergence of the Indian Caste System in India," 866. (ATLA accessed)

[76] James Massey writes, "...God in full solidarity with us, not just as any human being, but one who became the poorest of the poor (in real sense a Dalit), who lost His otherworldly identity completely for the sake of human beings." M. John also writes, first, we should appropriate

This hermeneutical tool helps dalit theology not to be theology of / for / from / to the dalits, but a theology '*with*' dalits in their broken condition.[77] In the words of S. Lourdunathan, "the task of theology of solidarity with reference to dalits problematic needs aim at more foundational approach in terms of reconstructing those systems of knowledge that subjugate both the dalits and the non-dalits into the self-same oneness of domination."[78] In this hermeneutical method, there is a shift from 'particularity to commonality.'[79] Since dalitism teaches communal harmony and respects others throughout history,[80] search for ways of framing inclusive dalit Christology would be through solidarity with the weaker sections and *samvad* with the dominant traditions.

3.5.3.2 Method of Analyzing Historical and Social Dalit Situation

The methodology of solidarity and *samvad*, as explained previously, can be rendered to formulate an inclusive dalit Christology in India. This comprehensive and deeper analytical framework can apply to dalit hermeneutics that deals with history, culture and religion of dalits. At the same it can also apply to the Christian faith confession that dalit seeks for hope and liberation.[81] According to George Oommen, "memory and identity are important components of dalit history."[82] The interaction between dalit world view and Scripture bring forth radical difference comparing with brahmanical ethics of casteism. Drawing out the framework for a pertinent dalit hermeneutics, Arul Raja proposes, "the religiosity latent in dalit culture should be activated and brought into dialogue with biblical

---

personally the spirit of his life of poverty and his profound self-identification with the poor and oppressed.... That will largely remove from the dalit community their sense of inferiority and want about themselves and then we need a radical inner conversion. M. John, "The Church in the Service of Dalits: Statistics and Policy," 123. Also James Massey, "Paradigm Shift in Theological Education," 84-85. Also *Down Trodden*, 59-65. Also Anthoniraj Thumma, *Voices of the Victims*, 38.

[77] Cf. Paulo Friere, *Pedagogy of the Oppressed* 30th ed. (London: Continuum, 2005), 38.

[78] S. Lourdunathan, "Theoretical Grounds for a Theology of Solidarity: Instantiating a Dalit Discourse," in *Building Theologies of Solidarity: Interfacing Feminist Theology with Dalit Theology and Tribal/Adivasi Theologies*, edited by Hrangthan Chhungi, Raj Bharath Patta and P. Mohan Larbeer (Bangalore: BTESSC/NCCI/SCMI, 2012), 33.

[79] Bhanu Samuel, "Dalit Theology: A Theology Towards Solidarity," in *Building Theologies of Solidarity: Interfacing Feminist Theology with Dalit Theology and Tribal/Adivasi Theologies*, edited by Hrangthan Chhungi, Raj Bharath Patta and P. Mohan Larbeer (Bangalore: BTESSC/NCCI/SCMI, 2012), 38.

[80] S. Anandan, "Dalit Non-Violence As a Means of Community Healing," in *Building Theologies of Solidarity: Interfacing Feminist Theology with Dalit Theology and Tribal/Adivasi Theologies*, edited by Hrangthan Chhungi, Raj Bharath Patta and P. Mohan Larbeer (Bangalore: BTESSC/NCCI/SCMI, 2012), 57.

[81] Franklyn J. Balasunderam, "Dalit Theology and other Theologies," in *Frontiers of Dalit Theologies*, 261-2.

[82] George Oommen, "Introduction," in *Local Dalit Christian History*, edited by George Oommen and John C. B. Webster (Delhi: ISPCK, 2002), 4-10.

religiosity."[83] "The liberative potential of the Bible" and "the resistive potential inherent in dalit religiosity"[84] would be a framework for dalit Christology. This social analysis from the dalit perspective should be seriously considered when one approaches to other dalit resources as well.

3.5.3.3 Inclusive Dalit Hermeneutical Approach to the Christological Resources

The critical study on the contemporary dalit faith confession brought the insufficiency or un-recognition of dalit resources for theologizing. Here, mainly two common dalit resources from the early faith community and contemporary dalit community can be taken into account as a significant resources in relation to construct an inclusive dalit Christology, such as textual resources and traditional resources. Textual resources include mainly three texts. Primarily the 'text' of the early faith community, secondly, texts carried by the dalit traditions in India and, finally 'other texts' of the dominant traditions that talk about dalit ways and means such as Vedas, Upanishads and so on. Traditional resources include the sources that pass through oral traditions such as the folklores of dalits, hymns and narratives of the early faith community and other brahmanical myths. The attempt here is to explain how to approach these decisive resources from dalit point of view that will help to stand distinct from other traditional way of approaching resources. Traditional way, for instance, includes brahmanical way of approaching these sources, or liberational way of approaching these resources. But dalit way of approaching these resources are distinct from castiest or classist approach. The inclusive dalit approaches to these resources are explained in some detail.

3.5.3.3.1 Inclusive Dalit Approach to Textual Resources

On the contrast to the traditional dalit faith confession, inclusive dalit methodology takes textual resources that are important for inclusive Christology. Traditional dalit theology that considers 'text' in the dalit context is absent.[85] However, the textual resources that dalit theologians deal with such as the Bible, Vedas and other religious writings for constructing dalit faith confession need a vigilant approach, since the 'text' was once a reason for their historical 'dalit'- broken condition. Moreover, we have a number of writings from dalits available now.

At the outset, therefore, the inclusive dalit approach would discard any caste or class interpretation of the text. The main aim of the inclusive dalit approach is to interpret the 'texts' for the full humanness of dalits, that is, an act of transforming

---

[83] A. Maria Arul Raja, "Towards a Dalit Reading of the Bible: Some Hermeneutical Reflections," in *Jeevadhara* 26/151 (1996): 31.

[84] Peniel Rajkumar, *Dalit Theology and Dalit Liberation*, 72.

[85] Traditionally, dalit context is considered as 'oral' context in nature, because of the increasing illiterate in the dalit communities. Therefore, dalit theologians were less concerned about the approach towards textual resources.

from brokenness to wholeness. In this act, three characteristics can be brought out. Primarily, dalit approach to 'text' is appropriateness than interpretation.[86] Value of a text, especially religious texts, in dalit context is understood by dalit way of appropriating it with their life. Because this appropriate nature of texts by dalits determine their condition of being dalit in many ways. For instance, dalits appropriated *Manu Smriti* into their context which made them slave to the text. In another instance, when dalits appropriated principles from biblical texts to their dalit context they found liberative impulses. Therefore, appropriating text in dalit context must be guided by the dalit hermeneutical principles. Secondly, dalit approach to textual resources is pragmatic or functional in nature. In the actual faith experiences of the dalit communities where the texts function in ways in which both the actual faith experience of the dalits and texts derives from and is dependent on each other.[87] They see 'text' has the power to act upon. Burning of *Manu Smriti* by dalit leaders is also needed to read in this line, since they understood the function of 'the text' (*Manu Smriti*) in the dalit context is negative and hegemonic. Therefore, dalit uncritical adoration of texts is questioned, since it can function quite opposite to dalit desire of being in full humanness. Thirdly, dalit approach to the textual resources is for their transformation. In short, Dalit's ideas about the appropriation of the texts are thoroughly functional and seek transformation of the dalit situation. Considering these wider characteristics of dalit approach toward texts, one needs to state, particularly, three textual resources and dalit approach towards it.

Textual resources from non-dalit tradition, such as Vedas, Ramayana, etc., are helpful to understand what others understood or misunderstood about dalits and their tradition. Dalit, while approaching to this secondary source for theologizing, needs the tool of critical suspicion of the text.[88] Since non-dalit traditions is the result of caste or class interpretation, there is always a chance to misrepresent what dalit is. Therefore, in addition, to critical suspicion to the text, dalit must engage in *samvad* with other dominant texts. This dialogue with dominant texts would clarify misrepresentations and can have solidarity with them to identify their weakness. Thus, dalit approach towards non-dalit textual resources not only clarifies the misconceptions, but also intervene in other traditions with dalit solutions.

Textual resources carried by the dalit tradition needs to be approached with the hermeneutic of suspicion. Because, the 'anti' nature of *dalitvad* has been working against non-dalit traditions. Therefore, there is always a chance to glorify

[86] Peniel Rajkumar, *Dalit Theology and Dalit Liberation*, 74.

[87] Sathinathan Clarke, *Dalits and Christianity: Subaltern Religion and Liberation Theology in India* (New Delhi: OUP, 1999), 30.

[88] "It is only that texts have been interpreted in support of oppressive values, but also that texts were created in support of the same." M. Gnanavaram, "Some Reflections on Dalit Hermeneutics," in *Frontiers of Dalit Theology*, edited by V. Devasahayam (New Delhi: ISPCK, 1997), 333.

whatever is dalit and total negation of non-dalits. This *dalitvad* approach towards dalit texts need to be critically looked at. Further, *samvad* with real or actual dalit and the representation in the dalit text needs to be continually maintained while approaching dalit texts. In addition to critical suspicion and *samvad*, in inclusive dalit approach, dalit text must always be solidarity with other texts. Since, solidarity is one of the characteristics of dalitism, it can identify with other texts which portray the dalitness and ways to become wholeness. In this juncture the biblical texts of the early faith community need to be analyzed as the third and important resource for dalit Christologising.

Biblical texts of the early faith community, as the primary datum for the formulation of authentic inclusive dalit faith confession in the context of 'dalitness', needs to be interpreted in dalit terms. Biblical texts supply ample resource for dalits to identify themselves with early faith community and be inspired to overcome brokenness to wholeness.[89] As Arul Raja states,

> Dalit reading of the Bible is a transformative/pragmatic approach which focuses- not on the author/redactor and his/her intention nor the deep structures of the external architecture of the text, but, on the flesh-and-blood persons of the dalit community hearing/ reading the text.[90]

He continues to write, "this reading-experience is defined by the intimate conversation between the totality of the history, social relationships, horizon and world view of the dalitness and that of the biblical text."[91] Thus, in addition to critical suspicion of the text, *samvad* and methodology of solidarity towards biblical texts, one can take advantage of the characteristics of dalit approach towards texts. They are appropriateness, pragmatic and transformative approaches. That means, not only biblical texts work in the dalit context, rather the dalit way of approaching the biblical text also gives meaning to the biblical text.

Thus, while considering appropriateness of biblical texts in the dalit context, dalits move from "exegetical activity to an interpretive activity."[92] It can be better described in terms of *appropriation* of the text as *interpretation* of the texts, as it transcends the convictions of textual interpretation.[93] Peniel Rajkumar writes,

---

[89] Monica Jyotsna Melanchthon, "Dalits, Bible and Method," in *SBL Forum*, http://www.sbl-siteorg/Article.aspx?ArticleID=459 assessed on 24/10/2014.

[90] A. Maria Arul Raja, "Some Reflections on a Dalit Reading of the Bible," 336. Cf. E.V. McKnight, *The Bible and the Reader: An Introduction to Literary Criticism* (Philadelphia: Fortress Press, 1985), XVIII.

[91] A. Maria Arul Raja, "Some Reflections on a Dalit Reading of the Bible," 336.

[92] I. John Mohan Razu, "The Promise and Possibilities of Hermeneutics: The Place of Dalits in the Private Sector," in *Frontiers in Dalit Hermeneutics*, edited by James Massey and Samson Prabhakar (Bangalore and Delhi: BTESSC/SATHRI and CDSS, 2005), 212.

[93] We can talk of 'trans-textual' and 'sensory' dimensions of the emancipatory appropriation of the bible by ordinary Christian dalit communities. The magical notion of the Bible testifies to dalit

> [T]he strength of the textual appropriation of the Bible by the dalits lies in such refiguring of important biblical characters in interaction with the experience of the dalits so as to reconfigure the communal identity of the dalit communities in an affirmative and identity-enhancing manner.[94]

Further, considering the functional characteristics of dalit approach to the texts, helps dalit Christology to be more liberative in terms of brokenness to wholeness. Devasahayam also has contributed a positive stimulator for reading the Bible from the Dalit liberative perspective.[95] It motivated dalit thinkers to re-read, re-interpret, and re-understand the Bible afresh from marginalized and in particular the dalit perspective.[96] This solidarity nature of the incarnate word in the context of dalitness becomes a transformative force.[97] Because, Jesus is the real text or canon, the Word in the biblical texts.[98] Christological concentration in reading the biblical text, then, becomes a paradigm for dalit transformative vision.

Christological concentrated reading can also be rendered to dalit writings, since both are characterized with narratives, stories, poems, etc.[99] In this dalit hermeneutics, Jesus plays a decisive role as the foundation and center of dalit theology.[100] Inferring Christological assumptions from the dalit textual traditions, one can enter into the dialogue with the issue of Jesus of the text and Jesus from the text, since the evidence for Jesus the Christ is almost exclusively literary.[101] Biblical text is one of the carriers of both historical Jesus and Christ of faith to the contemporary dalits. Therefore, is the Christ who derive from the text, or Jesus who is portrayed in the text is important for the dalits? 'Jesus of the text', that is, Jesus presented in the text is an expression of the early faith community in their 'dalit' situation. 'Jesus from the text', that is, Jesus one who is above the text,[102]

---

reception of the performative dimension of the Bible which is crucial to their understanding of the Bible as being emancipatory. Peniel Rajkumar, *Dalit Theology and Dalit Liberation*, 74.

[94] Peniel Rajkumar, *Dalit Theology and Dalit Liberation*, 75-76.

[95] V. Devasahayam, ed., *Frontiers of Dalit Theology* (New Delhi: ISPCK, 1997).

[96] Jeremiah Anderson, "An Explorative Search for Some Relevant Directions in Dalit Theology in the Context of Emerging Christian Liberation Theologies in India," 99.

[97] James Massey, "Introduction," in *Dalit World-Biblical World: An Encounter*, edited by Leonards Ferdinanda and James Massey (New Delhi: CDS & Vidyajoti, 2007), 18-19.

[98] V. Devasahayam, "Introduction to Bible Studies," in *Frontiers of Dalit Theology*, edited by V. Devasahayam (New Delhi: ISPCK, 1997), 4.

[99] See the scholarly essay in Abraham Ayrookuzhy and Paul Chirackarodu, *Dalit Sahityam: Oru Padanam* (Mal) (Thiruvalla: CSS/CISRS, 1995), 9-35 especially 28.

[100] James Massey, "Introduction," 18-19.

[101] Christopher Tuckett, "Sources and Methods," in *The Cambridge Companion to Jesus*, edited by Markus Bockmuehl (New York: Cambridge University Press, 2001), 121.

[102] In a way, Jesus above the text goes in line with the *Mysterium Christi* of the early faith community, which deals with the mysteries of Jesus Christ.

is a universal phenomenon. Here, then, text becomes a mediator between the historical particularity of the universal Christ into 'dalit' context. Thus, 'Jesus of the text' becomes a model for the contemporary dalit faith confession to articulate the universal Jesus Christ, without negating its universality and particularity. In other words, Jesus of the text recorded in the scripture by the early dalit faith community and the universality of Jesus are not necessarily contradicting each other, but mutually complementing. Thus, the early faith confession was also a contextual faith reflection. Thus, any attempt to extremely depend on the 'text' than Jesus himself for dalit humanness would be a 'back-to-bondage situation.'

3.5.3.3.2 Inclusive Dalit Approach to Traditional Resources

When one considers the term 'tradition' as living tradition, the whole approach towards traditional sources needs revision. Wolfgag M. W. Roth writes, "[t]radition does not mean so much a fixed and formulated system of laws and beliefs, creeds and thought forms, but living Christian tradition as it finds expression in the ongoing pilgrimage of the Church."[103] Tradition as a source for inclusive dalit confession includes oral transmissions of songs, stories, etc., on the one hand, can be termed as oral tradition, while language, symbols, metanarratives, etc., on the other as dalit cultural and religious traditions. Such tradition is characteristics of both early faith community and Indian dalit community. How to approach these rich and vast traditional resources for the fuller humanness of dalits?

In order to approach dalit traditions, that include oral, cultural and religious traditions, for expressing inclusive faith confession in dalit context, one can render paradigm from the early faith community, which expressed their complete faith confession in their oral context (that is pre-literal context). Jesus Christ who was expressed, before the textual expression, by the early faith community was in oral form. The oral context of the early faith community includes hymns, narratives, usage of various titles, etc., in the occasions of worship inside the church and public witness outside the church (See previous chapter). It is, then, both pre-text and post-text of the early faith community's oral tradition is the source for dalit theology. Pre-text means the confession that was existed before the formation of particular text like epistles or gospels. That is to say, pre-text Jesus was a Christological expression of the early faith community before any written expression (text) was formed. This precedence of the oral Jesus Christ is more concrete resource for Christologizing in dalit context. The post-text oral tradition means that, the tradition on Jesus Christ, which is developing in the forms of apostolic traditions and creeds. The oral Christological tradition was appropriated

[103] Wolfgang M. W. Roth, "Thought Patterns-Fetters or Opportunities?," in *Voices in Today's Theological Debate*, edited by Horst Bürkle and Wolfgang M.W. Roth (Luknow: Luknow Publishing House in collaboration with Delhi/Madras: ISPCK, CLS, 1972), 43.

into different occasions of the early faith communities' life contexts such as of hymns, kerygma and so on and became integral part of the community's culture.

Textual Jesus, in one sense, is the end result of oral Jesus. Individual stories in the gospel narrative were personal encounter of particular individual/community. When these events were put into a systematic structure as gospels and letters, the biblical texts also became a parallel source book for Christology. Regarding the commonality in the content of the oral faith confession with the textual faith confession, the methodology to interpret traditional resources would be similar with the textual approach. Such as critical suspicion, *samvad* and solidarity with the oral tradition of the early faith community. For instance, the confession of the early faith community of Jesus as the Christ must be critically looked at in its oral context in which it confessed, such as in worship or public witness. Further, the carrier of traditional resources can also come under these approaches, such as creeds, hymns, etc. This approach could help dalit Christology to be more meaningful and authentic to the dalit context and faithful to the confession of the early church.

These fervent oral traditions reflected in the early faith confession by the early faith community written down, later, in gospels, epistles and futuristic hope in Apocalyptic writings. Further, the councils of the church, and their creeds are important source for dalit liberational Christology. Thus, the oral context of dalits can be suitably utilize the oral traditions of the early faith community integrating with dalit oral traditions that transmitted through folksongs, stories, sayings and so on. Therefore, the methodology of solidarity and *samvad* are both working together to integrate both dalit oral traditions and the early faith community's tradition for the fuller liberation of dalits.[104]

Dalit cultural and religious traditions also have significant place in the formation of the inclusive dalit faith confession. Dalit cultural symbols have been utilized as a meta-narrative over against dominant traditions such as of *Hindutva* by Dalit movements that was continued by dalit theologians without recognizing its consequences.[105] Hence, Dalits attempt to express their collective experience and to reconfigure their subaltern subjectivity as distinct from dominant caste

[104] Commonly, in dalit Christology, creeds and other early faith confessions are taken less value since dalit theologians consider these as the product of dominant religious traditions. These sources played vital role in the early faith community to maintain their identity and solidarity with their 'dalit' situations. Creeds and other sources are the carriers of the content of the early faith confession are declaratory in nature and functional in its characteristics, not necessarily vested on dominant streams in the society. Therefore, dalit Christology can utilize the liberative sources for articulating dalit understanding of Jesus Christ.

[105] There are both cultural and religious symbols such as Guru, Avatar for former and Krishna and Rama, Bali for the later. However, these religious symbols have been taken as national cultural symbols of *Ramarajya* and quite opposite *Bali Rajya*. Dalit theology also goes along with such trends such as Abraham Ayrookuzhiel's Mahabali ideology. A. M. Abraham Ayrookuzhiel, "Dalit Theology: A Movement of Counter Culture," 96ff. Cf. Michael Amaladoss, *The Asian Jesus*, 8.

groups with counter-cultural images. For instance, their drums, so evocative of a people that have no voice in their society, a symbol of divine power, rather than the sacred 'word', the mantra of priestly ritual, as Rudolf Heredia writes.[106] In addition, it has been acknowledged that there is a performative trait in the religious experience of the subalterns traditions. V. V. Thomas writes, "In fact the dalits and the tribal people are partners in their brokenness, partners in their origin, partners in their subjugation, partners in the way they are defined, partners under the same oppressors, partners in their black future."[107] There is a strong collective component to this oral tradition as well as one can participate in subaltern hermeneutics, but cannot simply access them through cognitive tools.[108] In this situation, dalits have created and have to continue to create new texts (myths and stories- a remythologisation!) to liberate the oppressed.[109] In short, Dalit Christology is actively in dialogue with the dominant popular convictions with dalit cultural elements and religious tradition.

Summary of Findings

This chapter can summarize as thematic, functional and structural analysis of two major arguments in the contemporary dalit Christology. They are Jesus as the dalit par-excellence and pro-dalit liberator.

Thematically, the contemporary dalit Christology seems to propose a casteist Christ, who annihilates non-dalits. Further, the lopsided approach to Jesus Christ is visible in contemporary dalit faith confession which uncritical subscription only to 'historical quest for Jesus' because of the influence of liberation theology, not necessarily Christ of faith.

Functionally, the contemporary dalit Christology would serve *dalitvad*, in which Jesus could be an annihilator of all that is non-dalit and, thus leading to the disintegration among dalits.

Structurally, the contemporary dalit faith confession lacks potentiality of 'dalit' in its articulation, since it is either credulously subscribe structures from castiest and classist or from the early faith community such as of their creeds and dogmas to confess their faith.

Therefore, new directions and vistas are deduced by integrating the early dalit (Christian) community with the contemporary dalit discourses to re-historize, re-

---

106 Rudolf C. Heredia, "Search for Identity, Quest for Dignity...," 757.

107 V. V. Thomas, *Dalit and Tribal Christians of India: Issues and Challenges* (Kerala: Focus India Trust, 2014), x. Also Felix Wilfred, "Towards a Subaltern Hermeneutics beyond Contemporary Polarities in the Interpretation of Religious Tradition," *Jeevadhara* XXVI/151 (1996): 60.

108 Cf. R. S. Sugritharaja, *The Bible and Empire: Postcolonial Explorations* (Cambridge: CUP, 2005), 233-6.

109 M. Gnanavaram, "Some Reflections on Dalit Hermeneutics," 333. Cf. J. T. Appavoo, *Folklore for Change* (Madras: TTS, 1986). Also J. H. Anand, "Dalit Literature of the Literature of Protest," in *Dalit Solidarity*, edited by B. Dass and James Massey (Delhi: ISPCK, 1995), 177-184.

mythologize and re-philosophize/dalitise complete content of the faith confession in 'dalit' context with *samvad* and solidarity as the two tools. Then it would be an authentically 'inclusive dalit' Christology.

Evaluation

In the context of emergent dalit militant secular movements and dalit theology, it is the prime time to re-check the radicalism and possibility of the dalit Christology critically.

Jesus as the dalit and the liberator are two main arguments in the contemporary dalit Christology. However, the premises of these arguments show a castiestic and class interpretation respectively. This casteistic and class interpretation is a jeopardy in the 'dalit' context to interpret Jesus, which is a-caste and a-class. Dalit way of interpretation, source, structure is missing in the contemporary dalit faith confession.

The method of solidarity is one of the dalit ways of doing theology. In this sense, the early faith confession and contemporary dalit Christology can work together in different areas. But dalit way is not uncritical transliteration of the early faith confession. Rather, the attempt would be to translate and transform in dalit way of the raw-materials provided by the early faith community and dalit traditions of India. Jesus Christ as the confession of early Christian faith community does not demarcate historicity and ontology. The inclusiveness of historical particularity and universality of Jesus Christ helped the early Christians to identify with other broken people of their society and helped them to see and experience full humanness through their faith confession. The methodology of solidarity was the tool. Irrespective of differences of the community, full gospel is proclaimed and resisted divisions in the community. The extremity of any side (of Christology) is demarcated as heresy.

This early kerygma is transmitted to the present time through the text (scripture) and traditions (creeds and confessions). These new found sources for dalit Christologisation need to be carefully approached and interpreted. For instance, the contemporary uncritical dalit use of the text is questioned and suggested for 'con'-textual reading. Further, the abandoned source for dalit Christology such as creeds and confessions, took a re-sourcing in doing dalit theology. Since dalitism as an ancient and living philosophy of dalits could be easily identified with the creeds and confessions of the early church because of its oral context and the situations which both the communities had gone through. These communities underwent radical revision and oppression by contemporary hegemonic ideologies that resulted into a militant approach of annihilation of opposing ideology.

Exposing such lopsided drawbacks, the researcher points out to more of inclusive character of dalitism which respects life and 'otherness' in a given society. Dalitism as a parallel strand in Indian philosophy can dialogue with other existing ideologies with full eagerness and earnestness, since the affirmation of dalits as "the Indian people" is established over the last decade. An authentic Indian dalit Christology/theology cannot be exclusive in nature, when one considers the universality and diversity of dalitness, the criteria of being a dalit. Further, for a particular community of people, one cannot reduce the cosmic nature of Christology. Therefore, contemporary dalit faith confession lacks complete content of the early faith confession. The argument, in this research, is not for 'Christ of faith' alone, rather for a more balanced and inclusive dalit Christology in nature. Thus, a complete substance in dalit faith confession is a requirement for an authentic dalit Christology in India.

Conclusion

The contemporary dalit faith confession is critically looked at from different angles in this chapter. Even though Jesus is understood as dalit, the premises of this claim have castiestic interpretation that alerts us of the hegemonic structure of *dalitvad.* Jesus as the dalit liberator is another faith confession, but the premises of this argument tend to lean towards class interpretation in which the function and method would be annihilation and 'anti' in nature towards whatever is non-dalit. Thus, dalit method of solidarity is sought and applied to the resources of the early faith community and of the dalits. This would provide an integrated and inclusive dalit Christology. In order to construct praxis-oriented inclusive dalit Christology, there is a need to revise and reconstruct dalit Christology in line with the criticisms which have emerged. Then only the dalit Christology would able to reinvent itself as a more efficacious theology of liberation. This would help to have a scope to set out inclusive Christological agenda over against the images used by *dalitvad.*

4

Towards an Inclusive Dalit Christology

Introduction

The critique made in the previous chapter on the contemporary dalit Christological discourse demands an alternative and inclusive dalit faith confession truly based on the early faith confession and the concept of 'dalit'. This proposal for an inclusive dalit Christological formula aims to prevent extreme *dalitvad* in its articulation. *Dalitvad* excludes non-dalits in caste terms. So, this proposed inclusive dalit Christology seeks *samvad* with dominant traditions, and solidarity with weaker sections. The content of the faith confession is interpreted purely in dalit terms from the early faith confession of the church. Toward this attempt, primarily the concepts of inclusive, dalit and Christology are explained. Further, content, function and structure of the inclusive dalit faith confession are proposed here. This emerging trend would become a signpost for the aspirant students of dalit theology to ponder upon and advance it.

4.1 Methodological Framework of Inclusive Dalit Christology

Before analyzing the content of the inclusive faith confession, it is necessary to explain the terminology that constitutes the possible dalit faith confession, i.e., inclusive dalit Christology. It draws contour for the same.

4.1.1 'Inclusive' Identity in the Inclusive Dalit Christology

Identity of a dalit in inclusive Dalit Christology is inclusive and open in character. Inclusive identity is inclined to affirm similarities and complementarities with one another. This makes tolerance and flexibility in the faith affirmation.[1] Opposing to

[1] Rudolf C. Heredia, "Search for Identity, Quest for Dignity: The Dalit's Long March," *VJTR* 74/10 (Oct., 2010): 749.

inclusive identity, exclusive identity emphasizes differences and set up oppositions and polarities with the other, says Rudolf C. Heredia.[2] Dalit and their confession determine how 'dalit are', than caste and class, which are not the central points for this inclusive dalit faith confession. Therefore, the proposed inclusive dalit faith confession is positive in its outlook. It is positive because dalit is understood as open forum for 'all' who experience the condition of *dalitness*. The proposal is that the main focus should be all aspects of the dalit phenomenon, and based on this axis inclusive faith confession can have its own existence. There is a need for socio-cultural analysis of the dalit situation, at the micro level, and of the entire human situation, including the global, at the macro level as T. K. John argues in his one of the writings.[3]

Similarly, faith confession also invites for an 'inclusive community of faith'. The traditional dalit theology "affirms God's bias towards the socially ostracized and stigmatized groups."[4] But 'inclusive' dalit Christology includes 'all those who experience the condition of brokenness and wholeness' irrespective of their social, religious, cultural, economic, etc., backgrounds. For instance, former untouchables and the tribal people are considered as partners in their brokenness, origin, subjugation, under the same oppressors.[5] Thus, the proposed dalit faith confession is 'inclusive' in its approach, construction and application towards all those who experience of *dalitness*.

4.1.2 'Dalit' Condition in the Inclusive Dalit Christology

The question of dalit identity is another area of implementation of the inclusive Christology. The term dalit, as the research proposed, is a 'subjective non-caste' identity that shows only the condition of dalitness. This framework not only resist caste ideology but also transcends its scope even to the caste people. The identity of 'dalit' is inclusive, in the sense of brokenness and thus strives for wholeness. The term 'dalit' endeavors not to signify another caste/class identity but rather aspires to name a non-caste and non-class collective movement. Its objective to dismantle, not reinforce the caste system must constantly be reiterated.[6] Dalit "is a

---

[2] Rudolf C. Heredia, "Search for Identity, Quest for Dignity," 749.

[3] T. K. John, "Method of Collaboration in Theological Journey," in *Dalit-Tribal Theological Interface: Current Trends in Subaltern Theologies*, edited by James Massey and Shimreingam Shimray (Jorhat and New Delhi: TSC/WSC and CDS, 2007), 255.

[4] Dhyanchand Carr, "Dalit Theology is Biblical and It Makes the Gospel Relevant," in *A Reader in Dalit Theology*, edited by A. P. Nirmal (Delhi/Madras: ISPCK, Gurukul, nd), 82.

[5] V. V. Thomas, *Dalit and Tribal Christians of India: Issues and Challenges* (Kerala: Focus India Trust, 2014), x.

[6] Sathianathan Clarke, Deenabandhu Manchala and Philip Vinod Peacock, "Introduction," in *Dalit Theology in the Twenty First Century: Discordant Voices, Discerning Pathways*, edited by Clarke Santhinathan, Manchela Deenabandhu and Vinod Philip Peacock (New Delhi: OUP, 2010), 6.

casteless identity. It stands for the rejection of the caste system, totally."[7] This new found condition is defined by Mohan Larbeer as follows:

> [d]alit identity, as such, means, developing the dalit perspective, which means searching for a new identity, self-awareness, self-esteem and rejection of the stereotyped morals and values of the caste system.[8]

It gives dalits the consciousness, which implies a vision of the heritage of dalits' fore-parents. It is the beginning of a new search for our roots, to anchor us firmly to ourselves.[9] Larbeer shares the false identity as "any identification based on caste is a false identity."[10] He writes another false identity. Leaders of dalit movements claim that "we were the rulers," and they also say that they once stood side by side with other castes and that they had descended from high society. This attitude again establishes the hierarchy complex rather than demolish it once and for all.[11] Therefore, in the inclusive dalit Christian faith confession 'dalit' is taken as a-caste, and a-class identity, and also as having a genuine historical tradition of India, nourished by the margins/weaker sections of the land.[12]

4.2 'Christology' in Inclusive Dalit Terms

The Christology is not only transform caste system rather works into the 'inclusiveness' of dalitism of the past and turns into present reality. The communalization of Jesus Christ in the contemporary dalit faith confession is disregarded in this 'inclusive' dalit Christology. It projects a confession of 'wholeness' as the word dalit denotes. In addition, Christology is not to be understood in terms of power, but what is humble and frailly human. That means, inclusive dalit Christology challenges the oppressors or non-dalits to have solidarity with 'dalits.' To oppressors, inclusive dalit Christology is a call to make sacrifices on behalf of poor- "*a dalit Christology for non-dalit people.*" Power is seen in love and acts of love, not in status or in relation to oppression. For instance, Jesus as the Son of God is to be dedicated totally to the purpose of God,

---

[7] P. Mohan Larbeer, "Dalit Identity- A Theological Reflection," in *Frontiers of Dalit Theology*, edited by V. Devasahayam (New Delhi: ISPCK, 1997), 377.

[8] P. Mohan Larbeer, "Dalit Identity- A Theological Reflection," 378.

[9] P. Mohan Larbeer, "Dalit Identity- A Theological Reflection," 378.

[10] P. Mohan Larbeer, "Dalit Identity- A Theological Reflection," 378-379.

[11] P. Mohan Larbeer, "Dalit Identity- A Theological Reflection," 379.

[12] I think we have to go beyond the western perception of 'Hinduism' as a religion here in India. The origin of the term Hindu from 'Sindhu' is a geographical derivation. Thus, Hinduism is not a religion in strict sense, but a celebration of various school of thought and cults that harmoniously existed, but objected on various matters. Dalit (Buddhist/Jainist), one of the Indic tradition, also has excellent place in Indian tradition. Thus, Indian tradition (ancient real Hinduism, not Brahmanism) cannot be divisive but integrative, placing 'dalit' (old form) into real status in ancient 'Indic tradition' solves the problem. Cf. Bipin Chandra Pal, *An Introduction to the Study of Hinduism* (Calcutta: S. C. Ghose, 1908), 1-2.

even unto death on the cross.[13] Thus, the main aim of the inclusive dalit faith confession is to the conversion of both oppressors and oppressed. Conversion in the sense of radical leap of past between the future in which non-dalits repent of being hegemonic to a marginalized social tradition, oppressed repent from the hatredness towards their oppressors and maintains unity and equality for having healthy dialogues and interaction. For one's identity is never developed in the isolation of a walled-in consciousness but in interaction with significant others.[14]

With above conceptual clarification of 'inclusive dalit Christology', now we can discuss on the content of the dalit faith confession considering the early faith confession as criterion. This is done with a critical suspicion in terms of the tool hermeneutic of suspicion and *samvad* of dalitism. Since dalitism is a combatable philosophical strand of dalits, it can be used to discuss the divinity and humanity, historicity and mythical nature, and significance and relevance of Jesus Christ. Not discarding the content and validity of the early faith confession, here, the dalit faith confession re-doing Christology in dalit way. Three themes from the early faith confession are interpreted with dalit ways to re-mythologize, re-historize and re-dalitise. It uses the methodology of *samvad* between the early faith confession and the dalits at the same time keeps solidarity as prime value.

4.2.1 Dalit *Mysterium Christi*

The attempt here is to re-mythologize the unity of historical Jesus with the Christ of faith in dalit way. By doing so, the intrusion of the contemporary quest for historical Jesus to dalit Christology, as elsewhere said, is challenged. Inclusive dalit faith confession contributes to this field by emphatically asserting that historical Jesus is the Christ of faith and vice versa. Because, the early faith community shared their faith in mystical and mythical language in which mystery of Jesus is emphatically asserted. Myths are neither for believing nor for thinking. Myths are simply for entering into the content of the faith confession. True religious symbols are held together constitute myths.[15] The interrelation of myth and symbol is vital for religious symbolism and this inter-relation is most clearly and directly manifested in dalit religious moorings.[16] Myth is of the essence of dalit religion.[17] Religious myths are true because they are all-comprehending. Non-religious myths are false because they leave out of account some areas of human

---

[13] M. E. Prabhakar, "In Search of a Dalit Theology," in *Towards a Dalit Theology*, edited by M. E. Prabhakar (Delhi: ISPCK, 1988), 46.

[14] Rudolf C. Heredia, "Search for Identity, Quest for Dignity," 747.

[15] John G. Arapura, "Rediscovering the Meaning of the Symbol," in *Indian Voices in Today's Theological Debate*, edited by Horst Bürkle and Wolfgang M.W. Roth (Luknow: Luknow Publishing House in collaboration with Delhi/Madras: ISPCK, CLS, 1972), 91.

[16] John G. Arapura, "Rediscovering the Meaning of the Symbol," 91.

[17] John G. Arapura, "Rediscovering the Meaning of the Symbol," 90.

experience, some levels of human perception, arbitrarily, as John Arapura says.[18] The dalits have been acknowledged to be master in myth-making, they are myth-maker. It is here, we learn that although myth itself is important, myth-making is even far more important, since the latter tells a story that the former cannot tell, reveals a dimension that is altogether hidden. But the two, obliviously, cannot be separated.[19]

The person of Jesus in the dalit mythical interpretation trace back to dalit tradition. For example, the concept of Maveli over against Mahabali tradition of brahmanic dominance gives a symbolic representation of Jesus Christ of history as a present mythical/mystical figure of faith confession.[20] People believe that Maveli, a legendary king of Kerala, visits his people yearly to enquire their welfare. It is considered that his rule was a prosperous era in Kerala history. Onam is a festival related to the mythical return/visit of him every year from the underground of the earth, *Patalam*.[21] The characteristics of kingdom of Maveli are reflected mainly in dalit folklore as follows:

When *Maveli* rules over land
All people follow an equal band
As they live in joy and charm
Everyone is free from harm
There is no theft and no deceit
And no one speaks and untruth yet
Weights and measures are all correct
No one tries to cheat or corrupt
When *Maveli* rules over the land all
People form an equal band.[22]

The reign of Maveli was based on the principle of 'equality' (which in Malayalam *onnupole*), is the center stage of discussion here. The folksong envisions

---

[18] John G. Arapura, "Rediscovering the Meaning of the Symbol," 91.

[19] John G. Arapura, "Rediscovering the Meaning of the Symbol," 90.

[20] See Josfin Raj, "A Study on the Concept of Melchizedek Priesthood in the Book of Hebrews for Developing a Dalit Christology," (Bachelor of Theology Thesis, New Life Biblical Seminary, 2009).

[21] Onam is celebrated in the beginning of the month of *Chingam*, the first month of the Malayalam Calendar (*Kollavarsham*). This corresponds with the months of August-September of the Gregorian calendar. Cf. A. Sreedhara Menon, *The Legacy of Kerala*, 1982 (Kottayam: DC Books, 2008), 29.

[22] English translation by Dr. Ayyappapaniker in a *Short History of Malayalam Literature*, Department of Publications, Govt. of Kerala cited by'Kavalam Narayana Paniker, *Folklore of Kerala* (New Delhi: National Book Trust, 1991), 26. Cf. A. Sreedhara Menon, *Cultural Heritage of Kerala*, 1978 (Kottayam: DC Books, 2008), 90.

neither caste nor class differences.[23] This interpretation uncovers the original consciousness of *dalits* with their egalitarians system. It provides a shift from the exploitation of the innocent and weak by the oppressors.[24] This strong egalitarian reading can uplift dalits from the domination of the militant caste association and discrimination. *Maveli* is narrated as one who crushed all caste barriers, i.e., *sudalit*. Rhetorically *Maveli* figure is a restructuring of original privilege of the ancient dalit consciousness.[25] The golden age of *Maveli* is then generally seen as a historical antecedent and can be theologized in the current dalit consciousness. This theologizing can bring back the golden age of *dalits* in which they endowed with a sense of justice. This positive dalit consciousness develops a Christological paradigm of *Maveli* to liberate people from the wounded psyche.

If so then, the vision of messianic community by dalit theologians,[26] then, is not exclusive, but *inclusive of all* other similarly marginalized peoples and groups such as the Tribals, the women, who are the most backward and unorganized.[27] By rejecting pseudo Casteist-messiah, dalit would unearth, recapture, realizing, and recognizing the *Dalit Messiah* who has been present throughout dalit history.[28] This consciousness of the dalit community strengthens an inclusive Messianic identity.[29] This Messianic community, in the process of its liberation, will not be satisfied with 'land flows with the milk and honey' or even by winning the rights, reservations and privileges. On the other hand, its Messianic hope is continue to struggle towards and achieving the full humanness and the full divinity of all: in other words, achieving the very image of God with other people, argues Mohan Larbeer.[30] It is, in another word, a global consciousness of dalit theology-*manusharellam onnupole*.[31]

There are points of convergence and divergence in this inclusive dalit faith confession about dalit messiah. Larbeer writes,

> This messiah who resembles us, is black, flat noses and big nosed, dressed in rags, standing always near our slums to protect us. We have

[23] Cf. A. M. Abraham Ayrookuzhiel, "Dalit Theology: A Movement of Counter Culture," in *Towards a Dalit Theology*, edited by M. E. Prabhakar (Delhi: ISPCK, 1988), 96.

[24] Filippo Osella and Carolane Osella, *The Return of King Mahabali: The Politics of Morality in Kerala* (London: C. Hurst and Co. Publishers, 2001), 141.

[25] A. Sreedhara Menon, *Cultural Heritage of Kerala*, 90.

[26] V. Devasahayam, "Theologising in Context," in *Frontiers of Dalit Theology*, edited by V. Devasahayam (New Delhi: ISPCK, 1997), 25-26. Also Peniel Rajkumar, *Dalit Theology and Dalit Liberation: Problems, Paradigms and Possibilities*, Ashgate New Critical Thinking in Religion, Theology and Biblical Studies Series (Farnham, England: Ashgate, 2010), 54.

[27] P. Mohan Larbeer, "Dalit Identity – A Theological Reflection," 391.

[28] P. Mohan Larbeer, "Dalit Identity – A Theological Reflection," 390.

[29] P. Mohan Larbeer, "Dalit Identity – A Theological Reflection," 391.

[30] P. Mohan Larbeer, "Dalit Identity – A Theological Reflection," 391.

[31] Sathianathan Clarke, Deenabandhu Manchala and Philip Vinod Peacock, "Introduction," 13.

> many stories to tell about this Messiah's involvement in our struggles, and sufferings. This Messiah accepts us as we are; we can approach him any time, however badly dressed we may be. We can sleep, we can play, cry, fight, - whatever we do in the temple the Messiah accepts. In the same way our women are also accepted without any inhibitions. With this Messiah, there is no division, neither male or female. This messiah is on the road-side without cover overhead, like us. Our Messiah is rejected by the caste people, since our Messiah is identified with us. This Messiah is none other than our own ancestor, who died, who sacrificed his life for us. This Messiah is the one who kindles us and makes us realised our rights, and encourages us to realise each of ourselves and win our self-respect and our self-dignity.[32]

The unchangeable once-for-all-ness of the Gospel has to be reformulated so that Jesus Christ is acknowledged as the good news from God by people living in different ages and in different countries.[33]

4.2.2 Dalit Disclosed Jesus

Jesus was a disclosure of the condition of 'dalit' in its uttermost way by stating the God and human-forsakenness. The reversal of dalit faith confession, especially, the passion and death of Jesus has to come into forefront. That is, the reason for dalitness of Jesus Christ is not the act of oppressors, nor the willingness of Father, but rather His willingness to undergo such severity so that the wall of division is broken down and the way to Fatherhood may open to all, in spite of any differences.[34] Thus, Jesus is the disclosure of the way, the truth and the life.

Jesus reconciled both dalits and non-dalits on the cross. The non-dalits are repented of themselves to have solidarity with dalits like Cornelius (Acts 10), Zacchaeus (Luke 19), the tax collector and so on. The conversion does not mean the so-called conversion to other religions. Mere conversion to another religion cannot be a solution to the problems of dalits.[35] But rather, as Ambedkar has observed, it is the touchable that need to undergo greater conversion than the

[32] P. Mohan Larbeer, "Dalit Identity – A Theological Reflection," 390-391.

[33] J. R. Chandran, "Preface to Indian Edition," in *Indian Voices in Today's Theological Debate*, edited by Horst Bürkle and Wolfgang M.W. Roth (Luknow: Luknow Publishing House in collaboration with Delhi/Madras: ISPCK, CLS, 1972), v.

[34] Fatherhood of God and brotherhood of all was the concept of dalit traditions especially Phule emphasised. See 1.2.3.1. Dalit Movements in Pre-Independent India.

[35] Rudolf C. Heredia says that, "At times conversion to Christianity has meant a transfer of dependence from the more exploitative patronage of the landlord to the more benevolent paternalism of the missionaries.... Often such change as conversion did bring did not represent a complete liberation as might have been hoped for, but at least it was an indication of some positive improvement in their life chances." "Search for Identity, Quest for Dignity...," 757.

untouchable.[36] Therefore, the dalit theology must address oppressors, both within and outside of it, because those who oppress, oppose, or ignore the dalits have to that extent lost their own divinely created humanity,[37] not the so called dalits. Thus, the conversion must happen in two ways – the conversion of the oppressors and of the oppressed. The change of attitude towards the oppressors by oppressed to accommodate them in the greater struggle of emancipation. So this reciprocal conversion experience is a demand of disclosed Jesus. In the words of Alangaram,

> While we protest against all oppressions and unjust structures, we need a *metanoia* among our people without which a total liberation will be impossible. Overcoming division by unity, betrayal by trust, revenge by love and forgiveness are some of the essential and positive attitudes we need to cultivate among ourselves.[38]

Therefore, inclusive dalit Christology is disclosed not only for dalits alone, but more emphatically to non-dalits, where first conversion and transformation need to happen. By rethinking the prepositions of dalit Christology - by, for and of - dalit people, is questioned because the inclusive dalit theology is for non-dalits who oppress them for those who have oppressed them in the historical past or all dalits in the literal dalit. It is the dalit theology:-

> Not by birth does one become an outcaste
> not by birth does one become a brahman
> by deeds one becomes an outcaste
> by deeds one becomes a brahman.[39]

Adding to this, not by birth one does become dalits. Then, dalit theology is not on the bases of hereditary caste, rather on the condition of brokenness into the wholeness- *dalitness* to *sudalit.*

'Being a Jew' is a phrase in the contemporary dalit Christology, usually passingly remarks on the historical Jesus.[40] The early confession and dalit confession deliberately overlooks the 'jewishness' of Jesus. Jesus hail from Jewishness, a then dominant 'elite' religious tradition.[41] It strengthens the point

---

[36] V. Devasahayam, "The Nature of Dalit Theology as Counter Theology," in *Frontiers of Dalit Theology* (Delhi/Madras: ISPCK, Gurukul, 1997), 56.

[37] James Massey, *Down Trodden: The Struggle of India's Dalits for Identity, Solidarity and Liberation* (Geneva: WCC Publication, 1997), 80.

[38] S. Alangaram, *Religions for Societal Transformation: Inter-Religious Dialogue from Subaltern Perspectives* (Bangalore: Asian Trading Corporation, 2006), 74.

[39] Vasalasutta 21. Cited in A. M. Abraham Ayrookuzhiel, "Dalit Theology: A Movement of Counter Culture, 96ff

[40] A. P. Nirmal, "Towards a Christian Dalit Theology," *A Reader in Dalit Theology*, edited by A. P. Nirmal and V. Devasahayam (Chennai: Gurukul, n.d.), 65-66.

[41] See Rebekah Simon-Peter, *The Jew Named Jesus: Discover the Man and His Message* (Nashville: Abingdon Press, 2013).

that purity and pollution or caste is not the criteria of determine who dalit is, but a person's *dalitness*, the condition of brokenness and strive for wholeness. Jesus' revelation in then dominant Judaism and his re-interpretation of the Law is created a new community in which the people become important than the structure and power.[42] Table fellowship of Jesus with despised people at the same time with the elites of the society is important here. He was not only dining with socially so-called 'out castes' but with elite classes of the community too.[43] Even he did not cease the privilege of entering into high table fellowship to woman of low reputation. The example of transformation of Zachaeues, a tax exploiter who had a meeting and eating with sinners and then shares all what he possess and taken away from poor.[44] The early faith community was carrying, in a sense, not Jewish Jesus but a people's Jesus with affirmative statements of historicity and mysteriosity in which an inclusive community is formed irrespective of religion, class, and so on with no discrimination. This community provided identification with *dalitness*, that is condition of brokenness and strive for wholeness. That is the total Christology. Further, it was a revelation that even inside (being a Jew) of a dominant religious structure and provided that there is meaningful dalitness in every castes of the society.

This is also a dalit Cosmic Christ. As M. M. Thomas and S. J. Samartha find the Cosmic Christ in major social and religious traditions in India,[45] the challenge before dalits is to find out the presence of Cosmic Jesus Christ in their dalit situations.

> Dalit Cosmic Christ is understood less in terms of the person Jesus but the mandate of the Christ to bring about a just and loving kingdom. God cannot be hemmed in; Jesus 'cannot exhaust fully the mystery and depth of God'. Such a cosmic Christology better reflects the religious experience of Dalits in reality rather than the abstractions of exclusive metaphysics that shapes so much of traditional Indian theology and preaching.[46]

---

[42] Cf. Gerhard Cohfink, *Jesus and Community: The Social Dimension of Christian Faith* (Augsburg: Fortress Press, 1984), 77.

[43] Michael F. Bird, *Jesus and the Origins of the Gentile Mission* (London: T&T Clarke, 1988), 104. Cf. James D. G. Dunn, *Jesus Remembered: Christianity in the Making*, Vol. 1 (Grand Rapids: Wm. B. Eerdmans, 2003), 602.

[44] Peniel Rajkumar, *Dalit Theology and Dalit Liberation*, 64.

[45] M. M. Thomas, *The Acknowledged Christ of Indian Renaissance* (Madras: CLS, 1970, third edition, 1991). Also S. J. Samartha, *One Christ- Many Religions: Towards a Revised Christology*, 2nd edition (New York: Orbis Books, 1991 published in India by Bangalore: SATHRI, 1994).

[46] Keith Hebden, *Dalit Theology and Christian Anarchism*, Ashgate New Critical Thinking in Religion (Farnham: Ashgate Publishing Limited, 2011), 146.

Jan Peter Schouten argues that the image of 'cosmic Christ' becomes a counter-reaction from Dalit theologians, found Jesus as "the earthly Jesus."[47] He blames dalit theology for 'killing cosmic Christ' and the image of Christ came 'down to earth again.'[48] We see a Christological reversal here. Chronologically, the down to earth Jesus (historical Jesus) is primary, and the early faith community found him as Cosmic Christ in their everyday activities. This would applicable to the dalits, as Jesus of Nazareth is the launching pad and Christ of Faith allows them to go beyond in their liberation, emancipation and integration.

Inclusive dalit Christology would also help to move from welfare measures to social justice. In the name of reservations, we have only perpetuated violence and inequality among dalits, for reservations define the dalit problem as a welfare problem not as a matter of social justice, Harry Emmanuel laments.[49] Does one need to declare his or her caste status to avail of benefits? Are reservations only a fight for minimum justice and human rights? - are the questions need further probing reflection. For the Indian Christian dalits, to know Jesus Christ is to realize that the God of Jesus Christ will save them from inhumanity, social oppression, economic exploitation and cultural subjugation.[50] In dalit thinking, Christ and God are integrally linked with the dalits' dehumanized social existence and their hope for a future in Christ.[51] This argument would help us to answer the following questions such as, how does 'Christological dalitness' is related to 'the people's dalitness' and vice versa? What is the way and means to relate 'dalitness of the people and of Jesus' dalitness? How Jesus' dalitness is significant to dalits' dalitness?

4.2.3 Inclusive Dalit Jesus

According to Sobirno, "the basic locus of Christology is the place where faith and life meet."[52] Every understanding and confession of Jesus Christ grows out of a particular situation and both reflect and speak to particular needs and aspirations.[53] A creed, a confession, a faith affirmation, therefore, must be the

---

[47] Jan Peter Schouten, *Jesus as Guru: The Image of Christ among Hindus and Christians in India,* Currents of Encounter, Studies on the Contact between Christianity and Other Religions, Beliefs, and Cultures, Vol. 36 Translated by Henry and Lucy Jansen (Amsterdam, New York: Rudopi, 2008), 265.

[48] Jan Peter Schouten, *Jesus as Guru*, 279.

[49] Quotas and reservations for dalits in general, and in some places also for dalit Christians, have had some positive impact. Harry Emmanuel, "Violence Against Dalits: An Indian Christian Response," *Violence and Its Victims: A Challenge to Philosophising in the Indian Context*, edited by Ivo Coelho (Bangalore: ATC, 2010), 331.

[50] M. E. Prabhakar, "Christology in Dalit Perspective," in *Frontiers of Dalit Theology*, edited by V. Devasahayam (New Delhi: ISPCK, 1997), 409.

[51] M. E. Prabhakar, "Christology in Dalit Perspective," 405.

[52] Jon Sobrino, *Christology at the Cross Roads* (New York: Orbis Books, 1985), 34.

[53] Daniel L. Migliore, *Faith Seeking Understanding: An Introduction to Christian Theology,* 2nd ed. (Grand Rapids: William B. Eerdmann Publishing Company, 2004), 168. Also R. S. Sugritharaja,

first exercise in laying bare the roots of the believing community. It is only when we recognize our roots, our identity, that are become truly confessional. A truly confessional theology, therefore, has to do with the question of roots, identity and consciousness.[54] While Nirmal deals with Deuteronomic creed (Deut. 26:5-12) to share the idea of 'no-people' referring to dalits,[55] it can be argued that it is a false identity. Because dalits, having a better place in ancient Indic spirituality, was a people with dignity and high regards. Therefore, dalit inclusive confessional theology would serve to such glorious heritage of 'dalits' of the past.

In the context of dalitness, the inclusive dalit Christology could positively influence. The wounded psyche results in feelings of fatalism and frustration, in feelings of powerlessness and loss of control over one's own life.[56] This has resulted into hatred towards oneself and others. A loss of self-worth and self-esteem is another result of centuries of socialization over dalit tradition especially with caste stigma. Recognition of dalitism as one of the composite culture of Indian tradition could bring forth the authentication of dalit Christology as inclusive Christology. The access to Jesus is not rested to particular people groups alone. This could provide ample resourcefulness to dalits to actively rejuvenate the history with Jesus of dalits radically elevated to a 'high' (in positive sense) Christology, as the early faith community experienced. This inclusive Dalit Christ would help to have solidarity and emancipator approach to any 'other' in Indian/dalit communities. The notion of *Ghar Vapasi* (back to home) of brahmanical tradition is called back by this dalit tradition. Because, it is a spontaneous self-assertion of *all* people who face dalitness is very part of nation India.

The early faith community was a catholic community under the personal tie of the apostles with faith confessions.[57] It is thus no wonder that the apostles placed this unity and catholicity of the church in the foreground and issued serious warnings against all division. This was a widespread danger as early as the first century. Judaistic and Gnostic, nomistic and antinomistic heresies entered the churches. Now it was indeed necessary that scandals and heresies should come (Matt. 18:7; I Cor. 11:19) in order to bring the church to self-conscious awareness of both its unity and the truth.[58] Thus, our dalit Christology is also a theology of unity and catholicity. What really characterizes the dalit situation is

"Prologue and Perspective," in *Asian Faces of Jesus*, edited by R. S. Sugritharaja (London: SCM Press, 1993), ix.

[54] A. P. Nirmal, "A Dialogue with Dalit Literature," in *Towards a Dalit Theology*, edited by M. E Prabhakar (Delhi: ISPCK, 1989), 77.

[55] A. P. Nirmal, "Towards a Dalit Theology."

[56] Philip Vinod Peacock, "Impact of the Context: Dalit Perspective," in *Dalit-Tribal Theological Interface: Current Trends in Subaltern Theologies*, edited by James Massey and Shimreingam Shimray (Jorhat and New Delhi: TSC/WSC and CDS, 2007), 142.

[57] Herman Bavinck, "The Catholicity of Christianity and the Church," 226.

[58] Herman Bavinck, "The Catholicity of Christianity and the Church," 227.

their condition of brokenness. Caste is not specific to the dalit situation since there are a number of castes which are not broken in nature. The acceptance and assertion of their humanity in a particular caste by affirming the equality of all castes, humanizes the caste.[59]

Dalits tend to see salvation as a historical process, in their context of suffering and struggles against "earthly oppression," Jesus Christ, the Saviour, is the one who gave life as a ransom for many and who will come again to establish God's justice on earth and fully liberate the oppressed from the misery of human sin and suffering. God in Jesus Christ is the liberator in history. Since dalit thought on Jesus Christ and God's saving act in and through Jesus is integrally linked with dalit dehumanized social existence and their hope for a future in Him, will be freed from all inhumanity and injustice.[60]

Then, dalit includes a larger religious framework.[61] A common heritage of oppression is one of the factors that should enable us to include people of other faiths.[62] Then, the inclusive dalit faith confession as multi-religious in application, the Lord Christ needs to be seen as the Lord of all people. He is not only the Lord of Christian dalit, but also for all those who experience dalitness – the whole of God's creation. Therefore, the dalit theology should go beyond the casteistic feelings, religious fundamentalism, and emotional stigma.

> Christ *is* Lord of all, and the salvation of the world *is* accomplished, yet men are called to accept the gospel; all men [*sic*] are children is fulfilled only in relationship to Christ; all are reconciled to God in Christ and a supreme destiny is given to all, yet that destiny is to be attained through conditions laid down in the gospel; Christ comes to all men and takes them all to himself yet insists that "the gate is narrow and the way is hard, that leads to life, and those who find it are few.[63]

4.3 Characteristics of Inclusive Dalit Christology

The proposed inclusive dalit Christology is having characteristics, which leads further into the content of the dalit faith confession. It also discusses how proposed

[59] "The humanization of caste transforms it into a socio-cultural ethnic identity and annihilates the brahmanic understanding of caste wherein the humanity of communities in India is graded resulting in graded inequality and hierarchy in society." Dionysius Rasquinha, *The Dalit Quest*, 130.

[60] M. E. Prabhakar, "Christology in Dalit Perspective," 405.

[61] Sundar Clarke, "Dalit Movement- Need for a Theology," in *Towards a Dalit Theology*, edited by M. E. Prabhakar (Published for CISRS and CDLM by Delhi: ISPCK, 1988), 32.

[62] Sundar Clarke, "Dalit Movement- Need for a Theology," 33.

[63] L. Thornton, *The Domination of Christ*, 10 mentioned in Richard W. Taylor, "Christ Acting in Our Society," in *Indian Voices in Today's Theological Debate*, edited by Horst Bürkle and Wolfgang M.W. Roth (Luknow: Luknow Publishing House in collaboration with Delhi/Madras: ISPCK, CLS, 1972), 168.

inclusive dalit Christology can supplement and correct the contemporary dalit faith confession.

4.3.1 Fulfilling Meaning of the term Dalit

The inclusive dalit confession, as suggested here, would help to fulfill the meaning of the term dalit itself – brokenness and wholeness. Broken condition is the nature of dalit. Jesus, dalit *par-excellence* is undergone through this broken situation and become complete dalit. This traditional view of the dalit Christology is supplemented by the inclusive faith confession, when one considers Jesus' act of 'wholeness'. Because the early faith confession was given attention to the broken condition of Jesus (i.e., emptied himself and become flesh, suffering and death), only because they experienced the presence of resurrected Christ (i.e., the totality of Jesus). It is the complete confession of the faith confession too.[64] Therefore, when Jesus is identified as dalit *par-excellence* in contemporary dalit context, it is not only the condition of brokenness in his earthly life is projected. But rather, Jesus' act of making wholeness is also need to emphasis. Thus, primarily, the inclusive faith confession fulfills the meaning of the term dalit inclusively.

4.3.2 Sharing or Contain the Complete Faith Confession

By fulfilling the meaning of the term dalit, the inclusive dalit faith confession shares complete faith confession. As elsewhere mentioned, by believing the liberative power in Jesus of Nazareth, contemporary faith confession gave importance to the humanity of Jesus Christ alone. They found appropriateness towards the incidents of Jesus of Nazareth in the biblical texts and their dalit realties.[65] However, Jesus of the text is narrated in the context of the early faith community's dalit context. Here, in inclusive dalit faith confession, Christ can be experienced not only texts, but also in their day to day life as resurrected one over any oppression and would transcend into *high Christology of Liberation*. Thus, inclusive dalit faith confession, regarding the importance of humanity of Jesus, regards divinity of Jesus is equally important-as well as-thus complete the faith confession.

4.3.3 *Sudalit* from Exclusive Caste-Class Nexus

Another meaning associated with the term 'dalit' is 'manifested or displayed'. It is the understanding that through dalit that God will manifest and display His salvation. It is precisely in and through the weaker, the downtrodden, the crushed, the oppressed and the marginalized that God's saving glory is manifested or displayed.[66] This is because brokenness belongs to the very being of

[64] See 2.4.3 Christological-Thematic Analysis.

[65] Peniel Rajkumar, *Dalit Theology and Dalit Liberation*, 74.

[66] Cf. Dionysius Rasquinha, *Towards Wholeness from Brokenness- The Dalit Quest: A Historical Analysis and Theological Response* (Delhi: ISPCK, 2013).

God.[67] God's divinity and humanity are both characterized by this dalitness as M. E. Prabhakar.[68] One of the main features of *dalitness* is the experience of exclusion. When dalitism is identified unique competitive property of dalits in India, than class or caste interpretations, it will be the experience of "rejected stone becomes the key-corner stone."[69] While inclusive dalit Christology is based on dalitism, it could allow dalits to have access to other Indian resources. The wall of caste-class is not a barrier for theologizing. The integrated model could bring dalit philosophy and culture into the format and could be made available to dalits and educational syllabus could be related to dalit and their culture.

4.3.4 Dehumanization to Consciousness of *Sud*-Dalit[70]

Traditional understanding of being dalit is based on purity and pollution of brahmanical tradition. Purity and pollution demarcation negatively affected the consciousness of dalits, that is, it lead dalit consciousness into a level of dehumanized status.[71] Here, the inclusive dalit faith confession, which purely from dalit perspective, transcends the purity and pollution demarcation of brahmanical clutches and brings pure consciousness of being dalit, that can be termed as *sud*-dalit consciousness. Because the dalit consciousness is not only the consciousness of oppression, but a proud stream of thought emerged from the margins of the society continuously dialogue with other traditions. Then it would also help to overcome the wound that infiltrated by the brahmanical traditions. This radical approach towards dalit could help dehumanized consciousness to a *sud* and humanized consciousness by recognising the value of being dalit.

Thus, the inclusive dalit faith confession could create a rational mind-set against exploitation. This would lead to emancipation, which will be an internal process primarily. It is a process of liberation from the old internalized prejudices-physical, social, economic or political. It presupposes a knowledge of the how's and why's of the dehumanisation process, the persons and structures involved in it. It calls for a collective action. What is needed, therefore, is not merely 'education' but the creation in dalits of a rational mind set against exploitation.[72] In addition, this confession would work for a purified cultural consciousness. We need to respect the otherness of the other and yet take the other into ourselves. The so-called mainstream cultures are not complete without the subaltern cultures. One needs to address the question of the identity of dalits as dignified co-humans. All this is

---

[67] Anthoniraj Thumma, *Springs from the Subalterns: Patterns and Perspectives in People's Theology* (Delhi: ISPCK, 1999), 8.

[68] M. E. Prabhakar, "Christology in Dalit Perspective," 422.

[69] Anthoniraj Thumma, *Springs From the Subalterns*, 12.

[70] The term *sud* means purified one. Then, by using *sud*-dalit, here means the consciousness of dalits which is purified.

[71] Anthoniraj Thumma, *Springs from the Subalterns*, 6.

[72] Harry Emmanuel, "Violence Against Dalits...," 329.

not possible unless we uphold the history and culture of dalits and purify it from biased structures and ideologies of caste and class nexus.[73]

4.3.5 *Dalitism* is the Backbone of Inclusive dalit Christology

Inclusive dalit Christology is involved in reassessment and reversal of inherited notions through a process of ideological and hermeneutical suspicion.[74] Caste system that determined who a dalit is, negated in this inclusive faith confession. Since caste system maintains that dalits are responsible for their plight and caste also lead us to think that dalits has to change and adopt cleaner life style to free from untouchability.[75] Caste system conserves Brahmins only can mediate divine grace and help in the process of forgiveness for the dalits.[76] The caste consciousness sabotages any collaborative communal endeavor.[77] The authentic inclusive Indian dalit Christology provides the guidelines to do away with casteistic ideology. The protests either for or against the reservation policy has shown how deeply divided this country is on the basis of caste.[78] The inclusive dalit Christology cannot be sidelined with 'for or against' but 'inclusive and emancipatory' would be its assertion. The structure of casteism divides and rules, but dalitism (the source of dalits) would integrate and liberate people. Dalitism takes control of the situation than allowing others to dominate. Because, dalitism is a popular and pro-people oriented 'ism' provides better viability in theologizing.

The inclusive dalit faith confession would shift dalit consciousness from victim mind set to protagonist. The dalit struggle must be seen not only as a matter of exposing atrocities and fighting for human rights, but as aiming towards the creation of a casteless humanity. And dalits have to move from seeing themselves as victims to being subjects and protagonists in the building of a new humanity.[79] Thus, the inclusive dalit Christology can create within the dalits a realization, a 'consciousness' of their own intrinsic worth, 'their full humanness' through Christ than any derogatory consciousness of caste and class.

4.3.6 Universality and Indigenity:[80] Structural Implication

The faith of the inclusive dalit confession would be characterized with both universality and indigenous. It is universal in relation to the content of the faith confession, in which the 'Cosmic Christ,' 'Lord of all' is emphasized and it is

---

[73] Harry Emmanuel, "Violence Against Dalits...," 329.

[74] V. Devasahayam, "The Nature of Dalit Theology as Counter Theology," 55.

[75] V. Devasahayam, "The Nature of Dalit Theology as Counter Theology," 55-56.

[76] V. Devasahayam, "The Nature of Dalit Theology as Counter Theology," 56.

[77] V. Devasahayam, "The Nature of Dalit Theology as Counter Theology," 58.

[78] Philip Vinod Peacock, "Impact of the Context: Dalit Perspective," 132.

[79] Harry Emmanuel, "Violence Against Dalits...," 330.

[80] Indigeneity is derived from 'indigenous' which means born or produced naturally in a land or region; native or belonging naturally to (the soil, region, etc.), from *indu*, an old Latin root

indigenous in relation to its interpretation of the universal confession into local dalit situations. Faith is not a self-evident category; but here faith means essentially the totality of personal and corporate commitment to Christ and his mission. It is important to distinguish between the once-for-all event in Christ, which has generated the faith of the Church, and interpretation of the event and the faith. In the event and commitment of the Church to the faith, there is universality.

No particular formulation of the Christian faith is adequate for all times and situations. Nor does anyone's formulation exhaust the full meaning of the truth as known in the Christian faith.[81] Thus, it is most important that both the dimensions of universality and indigeneity should be held together. This would mean that no particular formulation of Christology can claim universal and perennial validity, since there is no perennial theology.[82] We may speak of a contextual theology only in the sense that we mean the interpretation of the universal Gospel in terms in the relevant to the particular situation. If we understand it right, Russel Chandran says, "the principle of a contextual theology will give to inclusive Christian faith the greater power and relevance than the theology which seeks to be of perennial significance."[83]

4.3.7 Response to Wounded Dalit Psyche

Wounded psyche of the dalits is considered the result of age long caste oppression, which is also a reason for the condition of being broken. The inclusive dalit faith confession, as already argued, is not only intended for oppressed, but also for the oppressors. It demands response from the oppressors in their hegemonic action. The confession of Centurion at the feet of the cross – He is the real Son of God (Matt. 27:54)- exemplifies the conversion of the oppressors. Zacchaeus, a tax exploiter is another example. Further, the transformative approach of dalits to the event of Jesus Christ would bring healing to the inner consciousness of the dalits and the makers of the dalits (oppressors). It is not a palliative approach to wounded psyche of dalits, but a radical call for *metanoia* of oppressors.[84] It would release from a socio-psychological stigma.

Further, the inclusive dalit Christology is rooted in dalit culture and dalit identity. It seeks to challenge caste consciousness and caste culture within and outside of the church. It conceives itself as a means of humanization and enables

---

meaning 'within' (like the Greek *endon*) and *gignere* meaning "to beget." http://www.definition-of.com/indigeneity accessed on 23/10/2014.

[81] J. Russel Chandran, "The Theological Task of the Church in India," in *Indian Voices in Today's Theological Debate*, edited by Horst Bürkle and Wolfgang M.W. Roth (Luknow: Luknow Publishing House in collaboration with Delhi/Madras: ISPCK, CLS, 1972), 113.

[82] J. Russel Chandran, "The Theological Task of the Church in India," 113.

[83] J. Russel Chandran, "The Theological Task of the Church in India," 113.

[84] S. Alangaram, *Religions for Societal Transformation*, 74.

all to participate in the glorified humanity of the Risen Lord.[85] Thus, inclusive dalit faith confession can strengthen the identity of dalits as dignified human being.

4.3.8 Avoiding Christological Isolation

The readiness of Indian theologians to address themselves independently to questions of their own society and its religious heritage does not seem to lead, as far as one can see, into the one-sided isolation of a so-called indigenous theology.[86] It cannot be overlooked that the contribution from India is shaped by its Indian origin. This does not mean that they are "only valid for India." Clarke says that Dalit Christian communities may have concretized and contextualized the Christian gospel into their own particular historical context but this has not enabled them to broaden the scope of this good news to build community solidarity with similar oppressed communities.[87] The new interest in one's own situation has given to these endeavors ecumenical relevance. Only through this involvement such a theology "come of age" could come into being, a theology which now challenges the theologians of the West to a debate in full partnership.[88] Horst Bürkle writes these in relation to the debate between Indian Christian theology and western theology. Here, we have to re-define his Indian theology or else has to re-read his words from dalit-brahmanical theology, calling for an ecumenical oriented theology than opposing one.[89]

Other possible impacts of inclusive dalit faith confession in the dalit context would be self-empowerment, experience of honour and dignity, being included in human relationship with personal choices of work with creativity, eradication and annihilation of every form of hierarchy, appropriation of participatory roles in every realm, equal opportunities in every realm and availability of the means needed for dignified life.[90] Poverty, division based on geography and social division are some of the important areas where the methodology of solidarity becomes important to make a holistic outlook of dalit faith confession. In addition, structurally, functionally and other characteristics of the inclusive dalit Christology's impact is envisioned here.

---

85 V. Devasahayam, "Introduction," to *Frontiers of Dalit Theology*, xii.

86 Horst Bürkle, "Introduction to German Edition," in *Indian Voices in Today's Theological Debate*, edited by Horst Bürkle and Wolfgang M.W. Roth (Luknow: Luknow Publishing House in collaboration with Delhi/Madras: ISPCK, CLS, 1972), xvi.

87 Clarke, "Subaltern, Identity Politics, and Christian Theology in India," 273.

88 Horst Bürkle, "Introduction to German Edition," xvii.

89 Horst Bürkle, "Introduction to German Edition," xvii.

90 A. Maria Arul Raja, "Dalit Layers of Consciousness in Dialogue with Biblical World," in *Dalit-Tribal Theological Interface: Current Trends in Subaltern Theologies*, edited by James Massey and Shimreingam Shimray (Jorhat and New Delhi: TSC/WSC and CDS, 2007), 196-197.

In short, the proposed inclusive dalit Christology would address the issue of isolation, parochialism and other structural flaws of contemporary dalit Christology and become an authentic Indian *dalit* Christology/theology.

4.4 Inclusive Dalit Christology and Other Liberation Theologies

The proposed inclusive dalit Christology does not isolate from other theological enterprises, especially liberation theologies. Common platform for both dalit and other liberation theology is praxis of liberation from the situation of oppression. According to Gutiérrez true "liberation" has three main dimensions: First, it involves political and social liberation, the elimination of the immediate causes of poverty and injustice. Second, liberation involves the emancipation of the poor, the marginalised, the downtrodden and the oppressed from all "those things that limit their capacity to develop themselves freely and in dignity." Third, liberation theology involves liberation from selfishness and sin, a re-establishment of a relationship with God and with other people.[91] In a way, Latin American liberation theology stands along with proposed inclusive theology in relation to the approach towards both people who experience the dalit condition of brokenness and the oppressors. Gustavo writes, "A spirituality of liberation will center on *conversion* to the neighbour, the oppressed person, the exploited social class, the despised race, the dominated country. Our conversion to the Lord implies this conversion to the neighbour."[92] The conversion of oppressor also demanded in both theologies.

However, as elsewhere I have pointed out that liberation theologies focus only on the historical Jesus and actively promotes historical quest by ignoring Christ of faith. Christ of faith, it seems, the product of oppressors, does not have much relevance to liberation theologizing process. Traditional dalit theology also follows such pattern. Here, the proposed inclusive Christology overcomes such division of Jesus of history and the Christ of faith. Only a Christology which gives equal importance to Jesus of history and Christ of faith is authentic and complete. For inclusive Christology resources are taken from both Jesus of history and Christ of faith, since the Christ of faith is the byproduct of *dalitness* of the early Christian community. Thus, Christian creeds, dogmas, hymns, etc., become radical sources for theologizing unlike other liberation theologies.

In addition, "preferential option for the poor" is another dictum of liberation theology. The definition of poor is given from the context of poverty – a economic approach to interpret the condition to brokenness. However, the proposed inclusive dalit Christology or theology goes beyond economic or class interpretation on the condition of brokenness. The term dalit, instead of poor,

---

[91] Gustavo Gutiérrez, *A Theology of Liberation: History, Politics and Salvation*, translated and edited by Sister Caridad Inda and John Eagleson (London: SCM Press, 1974).

[92] Gustavo Gutiérrez, *A Theology of Liberation*, 204.

means *oppression in an undefined character.* It comprises of condition of poverty, but not limited to it. It goes further to mean the vulnerability of dalit condition.

Summary of Findings

Inclusive dalit faith confession can be summarized as follows.

Inclusive dalit Christology is 'inclusive' and at the same time 'dalit' in its etymological meaning. The complete content of the Christian confession can be interpreted in dalit way with dalit tools of *samvad* and solidarity.

Inclusive dalit faith confession regards the content of the early faith community as valid and suite for reflection in any 'dalit' contexts. The confession should not be opposing to any other culture but rather challenging for a continues *samvad* and seeks solidarity with others.

Dalit way of expressing *mysterium Christi* and disclosed Jesus, in one way, is mythical and on the other way, is existential. Because, dalit myth making would help them to get out of caste/class consciousness and existential interpretation would help them to frame dalit outlook.

Implication of this 'inclusive dalit faith confession' is structurally, universality and indigenity and functionally, it is the experience of *sudalits* in which removing any caste/class consciousness and restoring original dalit consciousness- from brokenness to wholeness.

Evaluation

The contemporary trends in dalit theology is that, "...while earlier dalit theology would reach out to the dalit movements, we now find that dalit movements are reaching out to embrace dalit theology as a valid vehicle for the articulation of dalit experience."[93] In such context, dalit movements should get right directions from our theologizing. Than uncritically subscribing to dalit movement's non-caste ideologies, it is better to have a 'Christian' in our theologizing, that is why a theologian is called to be. Our theologizing should not be a reason for "hegemonic act on caste people." It is not the caste people who do evil, but the Satanic structure that built around them. The call of dalits/theologians is not to destroy the people, but the walls that protect them to act- Jericho Walls.

Now it is the time to revise such course of theologizing and reach the brahmanic philosophical system with the dalit theology and find rooms that annihilate caste identity and establish a collaboration and proposed caste-less society as such [co-related dalit theology]. This will not harm as Arvind P. Nirmal had alerted us. Because it is not brahmanic system coming to dalit structure, but rather it is the dalit cultural heritage that seeks *samvad* with the so-called elite system. That would strengthen the confidence and consciousness of dalits as well.

---

[93] Sathianathan Clarke, Deenabandhu Manchala and Philip Vinod Peacock, "Introduction," 11.

Dalit theology is engaged in teaching or education in order to felicitate a conceptual understanding as well as commitment to a liberational praxis.[94] Dalit theology aims to conscientizing people to this subtlety.[95] It aims at providing comfort to those who are afflicted by their participation in the liberative struggles and encouraging them to go forward trusting in the Risen and Ascended Jesus, who goes ahead of us.[96]

No Christology can be described as ecumenical without being particular, that is, without being rooted in the fact of Jesus of Nazareth to whom the early faith confession bear testimony as "the Christ, Son of the living God," (Matt. 16:16).[97] Dalit theology has a role to play in raising the consciousness of the Christian unity as a whole that undergirded the support for existing political, social, economic, religious and cultural orders, including caste-based division.[98] Therefore, dalit Christology can never be a narrow, individualistic, nationalistic or parochial enterprise.[99]

The inclusive dalit Christology would be authentic, because it bases deep roots into the earlier possible dalit traditions such as Lokayata/Charvaka. Further, it is the Indian because it is the voice of silenced/ignored tradition of early inhabitants of the land India. It is 'inclusive dalit' because it does not subscribe 'caste' situation, but condition of brokenness. Thus the methodology of solidarity would bring both caste and outcaste, who experience dalitness to emancipate for the *sudalit* – removal of dalitness and work for a nation of love, peace, harmony and humanness.

Conclusion

The proposed 'inclusive dalit Christology' is mainly characterized by 'inclusivism', and 'dalit in interpretation' of the mystery, revelation and significance of Jesus Christ. Dalit world makes myths to preserve the complete content of the faith confession with a view of praxis. Here, in the inclusive dalit faith confession, the myth/symbols like *Maveli* can be used to explain the *mysterium Christi*. It is a dalit way of doing Christology, which does not divide Jesus into person and his work or dividing historical Jesus and Christ of faith. This would also serve as a method for doing dalit Christology in the midst of extreme *dalitvad* and dalitness. Major characteristics of this inclusive faith confession would be its structural application, as the tension between universality of the content of the

[94] V. Devasahayam, "The Goals of Dalit Theology," in *Frontiers of Dalit Theology* (Delhi/ Madras: ISPCK, Gurukul, 1997), 72.

[95] Dalit subtlety is constantly coopt dalits with a view to making them serve the interests of caste people.

[96] V. Devasahayam, "The Goals of Dalit Theology," 73-74.

[97] S. J. Samartha, *One Christ- Many Religions*, xi-xii.

[98] James Massey, *Down Trodden*, 80.

[99] S. J. Samartha, *One Christ- Many Religions*, xi.

faith confession and the indigenity of the context of dalits exist. Functionally, the dalit faith confession envisions dalit to *sudalit-* from caste/class to casteless and classless dalit community. Thus, the proposed inclusive dalit Christology would reverse the contemporary communal dalit Christ into universal, cosmic Christ of faith where love, equality, and justice prevail. Thus, the dalit faith confession is complete and viable for 'any dalit' in any given 'dalit context.'

Conclusion

Who is dalit? Now the question remains in the heart of the readers, at least with introduction and conclusion readers. They are 'broken people'. But this statement is incomplete. They are not 'simply' broken, but people who strive for wholeness. We find Christ with or in them. He is inclusive. He is with the people who are broken and who initiate for achieving reconciliation between oppressed and oppressors. The healing ministry must be for both oppressed and oppressors. No enemy is here. The problem will be solved once this vision comes true. The so-called structural issue will also be solved once oppressed and oppressors come in a round table fellowship with Jesus – the inclusive Christ. This book is an attempt to do so.

Most of the dalit movements aroused with such inclusive motif, but failed to be inclusive in its agenda and visions. It remained to be a separatist, during contemporary time, in its extreme separation from the national life, as some laments. The real nature of 'dalitism' is to have solidarity with the weaker sections, respecting the life of others and keeping the humanitarian values. Over the course of time, the extremity of 'dalitism' overshadowed in the Indian context and can be named as *dalitvad*. It creates caste conflicts and class struggles that even disintegrate the nation India, i.e., from dalit *desiyatha* to *dalitsthan*. This caste and class interpretation has also shown its influence in the dalit theology that emerged during 1970s by claiming that it is authentically an Indian theology. The original dalit vision has to rejuvenate so that inclusive community can be built in Indian context. Dalit, in such vision, means not a caste or a class identity of people groups, but an inclusive term that denotes 'all' who experience the condition of brokenness and strive for wholeness. This definition unites contemporary dalits and the early faith community. The early faith community confessed their faith confession in the context of their dalitness. The community was *broken* by hostile Greco-Roman-Jewish, cultural-political imperialism and religious fundamentalism. However, they strive for *wholeness* with their faith confession. The faith confession, as the center of community life, becomes a radical liberative phenomenon for their broken conditions.

What is dalit faith confession? As any (doing) theological activity, it must be faithful to the first witness of the gospel and should be concretely grounded in present realities. It is epitomized in the faith confession of early faith community in their dalit condition. The complete content of the faith confession is both historical Jesus and whom now they experience as the Christ of faith in their brokenness and attempt of wholeness. Therefore, any divisiveness based on the person, nature, and work of Jesus Christ, etc., is discouraged. However, the complete confession could express in a structural limited way only. That is to affirm that the message is universal, but the carriers of the universal is limited and can be revised or changed. Using creatively and critically the imageries of Greco-Roman-Jewish oppressors, the complete content of the faith confession was preserved in the new wineskins of the oppressors by the oppressed. Without changing the content and creatively using the dominant imageries to their content, the early community of faith continued to be inclusive, integrative and in solidarity with the weaker sections of then society. It was, in a sense, celebration of all those who were 'dalits'. At the same time, the community had been doing healthy dialogues, *samvad*, with then dominant structures.

But what happened to the contemporary dalit faith confession? The traditional dalit Christology understands Jesus Christ as the dalit *par-excellence* and pro-dalit liberator. Even though this dalit way of looking at Jesus is acceptable, the foundation in which it is constructed is not dalit, but caste and class interpretations. It is dangerous phenomenon in Christian theologizing. When Jesus is interpreted in caste terms, especially of low caste, Jesus become a local dalit deity and loses universal content of the faith confession and its application. This also leads to caste conflicts, since 'exclusive' Christ looks to inflict a sense of 'terror' to those who are non-dalits. This jeopardy of caste and class interpretation of Jesus would only increase disintegration and conflicts within India. The 'dalit' meaning and the early faith confessional material provide an alternative way of looking at the faith confession. Dalit tradition is a way of solidarity, inclusiveness, respect for life, encourages *samvad* with other traditions for complementing the rich socio-cultural varieties. In this sense, dalit faith confession must not be a Christology of exclusivism, or a Christology for particular caste, or a Christology that functions as 'anti' to other traditions. The dalit Christology must be 'inclusive' in its content and application.

Who is inclusive Christ for the Broken People? Final part of the book elaborates the proposed inclusive dalit Christology in detail. It is 'inclusive' because of the characteristic of dalit which is inclusive – *all* that is broken. The proposed inclusive dalit Christological articulation embraces all those who experience the condition of brokenness and strive for wholeness as the term 'dalit' represents. The inclusive paradigm of Christology also considers the complete content of the early faith confession as necessary and inevitable, such as the Jesus of Nazareth and Christ of faith, because it is the complete faith confession helped the early 'dalit' community to have a distinct and relevant identity and consciousness. Mysterious characteristics of Christ, historical particularity of Jesus and His relevance to any contexts makes the dalit Christology 'inclusive'.

In this attempt of inclusive Christology, dalits need to re-mythologize, re-historicize, and re-dalitise the complete faith confession in dalit way. This revision can be seen in the dalit paradigm of *Maveli*, a mythical character, who is re-understood/re-mythologized by the dalits from re-historical sources for the unraveling the humanness in dalits. A person is dalit, not because of birth in a particular caste, but the oppression and exploitation in any sort makes a person dalit. Here, then, the methodology of exclusivism is turned to be methodology of solidarity and *samvad*, since dalit transcends any caste ideology. This change of approach towards dalit Christology becomes authentically Indian and people's Christology. This inclusive dalit faith confession is complete in its content, liberates from caste-class nexus, provides a pure (*sud*) dalit consciousness. It brings a healing to the wounded psyche of dalits by transcending the existing isolation in theological expression.

The complete humanness is the aim of the inclusive dalit Christology. Major characteristics of this inclusive faith confession would be its structural application, as the tension between universality of the content of the faith confession and the indigenity of the context of dalits. Functionally, the dalit faith confession envisions dalit to have a *sud-dalit* consciousness - from caste/class to casteless and classless dalit community. It points out to the fact that all contextual theologizing process must be guided with content of the faith, carrier of the faith and function of the faith. Any attempt to reduce the Christ of faith and glorify historical Christ alone is a limitation of liberation theology. By inclusive dalit Christology, we overcome such limitation and find the raw-material for Christ of faith is radical enough to christologize in any dalit (broken) condition of the people and their attempt of wholeness (dalit).

In short, inclusive dalit faith confession is faithful to the early faith confession in its approach of universality of its claims, at the same time able to accommodate all the people who experience dalitness to have solidarity with them, and *samvad* with all that is not dalit. This would bring a harmonious living in the context of caste and class ridden societies of India.

Bibliography

Books

"Annexures: The Statement of the New Delhi Seminar: Hermeneutics- October 2004." In *Frontiers in Dalit Hermeneutics*. Edited by James Massey and Samson Prabhakar. Bangalore and Delhi: BTESSC/SATHRI and CDSS, 2005.

Alackapally, Sebastian. "A Philosophy of Education for Dalit Assertion." In *Indigenous Philosophizing: Indian Horizons*. Dharmaram Philosophy Series: 5. Bangalore: Dharmaram Publications, 2010.

Alangaram, S. *Religions for Societal Transformation: Inter-Religious Dialogue from Subaltern Perspectives*. Bangalore: Asian Trading Corporation, 2006.

Alcock, S. E. "Greece: A Landscape of Resistance?." In *Dialogues in Roman Imperialism: Power, Discourse, and Discrepant Experience in the Roman Empire*. JRA Supp. Series, No. 23. Edited by D. J. Mattingly. Portsmouth: JRA, 1997.

Allison, Dale C. *Jesus of Nazareth: Millenarian Prophet*. Minneapolis: Fortress Press, 1998.

Amaladoss, Michael. *The Asian Jesus*. Chennai/Delhi: IDCR/ISPCK, 2005.

Ambedkar, B. R. *Writings and Speeches*. Vol. III. Bombay: Government of Maharashtra, 1989.

Anand, J. H. "Dalit Literature is the Literature of Protest." In *Dalit Solidarity*. Edited by Bhagavan Das & James Massey. Delhi: ISPCK: 1995.

Anandan, S. "Dalit Non-Violence as a Means of Community Healing." In *Building Theologies of Solidarity: Interfacing Feminist Theology with Dalit Theology and Tribal/Adivasi Theologies*. Edited by Hrangthan Chhungi, Raj Bharath Patta and P. Mohan Larbeer. Bangalore: BTESSC/NCCI/SCMI, 2012.

Anderson, Jeremiah. "An Explorative Search for Some Relevant Directions in Dalit Theology in the Context of Emerging Christian Liberation Theologies in India." In *Building Theologies of Solidarity: Interfacing Feminist Theology with Dalit Theology and Tribal/Adivasi Theologies*. Edited by Hrangthan

Chhungi, Raj Bharath Patta and P. Mohan Larbeer. Bangalore: BTESSC/NCCI/SCMI, 2012.

Apparavo, James Theophilus. "Dalit Way of Theological Expression." In *Frontiers of Dalit Theology*. Edited by V. Devasahayam. New Delhi: ISPCK, 1997.

________. *Folklore for Change*. Madras: TTS, 1986.

Arapura, John G. "Rediscovering the Meaning of the Symbol." In *Indian Voices in Today's Theological Debate*. Edited by Horst Bürkle and Wolfgang M. W. Roth. Luknow: Luknow Publishing House in collaboration with Delhi/Madras: ISPCK, CLS, 1972.

Aune, D. E. "Christian Prophecy and the Messianic Status of Jesus." In *The Messiah: Developments in Earliest Judaism and Christianity*. The First Princeton Symposium on Judaism and Christian Origins. Edited by James H. Charlesworth. Minneapolis: Fortress Press, 1992.

Ayrookuzhiel, A. M. Abraham. "Dalit Theology: A Movement of Counter Culture." In *Towards a Dalit Theology*. Edited by M. E. Prabhakar. Delhi: ISPCK, 1988.

________. "Dalit Theology: A Movement of Counter-Culture." In *Towards a Dalit Theology*. Edited by M. E. Prabhakar. Delhi: ISPCK, 1989.

________ and Paul Chirackarodu. *Dalit Sahityam: Oru Padanam* (Mal). Thiruvalla: CSS/CISRS, 1995.

Azariah, M. "The Church's Healing Ministry to Dalits." *Towards a Dalit Theology*. Delhi: ISPCK, 1988.

Bakshi, P. M. *The Constitution of India with Comments and Subject Index*. 1st Edition 1991, 3rd Edition 1996. Delhi: Universal Book Traders, reprint 1999.

Balasundaram, Franklyn J. "Dalit Theology and Other Theologies." In *Frontiers of Dalit Theology*. Edited by V. Devasahayam. New Delhi: ISPCK, 1997.

Balasuriya, Tissa. *Mary and Human Liberation: The Story and the Text*. Edited by Helen Staton. Harrisburg: Trinity Press, 1997.

Bardhan, A. "Caste-Class Situation in India." In *Caste and Class in India*. Edited by K. L. Sharma. Jaipur & New Delhi: Rawat Publications, 1994.

Barr, James. *Holy Scripture: Canon, Authority and Criticism*. Philadelphia: Westminster Press, 1983.

Bauckam, Richard. *Jesus and the Eyewitness: The Gospel as Eyewitness Testimony*. Grand Rapids, Michigan: William B. Eerdmans Publishing Company, 2006.

________. "The Future of Jesus Christ." In *The Cambridge Companion to Jesus*. Edited by Markus Bockmuel. Cambridge: CUP, 2001.

Behr, John. "Social and Historical Setting." In *The Cambridge History of Early Christian Literature*. Edited by Frances Young, Lewis Ayres, and Andrew Louth. Cambridge: CUP, 2004.

Bell, Daniel. *Communitarianism and its Critics.* Oxford: Clarendon Press, 1993.

Best, Ernest. "The Use of Creedal and Liturgical Materials in Ephesians." In *Worship, Theology and Ministry in the Early Church: Essays in Honor of Ralph P. Martin.* Edited by Michael J. Wilkin and Terence Paige. Sheffield: Journal for the Study of the New Testament (JSOT) Press, 1992.

Bethune-Baker, J. F. *An Introduction to the Early History of Christian Doctrine to the Time of the Council of Chalcedon* 1903. 6th Edition. London: Methuen & Co. Ltd, 1938.

Bettenson, Henry. Ed. *Documents of the Christian Church.* New York, London: Oxford University Press, 1967.

Bhattacharya, Neeladri. "Editorial Preface." In *Dalit Vision.* Tracts for the Times 8. Hyderabad: Orient Longman, 1995.

Bird, Michael F. *Jesus and the Origins of the Gentile Mission.* London: T&T Clarke International, 1988.

Borg, M. J. *Jesus in Contemporary Scholarship.* Valley Forge, P.A.: Trinity Press International, 1994.

Bornkamm, Günther. *Jesus of Nazareth.* Translated from German Edition of 1959 by Irene and Fraser McLuskey with James M. Robinson. Minneapolis: Fortress Press, 1995.

Bousset, Wilhelm. *Kyrios Christos: A History of the Belief in Christ from the Beginnings of Christianity to Irenaeus.* Translated by John E. Steely. Nashville: Abingdon Press, 1970.

Boyd, R. H. S. "The Philosophical Context of Indian Christian Theology with Special Reference to P. Chenchiah." In *Indian Voices in Today's Theological Debate.* Edited by Horst Bürkle and Wolfgang M.W. Roth. Luknow: Luknow Publishing House in collaboration with Delhi/Madras: ISPCK, CLS, 1972.

Bray, Gerald. *Creeds, Councils and Christ: Did the Early Christians Misrepresent Jesus?*, 1984. Scotland: Mentor, 1997 reprinted in 2009.

Brown, Francis. *A Hebrew and English Lexicon of the Old Testament,* 1907, Translated by Edward Robinson. Oxford: Clarendon Press, 1974.

Brown, Harold O. J. *Heresies: Heresy and Orthodoxy in the History of the Church.* Peabody: Hendrickson Publishers, 1988.

Brown, R. E, Carolyn Osick and Phem Perkins. "Early Church." *New Jerome Biblical Commentary.* Edited by Raymond E. Brown. Bangalore: TPI, 1991.

Bultmann, Rudolf. Etal. *Kerygma and Myth: A Theological Debate.* Edited by Hans Werner Bartsch. New York: Harper & Row Publishers, nd.

________. *Theology of the New Testament.* Translated by Kendrick Grobel. New York: Charles Scribner's Sons, 1951.

Burkett, Delbert. *An Introduction to the New Testament and the Origins of Christianity*. Cambridge: Cambridge University Press, 2002.

________. *The Son of Man Debate: A History and Evaluation.* Cambridge: CUP, 2004.

Bürkle, Horst. "Introduction to German Edition." as Example of an Ecumenically Oriented Theology." In *Indian Voices in Today's Theological Debate*. Edited by Horst Bürkle and Wolfgang M. W. Roth. Luknow: Luknow Publishing House in collaboration with Delhi/Madras: ISPCK, CLS, 1972.

________. "The Debate of the "Cosmic Christ" as Example of an Ecumenically Oriented Theology." In *Indian Voices in Today's Theological Debate*. Edited by Horst Bürkle and Wolfgang M. W. Roth. Luknow: Luknow Publishing House in collaboration with Delhi/Madras: ISPCK, CLS, 1972.

Caleb, Sunil. "Dalit Economic Condition as a Hermeneutical Tool in the Search for Dalit Liberation." In *Frontiers in Dalit Hermeneutics*. Edited by James Massey and Samson Prabhakar. Bangalore and Delhi: BTESSC/SATHRI and CDSS, 2005.

Carr, Dhyanchand. "Dalit Theology is Biblical and Its Makes the Gospel Relevant." In *A Reader in Dalit Theology*. Edited by A. P. Nirmal. Delhi/ Madras: ISPCK, Gurukul, np.

Chandran, J. R. "Preface to Indian Edition." In *Indian Voices in Today's Theological Debate*. Edited by Horst Bürkle and Wolfgang M. W. Roth. Luknow: Luknow Publishing House in collaboration with Delhi/Madras: ISPCK, CLS, 1972.

________. "The Theological Task of the Church in India." In *Indian Voices in Today's Theological Debate*. Edited by Horst Bürkle and Wolfgang M. W. Roth. Luknow: Luknow Publishing House in collaboration with Delhi/ Madras: ISPCK, CLS, 1972.

Charlesworth, James H. "Exploring Opportunities for Rethinking Relation among Jews and Christians." In *Jews and Christians: Exploring the Past, Present and Future*. Edited by James Charlesworth. New York: Cross Road, 1990.

________. "The Historical Jesus: How to Ask Questions and Remain Inquisitive." In *Handbook for the Study of the Historical Jesus*, Vol. 1: How to Study the Historical Jesus. Edited by Holmén and Stanley E. Porter. Boston, Leiden: Brill, 2011.

Chatterji, S. K. "Some Aspects of Dalit Ideology." In *Towards a Common Dalit Ideology*. Madras: Gurukul, nd.

________, "Why Dalit Theology?." In *Indigenous People: Dalits, Dalit Issues in Today's Theological Debate*, 1994. Edited by James Massey. Delhi: ISPCK, 2006.

Chirakkarode, Paul. "The Dalits and the Left in Kerala." *The Dalit Desiyata: The Kerala Experience in Development and Class Struggle*. Edited by A. M.

Abraham Ayrookuzhiel. Delhi: ISPCK, Published for Bangalore: CISRS, 1990.

Chiton, Bruce D. and Jacob Neuser. *Classical Christianity and Rabbinic Judaism: Comparing Theologies*. Grand Rapids, Michigan: Baker Academic, 2004.

Chungi, Harangthan. "Interfacing Tribal and Adivasi Theology with Feminist Theology for Building Theologies of Solidarity." In *Building Theologies of Solidarity: Interfacing Feminist Theology with Dalit Theology and Tribal/Adivasi Theologies*. Edited by Hrangthan Chhungi, Raj Bharath Patta and P. Mohan Larbeer. Bangalore: BTESSC/NCCI/SCMI, 2012.

Clarke, Santhinathan, Manchela Deenabandhu and Peacock Philip Vinod. Eds. "Introduction." To *Dalit Theology in the Twenty First Century: Discordant Voices, Discerning Pathways*. New Delhi: OUP, 2010.

Clarke, Sathianathan. *Dalits and Christianity: Subaltern Religion and Liberation Theology in India*. New Delhi: OUP, 1999.

________. "Subaltern, Identity Politics, and Christian Theology in India." In *Christian Theology in Asia*. Edited by Sebastian C. H. Kim. Cambridge: CUP, 2008.

Clarke, Sundar. "Dalit Movement- Need for a Theology." In *Towards a Dalit Theology*. Edited by M. E. Prabhakar. Delhi: ISPCK, 1988.

Cohfink, Gerhard. *Jesus and Community: The Social Dimension of Christian Faith*. Augsburg: Fortress Press, 1984.

Cone, James H. *A Black Theology of Liberation*. Philadelphia: J.B. Lippincott Company, 1970.

Conzelmann, Hans. *An Outline of the Theology of the New Testament*. New York: Harper & Row, 1969.

Crossan, John Dominic. "Context and Text in Historical Jesus Methodology." In *Handbook for the Study of the Historical Jesus*, Vol. 1: How to Study the Historical Jesus. Edited by Holmén and Stanley E. Porter. Boston, Leiden: Brill, 2011.

________. *The Birth of Christianity: Discovering What Happened in the Years Immediately After the Execution of Jesus*. New York: Harper Collins, 1998.

Crowland, H. *Cambridge Ancient History*. Vol. 1. Cambridge: CUP, 1967.

Cullmann, Oscar. *The Christology of New Testament*. Philadelphia: Westminster John Knox Press, 1963.

Cunningham, Scott. *Through Many Tribulations: The Theology of Persecution in Luke-Acts*. England: Sheffield Academic Press, 1997.

D'Souza, Joseph. *Dalit Freedom: Now and Forever: The Epic Struggle for Dalit Emancipation*. Centennial: Dalit Freedom Network, 2004.

Dangle, Arun. "Dalit Literature: Past, Present and Future." Translated by Avinash S. Pandit and Daya Agarwal. In *Poisoned Bread: Translations from Modern*

Marathi Dalit Literature. Edited by Arjun Dangle. Hyderabad: Orient Longman, 1992, reprinted 1994.

Devasahayam, V. "Doing Dalit Theology: Basic Assumptions." In *Frontiers of Dalit Theology*. Delhi/Madras: ISPCK, Gurukul, 1997.

________. "Formative Factors of Dalit Theology." In *Frontiers of Dalit Theology.* Delhi/Madras: ISPCK, Gurukul, 1997.

________. "Identity in Theology." In *Frontiers of Dalit Theology*. Delhi/Madras: ISPCK, Gurukul, 1997.

________. "Introduction to Bible Studies." In *Frontiers of Dalit Theology*. Edited by V. Devasahayam. New Delhi: ISPCK, 1997.

________. "Introduction." To *Frontiers of Dalit Theology*. Edited by Devasahayam. Delhi/Madras: ISPCK/Gurukul, 1997.

________. "New Thrusts of Dalit Theology." In *Frontiers of Dalit Theology.* Edited by Devasahayam. Delhi/Madras: ISPCK/Gurukul, 1997.

________. "The Goals of Dalit Theology." In *Frontiers of Dalit Theology*. Delhi/Madras: ISPCK, Gurukul, 1997.

________. "The Nature of Dalit Theology as Counter Theology." In *Frontiers of Dalit Theology*. Delhi/Madras: ISPCK, Gurukul, 1997.

________. "The Norms of Theology." *Frontiers of Dalit Theology*. Edited by V. Devasahayam. New Delhi: ISPCK, 1997.

________. "Theologising in Context." In *Frontiers of Dalit Theology*. Edited by V. Devasahayam. New Delhi: ISPCK, 1997.

Dirks, Nicholas B. *Castes of Mind: Colonialism and the Making of Modern India.* Delhi: Permanent Black, 2001.

Downing, Gerald. *Doing Things with Words in the First Christian Century*. New York, London: T&T Clark, 2004.

Dunn, D. Geoffrey. *Unity and Diversity in New Testament: An Inquiry into the Character of Earliest Christianity,* 1977. 2nd Edition. London: SCM Press, 1981.

________. "Remembering Jesus: How the Quest of the Historical Jesus Lost its Way." In *Handbook for the Study of the Historical Jesus*, Vol. 1: How to Study the Historical Jesus. Edited by Holmén and Stanley E. Porter. Boston, Leiden: Brill, 2011.

________. *Did the First Christians Worship Jesus? The New Testament Evidence.* London: SPCK, 2010.

________. *Jesus Remembered: Christianity in the Making.* Vol. 1. Grand Rapids: Wm. B. Eerdmans, 2003.

________. *Tertullian: Early Church Fathers.* London: New York: Routledge, 2004.

Ehrman, Bart D. *The New Testament: Historical Introduction to the Early Christian Writings.* Oxford: OUP, 2000.

________. *Apocalyptic Prophet of the New Millennium.* New York: Oxford University Press, 1999.

Elwell, Walter A, and Robert W. Yarbrough. *Encountering the New Testament: A Historical and Theological Survey.* 1998. 2nd Edition. Grand Rapids: Baker Academic, 2005.

Emmanuel, Harry. "Violence Against Dalits: An Indian Christian Response." *Violence and Its Victims: A Challenge to Philosophising in the Indian Context.* Edited by Ivo Coelho. Bangalore: ATC, 2010.

Engberg–Pederson, Troels. Ed. *Paul Beyond the Judaism/Hellenism Divide.* Louisville: Westminster John Knox Press, 2000.

Erickson, Millard J. *Christian Theology.* 2nd Edition. Grand Rapids, Michigan: Baker Books, 2002.

Faustine, S. "From Exile to Exodus: Christian Dalit Women and the Role of Religion." In *Frontiers of Dalit Theology.* Edited by V. Devasahayam. Delhi/ Madras: ISPCK, Gurukul, 1997.

Ferguson, Everett. *Background of Early Christianity.* 2nd Edition. Grand Rapids, Michigan: William B. Eerdmans Publishing Company, 1993.

Fiorenza, Elisabeth Schüssler. "Critical Feminist Historical Research." In *Handbook for the Study of the Historical Jesus,* Vol. 1: How to Study the Historical Jesus. Edited by Holmén and Stanley E. Porter. Boston, Leiden: Brill, 2011.

Fitzmyer, Joseph A. *To Advance the Gospel: New Testament Studies.* 2nd Edition. Grand Rapids and Michigan: William B. Eerdmans Publishing Company, 1998.

Fosdick, Harry Emerson. *The Man from Nazareth: As His Contemporaries Saw Him.* New York: Harper and Brothers, 1949.

Fragments from Reimarus: Consisting of Brief Critical Remarks on the Object of Jesus and His Disciples as Seen in the New Testament. Translated by G. E. Lessing. Edited by Charles Voysey. London and Edinburgh: William and Norgate, 1879.

Fredriksen, Paula. *Jesus of Nazareth, King of Jews: A Jewish Life and the Emergence of Christianity.* New York: Vintage Books, 1999.

Fuchs, E. *Studies in Historical Jesus.* Edited by A. Scobie. London: SCM Press, 1964.

Fuller, Reginald H. *The Foundations of New Testament Christology.* New York: Charles Scribner's, 1965.

Fyzee, Asaf A. A. "Islamic Law and Theology in India – Proposals for a Fresh Approach." In *Cultural and Religious Heritage of India: Islam.* Edited by Suresh K. Sharma and Usha Sharma. New Delhi: Mittal Publications, 2004.

Garrett, James W. *The New Testament Church and Heresy.* Tulsa, Oklahoma: Doulos Press, 2004.

Garrison, Roman. *The Greco-Roman Context of Early Christian Literature.* Sheffield: Sheffield Academic Press, 1997.

Gebara, Ivone and Maria Clara Bingemer. *Mary: Mother of God, Mother of the Poor.* Liberation and Theology Series. 7. Translated by Philip Berryman. USA/Maryknoll: Burns & Oates/ Orbis Books, 1989.

Gilbert, Gary. "Roman Propaganda and Christian identity in the Worldview of Luke-Acts." In *Contextualising Acts: Lukan Narrative and Greco-Roman Discourse.* Society of Biblical Literature: Symposium Series No. 20. Edited by Todd Penner and Caroline Vender Stichele. Atlanta: Society of Biblical Literature, 2003.

Gladstone, J. W. "Christian Missionaries and Caste in Kerala." In *Towards a Dalit Theology*. Edited by M. E. Prabhakar. Delhi: ISPCK, 1988.

Gnanavaram, M. "Some Reflections on Dalit Hermeneutics." In *Frontiers of Dalit Theology*. Edited by V. Devasahayam. New Delhi: ISPCK, 1997.

Grillmeier, Aloys. S.J. *Christ in Christian Tradition: From the Apostolic Age to Chalcedon (451)*. Translated by J. S. Bowden. London: A. R. Mowbray & Co. Limited, 1965.

Grogen, Geoffrey. *The Christ of the Bible and the Church's Faith.* Np: Mentor, 1998.

Gupta, S. K. *The Schedule Caste in Modern Indian Politics: Their Emergence as a Political Power.* Delhi: Munshiram Manoharlal, 1989.

Guru, Gopal. "The Language of Dalit-Bahujan Political Discourse." In *Dalit Identity and Politics.* Cultural Subordination and the Dalit Challenge. Vol. 2. Edited by Ghanshyam Shah. New Delhi: Sage Publications, 2001.

Gutierrez, Gustavo. *A Theology of Liberation*. Translated by Carida Inda and John Eagleson. Maryknol: Orbis Books, 1988.

Hahn, F. *The Titles of Jesus in Christology*. London: Lutterworth, 1969.

Haight, Roger. *Dynamics of Theology*. Bangalore: Claretian Publications, 2002.

Harnack, Adolf. *What is Christianity*. New York: G. P. Putnam's Sons, 1901. Reproduced by San Diego: The Book Tree, 2006.

Hebden, Keith. *Dalit Theology and Christian Anarchism.* Ashgate New Critical Thinking in Religion. Farnham: Ashgate Publishing Limited, 2011.

Hengel, Martin. *Between Jesus and Paul: Studies in the Earliest History of Christianity*. 1983. Eugene, Oregon: Wipf and Stock Publishers, 2003.

Heredia, Rudolf C. *Changing Gods: Rethinking Conversion in India*. New Delhi: Penguin Books, 2007.

Hgner, Donald A. "An Analysis of Recent 'Historical Jesus' Studies." In *Religious Diversity in the Greco-Roman World: A Survey of Recent Scholarship*. Edited by Dan Cohn-Sherbok and John M. Court. Sheffield: Sheffield Academic Press, 2001.

Hindley, J. C. "The Jesus of History: An Appraisal from India." In *Indian Voices in Today's Theological Debate*. Edited by Horst Bürkle and Wolfgang M. W. Roth. Luknow: Luknow Publishing House in collaboration with Delhi/ Madras: ISPCK, CLS, 1972.

Ho, Huang Po. *No Longer a Stranger: Towards the Reconstruction of Contextual Theologies*. Thiruvalla: CSS, 2007.

Horsley, A. "Jesus-in-Context: A Relational Approach." In *Handbook for the Study of the Historical Jesus*, Vol. 1: How to Study the Historical Jesus, edited by Holmén and Stanley E. Porter. Boston, Leiden: Brill, 2011.

Hrangkhuma, F. *Introduction to Church History*. Bangalore: TBT, 1996.

Hurtado, Larry W. *At the Origins of Christian Worship: The Context and Character of Christian Devotion*. New York: Guideposts, 1999.

Ilaiah, Kancha. "Dalitism vs Brahmanism: The Epistemological Conflict in History." *Dalit Identity and Politics: Cultural Subordination and the Dalit Challenge*. Vol. 2. Edited by Ghanshyam Shah. New Delhi: Sage Publications, 2001.

________. *Post-Hindu India: A Discourse on Dalit-Bahujan, Socio-Spiritual and Scientific Revolution*. New Delhi: Sage Publications, 2009.

________. *Why I am Not a Hindu: A Sudhra Critique of Hindutva Philosophy, Culture, and Political Economy*. 2nd Edition. Calcutta: Samy, 2005.

Iyer, V. R. Krishna. *Dr. Ambedkar and the Dalit Future*. Delhi: B. R. Publishing Corporation, 1990.

Jaffrelot, Christopher. "The BSP in Uttar Pradesh: Whose Party is It?." In *Dalits in Modern India: Vision and Values*. Edited by S. M. Michael. 2nd Edition. New Delhi: Sage Publications, 1999, 2007.

Jagersma, H. *A History of Israel from Alexander the Great to Bar Kochba*. London: SCM Press Ltd., 1998.

Jayakumar, Samuel. *Dalit Consciousness and Christian Conversion: Historical Resources for a Contemporary Debate*. Chennai: Mission Educational Books, 2004, First Published 1999.

John, M. "The Church in the Service of Dalits: Statistics and Policy." *Towards a Dalit Theology*. Delhi: ISPCK, 1988.

John, T. K. "Method of Collaboration in Theological Journey." In *Dalit-Tribal Theological Interface: Current Trends in Subaltern Theologies*. Edited by James Massey and Shimreingam Shimray. Jorhat and New Delhi: TSC/WSC and CDS, 2007.

Kamble, J. R. *Rise and Awakening of Depressed Classes in India*. New Delhi: National Publishing House, 1979.

Käseman, Ernst. *Essays in New Testament Themes*. Translated by Montague. London: SCM Press Ltd., 1964.

Kashyap, Subash C. *Our Constitution: An Introduction to Indian's Constitution and Constitutional Law*. 1994. 2nd Edition. New Delhi: National Book Trust, Reprint 2000.

Kasper, Walter. *Jesus the Christ*. New York: T&T Clark International, 2011, first edition 1976.

Kee, Howards C. *Christian Origins in Sociological Perspective*. London: SCM Press, 1980.

Keer, Dhanjay. *Mahatma Jotirao Phooley: Father of Indian Social Revolution*. Reprint 2002. Bombay: Popular Prakashan, 1964.

Kelly, J. N. D. *Early Christian Creeds*. 1960 3rd Edition. London, New York: Continumm, 1972.

________. *Early Christian Doctrines*. 1958. 4th Edition. London: Adam & Charles Black, 1968.

Khan, Salauddin. "Globalization, Dalits, Adivasis and Naxalite Movements." In *Dalits and Tribes of India*. Edited by J. Cyril Kanmony. New Delhi: Mittal Publications, 2010.

Knight, Jonathan. *Christian Origins*. New York: T&T Clark International, 2008.

Knox, John. *The Early Church and the Coming Great Church*. London: The Epworth Press, 1957.

Köstenberger, Andreas J. and Michael J. Kruger, *The Heresy of Orthodoxy: How Contemporary Culture's Fascination with Diversity has Reshaped our Understanding of Early Christianity*. Illinois: Crossway, 2010.

Kshirsagar, R. K. *Dalit Movements in India and Its Leaders*. New Delhi: M.D. Publications, 1994.

Lalpekhlua, L. H. *Contextual Christology: A Tribal Perspective*. Delhi: ISPCK, 2007.

Lampe, Peter. "Early Christians in the City of Rome. Topographical and Social Historical Aspects of the First Three Centuries." *Christians as a Religious Minority in a Multicultural City: Modes of Interaction and Identity Formation in Early Imperial Rome. Studies on the Basis of a Seminar at the Second Conference of the European Association for Biblical Studies (EABS) From July 8-12, 2001, in Rome*. Edited by Jürgen Zangenberg and Michael Labahn. New York, London: T&T Clark International, 2004.

Larbeer, P. Mohan. "Dalit Identity - A Theological Reflection." In *Frontiers of Dalit Theology*. Edited by V. Devasahayam. New Delhi: ISPCK, 1997.

The Law of Manu. In Sacred Books of the East Series: XXV. Translated by G. Bühler. Delhi: Motilal Banarsidass, Reprinted 1988, First published in 1886.

Lohse, Edward. *The Formation of the New Testament*. Translated by M. Eugene Boring. Nashville: Abingdon Press, 1981.

Longenecker, Richard N. *New Wine Into Fresh Wineskins: Contextualizing the Early Christian Confessions.* Peabody: Hendrickson Publishers, Inc., 1999.

Lourdunathan, S. "Theoretical Grounds for a Theology of Solidarity: Instantiating a Dalit Discourse." In *Building Theologies of Solidarity: Interfacing Feminist Theology with Dalit Theology and Tribal/Adivasi Theologies.* Edited by Hrangthan Chhungi, Raj Bharath Patta and P. Mohan Larbeer. Bangalore: BTESSC/NCCI/SCMI, 2012.

Mack, Burton L. *A Myth of Innocence: Mark and Christian Origins.* Philadelphia: Fortress Press, 1988.

Malhotra, Rajiv and Aravindan Neelakandan. *Breaking India: Western Interventions in Dravidian and Dalit Fault Lines.* New Delhi: Amaryllis, 2001.

Mani, Braj Ranjan. *Debrahmanising History: Dominance and Resistance in Indian Society.* New Delhi: Manohar, 2005.

Manichala, Deenbandhu. "Expanding the Ambit: Dalit Theological Contribution to Ecumenical Social Thought." In *Dalit Theology in the Twenty First Century: Discordant Voices, Discerning Pathways.* Edited by Clarke Santhinathan, Manchela Deenabandhu and Peacock Philip Vinod. New Delhi: OUP, 2010.

Martin, Ralph P. *Worship in the Early Church.* New York: Guideposts, 1975.

Massey, James. "History and Dalit Identity." In *Dalit Solidarity.* Edited by Bhagavan Das & James Massey. Delhi: ISPCK, 1995.

________. "History and Dalit Theology." *Frontiers of Dalit Theology.* Delhi/ Madras: ISPCK, Gurukul, 1997.

________. "Ingredients for a Dalit Theology." In *Towards a Dalit Theology.* Edited by M. E. Prabhakar. Delhi: ISPCK, 1989.

________. "Introduction." In *Dalit World-Biblical World: An Encounter.* Edited by Leonards Ferdinanda and James Massey. New Delhi: CDS & Vidyajoti, 2007.

________. *Down Trodden: The Struggle of India's Dalits for Identity, Solidarity and Liberation.* Geneva: WCC Publication, 1997.

________. *Roots: A Concise History of Dalits.* 2nd Rev. 1991. Published for CISRS, Bangalore by Delhi: ISPCK, 1994.

McClymond, Michael J. *Familiar Stranger: An Introduction to Jesus of Nazareth.* Grand Rapids, Michigan: William B. Eerdmans Publishing Company, 2004.

McDonald, James Ian Hamilton. *Kerygma and Didache: The Articulation and Structure of the Earliest Christian Message.* Society for New Testament Studies Monograph Series, 37. Cambridge: CUP, 1980.

McGrath, Alister E. *Studies in Doctrine.* Michigan: Zondervan Publishing House, 1997.

McKechnie, Paul. *The First Christian Centuries: Perspective on the Early Church.* Secunderabad: OM Books, 2001.

McKnight, E. V. *The Bible and the Reader: An Introduction to Literary Criticism.* Philadelphia: Fortress Press, 1985.

Mclay, R. Timothy. "Biblical Texts and the Scriptures for the New Testament Church." In *Hearing the Old Testament in the New Testament.* Edited by Stanley E. Porter. Michigan: William B. Eerdmans Publishing Company, 2006.

Meeks, Wayne A. *The First Urban Christians: The Social World of Paul.* 1983. 2nd Edition. New Haven and London: Yale University Press, 2003.

Mehta, J. L. *Advanced Study in the History of Medieval India.* Vol. 1 (1000-1526). New Delhi: Sterling Publishers, 1979.

Melanchthon, Monica Jyostna. "Dalit Readers of the Word." In *Frontiers of Dalit Hermeneutics.* Bangalore and New Delhi: BTESSC/SATHRI & CDSS, 2005.

Menon, A. Sreedhara. *Cultural Heritage of Kerala.* 1978. Kottayam: DC Books, 2008.

________. *The Legacy of Kerala.* 1982. Kottayam: DC Books, 2008.

Meyer, Ben. *The Early Christians: Their World Mission and Self-Discovery.* Delaware, Wilmington: Michael Glazier Inc., 1986.

Migliore, Daniel L. *Faith Seeking Understanding: An Introduction to Christian Theology.* 2nd Edition. Grand Rapids: William B. Eerdmann Publishing Company, 2004.

Mohan, P. Chandra. *Popular Culture and Socio-Religious Reform: Narayana Guru and the Ezhavas of Travancore.* Studies in History, Vol. 3. New Delhi: np., 1987.

Mookenthottam, Antony. *Indian Theological Tendencies.* Las Vegas: Peter Lang, 1978.

Moreland, Milton. "Jerusalem Community in Acts: Mythmaking and the Sociorhetorical Functions of a Lukan Setting." In *Contextualising Acts: Lukan Narrative and Greco-Roman Discourse.* Society of Biblical Literature: Symposium Series No. 20. Edited by Todd Penner and Caroline Vender Stichele. Atlanta: Society of Biblical Literature, 2003.

Moxnes, Halvor. "Landscape and Spatiality: Placing Jesus." In *Understanding the Social World of the New Testament.* Edited by Dietmar Neufeld and Richard E. DeMaris. London and New York: Routledge, 2010.

Muller, Max. *The Sacred Laws of the Aryas as thought in the Schools of Apastamba, Gautama, Vaishtha and Baudhayana.* Sacred Books of the East Series 2. Translated by Geroge Buhler. Delhi: Motilal Banarsidass, Reprint 1986, First Published by Clarendon Press 1879.

Munoz, Ronaldo. *The God of Christians*. Liberation and Theology Series 11. Translated by Paul Burns. USA/Maryknoll: Burns & Oates and Orbis Books, 1991.

Naicker, E. V. Ramasami. *The Words of Freedom: Ideas of a Nation*. New Delhi: Penguin Books, 2010.

Nath, Trilok. *Politics of the Depressed Classes*. Delhi: Deputy Publications, 1987.

Neufeld, Vernon H. *The Earliest Christian Confessions*. New Testament Tools and Studies Volume V. Edited by Bruce M. Metzger. Netherland: Brill Archive, 1963.

Nirmal, A. P. "Towards a Christian Dalit Theology." In *A Reader in Dalit Theology*. Edited by Arvind P. Nirmal. Madras: Gurukul Lutheran Theological College and Research Institute, nd.

________. "A Dialogue with Dalit Literature." In *Towards a Dalit Theology*. Edited by M. E Prabhakar. Delhi: ISPCK, 1989.

________. *Heuristic Explorations*. Madras: The Christian Literature Service for the Gurukul Lutheran Theological College and Research Institute, 1990.

________. "Doing Theology from a Dalit Perspective." In *A Reader in Dalit Theology*. Edited by Arvind P. Nirmal. Chennai: Gurukul Lutheran Theological College & Research Institute, np, reprint 2007.

Norris, Richard A. "Articulating Identity." *The Cambridge History of Early Christian Literature*. Edited by Frances Young, Lewis Ayres and Andrew Louth. Cambridge: CUP, 2004.

Oakes, Peter. Ed. *Rome in the Bible and the Early Church*. Grand Rapids: Baker, 2002.

Oesterlay, W. O. E. *The Jewish Background of the Christian Liturgy*. 1925. London: Oxford University Press, 1965.

Okure, Teresa. "Historical Jesus Research in Global Cultural Context." In *Handbook for the Study of the Historical Jesus*, Vol. 2: Study of Jesus. Edited by Holmén and Stanley E. Porter. Boston, Leiden: Brill, 2011.

________. "The Global Jesus." In *The Cambridge Companion to Jesus*. Edited by Markus Bockmuel. Cambridge: CUP, 2001.

Omvedt, Gail. "Ambedkar and After: The Dalit Movements in India." In *Social Movements and the State*. Readings in Indian Government and Politics – 4. Edited by Ghanshyam Shah. New Delhi: Sage Publications, 2002.

________. *Dalits and the Democratic Revolution: Dr. Ambedkar and the Dalit Movement in Colonial India*. New Delhi, London: Sage Publications, 1994.

________. *Dalits Visions: The Anti-Caste Movement and the Construction of an Indian Identity*. Third Revised Edition 2006. Hyderabad: Orient Longman, 1995.

________. *Jotirao Phule and the Ideology of Social Revolution in India.* New Delhi: Critical Quest, 2004.

Oommen, George. "Introduction." In *Local Dalit Christian History*. Edited by George Oommen and John C. B. Webster. Delhi: ISPCK, 2002.

Pal, Bipin Chandra. *An Introduction to the Study of Hinduism*. Calcutta: S. C. Ghose, 1908.

Pandiappallil, Joseph. "Need for an Inclusive and Integral Philosophy in the Indian Subcontinent." In *Indigenous Philosophizing: Indian Horizons*. Dharmaram Philosophy Series: 5. Bangalore: Dharmaram Publications, 2010.

Papandrea, James L. *Reading the Early Church Fathers*. New Jersey: Paulist Press, 2012.

Patankar, Bharat and Gail Omvedt. *The Dalit Liberation Movement in Colonial Period*. New Delhi: Critical Quest, 2004.

Peacock, Vinod. "Impact of the Context: Dalit Perspective." In *Dalit-Tribal Theological Interface: Current Trends in Subaltern Theologies*. Edited by James Massey and Shimreingam Shimray. Jorhat and New Delhi: TSC/WSC and CDS, 2007.

Pentecost, J Dwight. *Words and Works of Jesus Christ*. Michigan: Zondervan Publishing House, 1981.

Phan, Peter C. "Living for the Reign of God; Liberation Culture, Religions. A Theology of Liberation for the Asian Churches." In *Movement or Moment: Assessing Liberation Theology Forty Years After Medellin*. Studies in Theology, Society, and Culture, Vol. 1. Edited by Patrick Claffey and Joe Egan. Switzerland: Peterlang, 2009.

Porter, Stanley E. "The Context of Jesus: Jewish and/or Hellenistic?." In *Handbook for the Study of the Historical Jesus*, Vol. 2: Study of Jesus. Edited by Holmén and Stanley E. Porter. Boston, Leiden: Brill, 2011.

________. "The Role of Greek Language in Historical Jesus Research." In *Handbook for the Study of the Historical Jesus*, Vol. 1: How to Study the Historical Jesus. Edited by Holmén and Stanley E. Porter. Boston, Leiden: Brill, 2011.

Prabhakar, M. E. "Caste-Class, Patriarchy and Doing Dalit Theology." In *Frontiers of Dalit Theology*. Delhi/Madras: ISPCK, Gurukul, 1997.

________. "Christology in Dalit Perspective." In *Frontiers of Dalit Theology*. Edited by V. Devasahayam. New Delhi: ISPCK, 1997.

________. "Dalit Concerns in the Context of Religious Fundamentalism in India." In *Religious Fundamentalism: An Asian Perspective*. Edited by J. Augustine. Bangalore: SATHRI, CCA/WARC, 1993.

________. "In Search of a Dalit Theology." In *Towards a Dalit Theology*. Edited by M. E. Prabhakar. Delhi: ISPCK, 1988.

________. "Introduction." *Towards a Dalit Theology*. Delhi: ISPCK, 1988.

________. "The Search for a Dalit Theology." In *Indigenous People: Dalits, Dalit Issues in Today's Theological Debate*. First Edition 1994. Edited by James Massey. Delhi: ISPCK, Reprint 2006.

Pradhan, Atul Chandra. *The Emergence of the Depressed Classes*. Bhubaneshwar: Bookland International, 1986.

Prior, Michael. *The Bible and Colonialism: A Moral Critique*. Sheffield: Sheffield Academic Press, 1997.

Pule, Jotirao Govindraw. *Slavery in the Civilized British Government under the Cloak of Brahmanism*. Np: Pune City Press, 1873.

Punalekar, S. P. "Dalit Literature and Dalit Identity." In *Dalit Identity and Politics: Cultural Subordination and the Dalit Challenge*. Vol. 2. Edited by Ghanshyam Shah. New Delhi: Sage Publications, 2001.

Puniyani, Ram. *God Politics*. New Delhi: Vitsta, 2012.

________. "Rashtriya Swayamsevak Sangh: Politics as 'Culture'." In *Communal Violence and Minorities: Gujarat Society in Ferment*. Edited by Lancy Lobo and Biswaroop Das. New Delhi: Rawat Publications, 2006.

________. *Religion and Politics: Essays on Contemporary Issues*. Thiruvananthapuram: Mythri Books, 2009.

Puthenpurackal, Johnson. "Philosophising from Dalit Perspective." In *Subaltern Perspectives: Philosophising in Context*. Edited by George Thadathil. Bangalore: ATC, 2005.

Pylee, M. V. *An Introduction to the Constitution of India*. 5th Edition. New Delhi: Vikas Publishing House, 2007.

Raja, A. Maria Arul. "Some Reflections on a Dalit Reading of the Bible." In *Frontiers of Dalit Theology*. Edited by V. Devasahayam. New Delhi: ISPCK, 1997.

________. "Dalit Layers of Consciousness in Dialogue with Biblical World." In *Dalit-Tribal Theological Interface: Current Trends in Subaltern Theologies*. Edited by James Massey and Shimreingam Shimray. Jorhat and New Delhi: TSC/WSC and CDS, 2007.

Rajkumar, Peniel. *Dalit Theology and Dalit Liberation: Problems, Paradigms and Possibilities*. Ashgate New Critical Thinking in Religion, Theology and Biblical Studies Series. Farnham, England: Ashgate, 2010.

Rao, Anupama. *The Caste Question: Dalits and the Politics of Modern India*. Ranikhet: Permanent Black, 2009.

Rao, Ch. Vasantha. "Dalit Christians' Struggle for Justice in the Indian Sub-continent." In *Towards Theology of Justice for Life in Peace: Minjung-Dalit Theological Dialogue*. Edited by Kwon Jinkwan and P. Mohan Larbeer. Bangalore: BTESSC, 2012.

Rao, Katti Padma. *Caste and Alternative Culture*. Madras: The Gurukul Lutheran Theological College and Research Institute/Centre for Research on New International Economic Order, 1995.

Rao, N. Sudhakar. "The Structure of South Indian Untouchable Castes: A View." In *Dalit Identity and Politics*. Cultural Subordination and the Dalit Challenge. Vol. 2. Edited by Ghanshyam Shah. New Delhi: Sage Publications, 2001.

Rasquinha, Dionysius. *Towards Wholeness from Brokenness- The Dalit Quest: A Historical Analysis and Theological Response*. Delhi: ISPCK, 2013.

Rausch, Thomas P. *Who is Jesus? An Introduction to Christology*. Minnesota: Liturgical Press, 2003.

Razu, I. John Mohan. "The Promise and Possibilities of Hermeneutics: The Place of Dalits in the Private Sector." In *Frontiers in Dalit Hermeneutics*. Edited by James Massey and Samson Prabhakar. Bangalore and Delhi: BTESSC/ SATHRI and CDSS, 2005.

Richardson, Cyril C. "Introduction to Early Christian Literature and Its Setting." In *Early Christian Fathers*. Translated and Edited by Cyril C. Richardson. New York: Touchstone, 1996.

Robinson, James M. *A New Quest of the Historical Jesus*. Studies in Biblical Theology 1959. London: SCM Press Ltd., 1970.

________. *Jesus According to the Earliest Witness.* Minneapolis: Fortress Press, 2007.

Robinson, John A. T. "The Last Tabu? The Self Consciousness of Jesus." In *The Historical Jesus in Recent Research.* Sources for Biblical and Theological Study, Vol. 10. Edited by James D. G. Dunn and Scot Mcknight. Winona Lake, Indiana: Eisenbrauns, 2005.

Roth, Wolfgang M. W. "Thought Patterns-Fetters or Opportunities?." In *Voices in Today's Theological Debate*. Edited by Horst Bürkle and Wolfgang M.W. Roth. Luknow: Luknow Publishing House in collaboration with Delhi/ Madras: ISPCK, CLS, 1972.

Sadangi, Himansu Charan. *Dalits: The Downtrodden India.* Delhi: ISHA Books, 2008.

Samartha, S. J. *One Christ – Many Religions: Towards a Revised Christology*. 2nd Edition. New York: Orbis Books, 1991 Published in India by Bangalore: SATHRI, 1994.

Samuel, Bhanu. "Dalit Theology: A Theology Towards Solidarity." In *Building Theologies of Solidarity: Interfacing Feminist Theology with Dalit Theology and Tribal/Adivasi Theologies*. Edited by Hrangthan Chhungi, Raj Bharath Patta and P. Mohan Larbeer. Bangalore: BTESSC/NCCI/SCMI, 2012.

Samuel, Simon. *A Postcolonial Reading of Mark's Story of Jesus*. New York: T&T Clark, 2007.

________. "Decolonising the Biblical Studies." *Theological Research in the Global South: Prospects and Challenges*. Edited by P. G. George. West Bengal: South Asia Theological Research Institute, 2015.

Samuel, V. C. *The Council of Chalcedon Re-Examined: A Historical and Theological Survey*. Delhi: ISPCK, 2001.

Schaff, Philip. Ed. *The Creeds of Christendom with a History and Critical Notes*. 1931. Vol. 1: The History of Creeds. 6th Edition. Michigan: Baker Books, 1998.

Schillebeeckx, Edward. *Jesus: An Experiment in Christology*. Translated by Hubert Hoskins. New York: The Seabry Press, 1979.

Schouten, Jan Peter. *Jesus as Guru: The Image of Christ among Hindus and Christians in India.* Currents of Encounter, Studies on the Contact between Christianity and Other Religions, Beliefs, and Cultures, Vol. 36. Translated by Henry and Lucy Jansen. Amsterdam, New York: Rudopi, 2008.

Schürer, Emil. *The History of the Jewish People in the Age of Jesus Christ (175 B.C.-A.D. 135)*. Vol. II. Revised 1979. Edited by Geza Vermes, Fergus Millar and Matthew Black. Edinburgh: T&T Clark Ltd., 1986.

Schweitzer, Albert. *The Quest of the Historical Jesus: A Critical Study of Its Progress from Reimarus to Wrede*. Translated by W. Montgomery from *Von Reimarus zed Wrede.* 1906. Np: Suzeteo Enterprises, 2011.

Segundo, Juan Luis. *Jesus of Nazareth Yesterday and Today*. Vol. II The Historical Jesus of the Synoptics. Translated by John Drury. Maryknoll: Orbis Books, 1985.

Seif, Jeffrey L. *Origin of the Christian Faith*. Dallas: JSM publishing in cooperation with Christ for the Nations Institute, 1992.

Shah, Ghanshyam. "Anti-Untouchability Movements." In *Caste, Caste-Conflict and Reservations*. New Delhi: Ajanta, 1985.

________. "Dalit Movements and the Search for Identity." *Dalit Identity and Politics: Cultural Subordination and the Dalit Challenge*. Vol. 2. Edited by Ghanshyam Shah. New Delhi: Sage Publications, 2001.

________. "Introduction: Dalit Politics." In *Dalit Identity and Politics: Cultural Subordination and the Dalit Challenge*. Vol. 2. Edited by Ghanshyam Shah. New Delhi: Sage Publications, 2001.

Sharma, Arvind. *Reservation and Affirmative Action: Models of Social Integration in India*. New Delhi: Sage Publication, 2005.

Sharma, R. S. *Rethinking India's Past*. New Delhi: Oxford University Press, 2009.

Shrirama. "Untouchability and Stratification in Indian Civilization." In *Dalits in Modern India: Vision and Values*. Edited by S. M. Michael. New Delhi: Vistaar Publications, 1999.

Simon-Peter, Rebekah. *The Jew Named Jesus: Discover the Man and His Message.* Nashville: Abingdon Press, 2013.

Singaram, Charles. "Can Dalit Theology be Systematized? A Tentative Proposal." In *Moving Forms of Theology: Faith Talk's Changing Contexts.* Edited by Israel Selvanayagam. Delhi: ISPCK, 2002.

________. *The Question of Method in Dalit Theology: In Search of Systematic Approach to the Practice of an Indian Liberation Theology.* Delhi: ISPCK, 2008.

Singh, Herbert Jai. "Toward a Relevant Gospel in India." In *Indian Voices in Today's Theological Debate.* Edited by Horst Bürkle and Wolfgang M. W. Roth. Luknow: Luknow Publishing House in collaboration with Delhi/ Madras: ISPCK, CLS, 1972.

Sobrino, Jon. *Christology at the Cross Roads.* New York: Orbis Books, 1985.

Stambaugh, John E. and David L. Balch. *The New Testament in its Social Environment.* Philadelphia: Westminster John Knox Press, 1986.

Stanton, G. N. *Jesus of Nazareth in New Testament Preaching.* Society for New Testament Studies Monographs Series. 27. Cambridge: CUP, 1974.

Stauffer, Ethelbert. *New Testament Theology.* Translated by J. Marsh. London: SCM Press, 1955.

Stephenson, Andrew. *The History of Christianity: From the Origin of Christianity to the Time of Gregory the Great.* Vol. 1. Boston: Richard G. Badger, 1919.

Sugritharaja, R. S. "Prologue and Perspective." In *Asian Faces of Jesus.* Edited by R. S. Sugritharaja. London: SCM Press, 1993.

________. *The Bible and Empire: Postcolonial Explorations.* Cambridge: CUP, 2005.

Taylor, Richard W. "Christ Acting in Our Society." In *Indian Voices in Today's Theological Debate.* Edited by Horst Bürkle and Wolfgang M. W. Roth. Luknow: Luknow Publishing House in collaboration with Delhi/Madras: ISPCK, CLS, 1972.

Taylor, Vincent. *The Person of Christ in New Testament Teachings.* London: Macmillan & Co., 1958.

Thangaraj, M. Thomas. *The Crucified Guru.* Nashville: Abingdon Press, 1994.

Thomas, M. M. *The Acknowledged Christ of the Indian Renaissance.* Madras: CLS, 1970. Third Edition, 1991.

Thomas, V. V. *Dalit and Tribal Christians of India: Issues and Challenges.* Kerala: Focus India Trust, 2014.

Thumma, Anthoniraj. *Dalit Liberation Theology: Ambedkarian Perspective.* Delhi: ISPCK, 2000.

________. *Springs from the Subalterns: Patterns and Perspectives in People's Theology.* Delhi: ISPCK 1999.

________. *Voices of the Victims: Movements and Models of People's Theology*. Delhi: ISPCK, 1999.

Torrance, Alan. "Jesus in Christian Doctrine." *The Cambridge Companion to Jesus*. Edited by Markus Bockmuel. Cambridge: CUP, 2001.

Torrance, T. F. *Theology in Reconstruction*. London: SCM Press, 1965.

Tuckett, Christopher. "Sources and Methods." In *The Cambridge Companion to Jesus*. Edited by Markus Bockmuchl. New York: Cambridge University Press, 2001.

Tyson, Joseph B. *The New Testament and Early Christianity*. New York and London: Macmillan Publishing Company, 1984.

Upadhyay, B. "The Incarnate Logos." In *The Writings of Brahmabandhab Upadhyay*, Vol. 1. Library of Indian Christian Theology – 6. Edited and annotated by Julius Lipner and George Gispert-Sauch. Bangalore: The United Theological College, 1991.

Vedartha-Sangraha of Sri Ramanujacarya. Translated by S. S. Raghavachar. Mysore: Sri Ramakrishna Ashram, 1978.

Vengal Chakkarai, Vol. 1. Edited by P.T. Thomas. Madras: CLS, 1981.

Vijayakumar, W. K., "A Historical Study of Buddhism in India." In *Ambedkar and the Neo-Buddhist Movement*. Edited by Wilkinsin and Thomas. Bangalore: CISRS/CLS, 1972.

Watson, Francis. "The Quest for the Real Jesus." In *The Cambridge Companion to Jesus*. Edited by Markus Bockmuchl. New York: Cambridge University Press, 2001.

Webster, John C. B. "Who is a Dalit?." *Dalits in Modern India: Vision and Values*. Edited by S. M. Michael. New Delhi: Vistaar Publications, 1999.

Whittaker, C. R. "Imperialism and Culture: The Roman Initiative." In *Dialogues in Roman Imperialism: Power, Discourse, and Discrepant Experience in the Roman Empire*. JRA Supp. Series, No. 23. Edited by D. J. Mattingly. Portsmouth: JRA, 1997.

Wilfred, Felix. *The Sling Utopia: Struggles for a Different Society*. Delhi: ISPCK, 2005.

Williams, D. H. *Evangelicals and Tradition: The Formative Influence of the Early Church*. Grand Rapids, Michigan: Baker Academics, 2005.

Williams, Roman. "A History of Faith in Jesus." In *The Cambridge Companion to Jesus*. Edited by Markus Bockmuel. Cambridge: CUP, 2001.

Wilson, K. "An Approach to Christian Dalit Theology." In *Towards a Dalit Theology*. Edited by M. E. Prabhakar. Delhi: ISPCK, 1989.

________. *The Twice-Alienated: Culture of Dalit Christians*. Hyderabad: Booklinks Corporation, 1982.

Winslow, J. C. *Narayan Vaman Tilak: The Christian Poet of Maharashtra*. Calcutta: Association Press, 1923.

Witherington III, Ben. *Jesus the Seer: The Progress of Prophecy*. Peabody: Hendrickson, 1999.

________. *The Jesus Quest: The Third Search for the Jew of Nazareth*. 2nd Ed. Illinois: InterVarsity Press, 1997.

Wright, N.T. *The Last Word: Beyond the Bible Wars to a New Understanding of the Authority of Scripture*. New York: HarperSanFrancisco, 2005.

Yagati, Chinna Rao. *Dalit's Struggles for Identity: Andhra and Hyderabad, 1900-1950*. New Delhi: Kanishka Publication, 2003.

Yoder, John Howard. *Preface to Theology: Christology and Theological Method*. Michigan: Brazos Press, 2002.

Young, John. *The Christ of History: An Argument Grounded in the Facts of His Life on Earth*. New York: Robert Carter & Brothers, 1857.

Zelliot, Eleanor. *From Untouchable to Dalit*. New Delhi, 1992.

Dictionaries

Bultmann, Rudolf. "πιστεύω κτλ." In *Theological Dictionary of the New Testament* Vol. VI. Edited by Gerhard Kittel and Gerhard Frierich (Michigan: Wm. B. Eerdmans Publishing Company, 1968): 174-228.

Carroll, M. Daniel. "רלל." In *New International Dictionary of Old Testament Theology and Exegesis*. Vol. 1. Edited by Williem A. Van Germeren (Michigan: Zondervan Publishing House, 1997): 951-954.

Fabry, Bonn. " בַּל." In *Theological Dictionary of Old Testament* Vol. III 1978. Edited by G. Johannes Botterweck and Helmer Ringgren (Grand Rapid, Michigan: William B. Eerdmans Publishing Company, reprint 1988): 208-230.

Highton, Mike. "Christology." *The Cambridge Dictionary of Christology*. Edited by Ian A. McFarland and Etal. (Cambridge: Cambridge University Press, 2011): 99-101.

Johnson, S. E. "Lord (Christ)." *The Interpreters' Dictionary of the Bible: An Illustrated Encyclopedia* Vol. 3. (New York: Abingdon Press, 1962): 151.

McKim, Donald K. *Westminster Dictionary of Theological Terms*. London: Westminster John Knox Press, 1996.

Plenis, J. David. "Poor, Poverty." In *The Anchor Bible Dictionary*. Vol. 5. Edited by David Noel Freedman (New York: Doubleday, 1992): 402-414.

Wikgren, A. "Maranatha." *The Interpreters' Dictionary of the Bible: An Illustrated Encyclopaedia,* Vol. 3. (New York: Abingdon Press, 1962): 262.

Wolf, C. U. "Poor." In *The Interpreter's Dictionary of the Bible: An Illustrated Encyclopaedia*. Vol. 3, 1962. Edited by George Arthur Buttrick (Nashville: Abingdon Press, 15th Printing 1985): 843-844.

Encyclopaedia

"Jagjivan Ram: Champions of Dalits-Post Ambedkar." In *Encyclopedia of Dalits*. Vol. 4, 112.

Bassett, Paul M. "Faith." In *Encyclopaedia of Early Christianity*. Edited by Everett Ferguson. (New York and London: Garland Publishing, 1990): 337-342.

Dragas, George D. "Greece, Greek." In *Encyclopaedia of Early Christianity*. Edited by Everett Ferguson (New York and London: Garland Publishing, 1990): 392-393.

Holwerda, D. E. "Poor." In *The International Standard Bible Encyclopaedia*. Vol. 3. Rev. 1915. Edited by Geoffrey W. Bromiley. Grand Rapids, Michigan: William B. Eerdmans Publishing Company, 1986): 905-908.

Parwan, Sanjay. and Paramanshi Jaideva. Eds. "Introduction." In *Encyclopaedia of Dalits in India*. Vol. 1: General Studies. Edited by Sanjay Parwan and Paramanshi Jaideva (Delhi: Kalpaz Publication, 2002): 11.

________. "Introduction." *Encyclopaedia of Dalits in India: Leaders*. Vol. 4. (Delhi: Kalpaz Publications, 2002): 11.

Journals

Balasundaram, Franklyn J. "Dalit Struggle and its Implication for Theological Education." *BTF* XXIX/3&4 (Sept. & Dec., 1997): 69-91.

Bavinck, Herman. "The Catholicity of Christianity and the Church." *Calvin Theological Journal* 27/2 (1992): 220-51.

Blaising, Craig A. "Creedal Formation as Hermeneutical Development: A Reexamination of Nicaea." *Pro Ecclesia* XIX/ 4 (from ATLA accessed on 21-08-13): 371-388.

Clarke, Satyanathan. "Subaltern Cultures as Resource for People's Liberation: A Critical Enquiry into Dalit Culture Theory." *Religion and Society* 44/4 (December, 1997): 89-94.

Donaldson, Terence L. "Gentile Christianity" as a Category in the Study of Christian Origins." *Harvard Theological Review* 106/4 (Oct, 2013): 433-458.

Dutta, Mohua. "Bhakti Movements: A Socio-Religious Struggle of the Marginalized Society." *Indian Journal of Applied Research* 4/8 (Aug., 2014): 685-687.

George, Samuel. "Jesus of History and Gospel-Culture Debate in India." *Master's Journal of Theology* 2/2 (Oct., 2012): 74.

Gnanavaram, M. "Dalit Theology and the Parable of the Good Samaritan." *Journal for the Study of the New Testament* 50 (1993): 59-83. Accessed through ATLA on 09-10-2014.

Heredia, Rudolf C. "Search for Identity, Quest for Dignity: The Dalit's Long March." *VJTR* 74/10 (Oct., 2010): 744-760.

Hoffman, Daniel. "The Authority of Scripture and Apostolic Doctrine in Ignatius of Antioch." *Journal of the Evangelical Theological* Society 28/1 (March. 1985): 71-75.

Iverson, Kelly R. "A Centurion's "Confession": A Performance-Critical Analysis of Mark 15: 39." *Journal of Biblical Literature*, 130/2 (Summer, 2011): 320-350.

Judge, E. A. "The Early Christians as a Scholastic Community." *Journal of Religious History* 1/61 (1960): 4-15.

Keith, Graham. "The Formulation of Creeds in the Early Church." *Themelios* 24/1(October, 1998): 13-35.

Lazenby, Henry F. "The Mythical Use of the Bible by Evangelicals." *JETS* 34/4 (Dec., 1991): 485-494.

Massey, James. "A Vision of a Dalit." In *NCCR* CXII/7 (Aug., 1994): 573.

________. "Christian Dalits: A Historical Perspective." In *Journal of Dharma* 1/1 (Jan.-March, 1991): 44-45.

Melanchthon, Monica Jyotsna. "Dalits, Bible and Method." In *SBL Forum*. Available in http://www.sbl-siteorg/Article.aspx?ArticleID=459. Accessed on 24/10/2014.

Oinam, Bhagat. "Philosophy in India: An Agenda for an Alternative Mode of Philosophising." *Journal of Indian Council of Philosophical Research* XXVIII/2 (April-June, 2011): 75-90.

Osthathios, Geevarghese Mar. "Cosmic, Communitarian and Kenotic Dimensions of the New Man in Christ," 177-185. Available from http://www.biblicalstudies.org.uk/pdf/ijt/27-3-4_177.pdf accessed on 12-02-15.

Prabahakar, M. E. "Beginning and Growth of Dalit Studies in the CISRS and its Joint Programmes. *Religion and Society* XL/1&2 (March-June, 1993): 95-128.

Prasad, L. "Gems from India: Dalit." *VJTR* 65/4 (April, 2001): 320.

Raja, A. Maria Arul. "Living Streams Across the Parched Land: Some Tenants of Dalit Spirituality." in *CTC Bulletin*. 1-8. Available at http://daga.dhs.org/cca/resourse/ctc/ctc01-04/ctc0104d.htm.

________. "Towards a Dalit Reading of the Bible: Some Hermeneutical Reflections." *Jeevadhara* 26/151 (1996): 29-34.

Rasquinha, Dionysius. "A Critical Reflection on the Meaning of Dalit Christian Theology." *VJTR* 66/4 (April, 2002): 251-269.

Ryerson, Charles A. "Meaning and Modernisation in Tamil Nadu: Tamil Nationalism and Religious Culture." *Religion and Society* XVII/4 (Dec., 1970): 231-249.

Saliba, Issa A. "The Bishop of Antioch and the Heretics: A Study of a Primitive Christology." *The Evangelical Quarterly* (ATLA Series accessed on 21-08-2013): 65-76.

Sanday, W. "Recent Research on the Origin of the Creed." In *The Journal of Theological Studies* 3-20. Accessed from http://www.biblicalstudies.org.uk/pdf/jts/001_003.pdf on 21-11-14.

Sharma, Arvind. "Dr. B. R. Ambedkar on the Aryan Invasion and the Emergence of the Indian Caste System in India." 866. (ATLA accessed).

Varavukala, Jojo. "Dalitharenna Daivajanam," (Mal) *Jeevadhara* XXXV/ 206 (April, 2005): 117-119.

Wilfred, Felix. "Towards a Subaltern Hermeneutics Beyond Contemporary Polarities in the Interpretation of Religious Tradition." *Jeevadhara* XXVI/151 (1996): 45-63.

Winn, Adam. "Tyrant or Servant? Roman Political Ideology and Mark 10.42-45." *Journal of the Study of the New Testament* 36/4 (June, 2014): 325-352.

Wolf, H. H. "Toward an Ecumenical Theology." *The Ecumenical Review* XIII/2 (1961): 216.

Index